For Service to Your Country

For Service to Your Country

The Insider's Guide to Veterans' Benefits

PETER S. GAYTAN

and

MARIAN EDELMAN BORDEN

FOREWORD BY SENATOR BOB DOLE

CITADEL PRESS

Kensington Publishing Corp.
www.kensingtonbooks.com

CITADEL PRESS BOOKS are published by

Kensington Publishing Corp.
850 Third Avenue
New York, NY 10022

All Kensington titles, imprints, and distributed lines are available at special quantity discounts for bulk purchases for sales promotions, premiums, fund-raising, educational, or institutional use. Special book excerpts or customized printings can also be created to fit specific needs. For details, write or phone the office of the Kensington special sales manager: Kensington Publishing Corp., 850 Third Avenue, New York, NY 10022, attn: Special Sales Department; phone 1-800-221-2647.

First printing: July 2008

10 9 8 7 6 5 4 3 2 1

Printed in the United States of America

Library of Congress Control Number: 2008922837

ISBN-13: 978-0-8065-2872-4
ISBN-10: 0-8065-2872-9

With respect and admiration for men
who served their country with honor and pride:

SSgt. Albert John Pikes, U.S. Army WWII
Sgt. David Earl Poore, U.S. Army WWII
—PSG

and

Captain Carol Edelman, U.S. Army WWII
Major Melvin N. Borden, M.D., Army Air Force WWII
—MEB

Contents

Foreword

by Senator Bob Dole

Our nation's Founding Fathers understood that every American owes a lifetime debt to those who put their own lives in danger to preserve our liberty. Each year we mark Veterans Day with solemn ceremonies. In speeches and editorials, we salute those who have died in defense of our country. We stand in respectful silence as a wreath is laid and Taps is played at the Tomb of the Unknown Soldier. We are struck by the poignant images of rows of gleaming marble headstones marking the final resting places of our fallen heroes at Arlington National Cemetery and elsewhere. Each year, as President Dwight D. Eisenhower wrote in the first Veterans Day proclamation, we must "solemnly remember the sacrifices of all those who fought so valiantly, on the seas, in the air, and on foreign shores, to preserve our heritage of freedom."

These annual ceremonies are important. They recall the ultimate sacrifice of those who have served. But it is also an opportunity to remember the 25 million veterans and their families who are still with us and to whom we owe a great deal.

For those who have survived but have suffered injuries in the line of duty, we must provide appropriate compensation and a lifetime of health care. For those whose careers were interrupted when they answered the call to serve, we must make available educational opportunities to prepare them for lives outside of the armed forces. For those who have served honorably, we could offer low-cost loans so that they can own their own homes. And at the end of their lives, we owe our veterans final burial rites and resting places that reflect the respect and honor of the nation that they have served.

Today's VA, like the world around us, is more complicated and complex than the agency used by your father and grandfather. But the mission is the same: To provide for the care and welfare of our nation's veterans and their families. Because of your service, you may be eligible for health, education, housing, and burial programs.

This book, *For Service to Your Country*, will help simplify the paperwork and bureaucracy that accessing these benefits entail. It's an insider's guide to the benefits that the Federal government, state governments, and private sector provide qualified veterans.

To the veterans who pick up this book, these benefits are not charity. Take advantage of these opportunities if you are eligible. You've earned them and deserve them. The greatest privilege of my life has been to wear the uniform of our country in a righteous cause. Whatever we may be today as a nation, it is because many generations of Americans were willing to make the greatest of sacrifices. You have earned the thanks of a grateful nation and I'm proud to salute you.

ROBERT J. "BOB" DOLE is a former U.S. Senator and Co-Chair of the President's Commission on Care for America's Returning Wounded Warriors

Introduction

> To care for him who shall have borne the battle and for his widow and his orphan.

Abraham Lincoln made that solemn promise in his second inaugural address on March 4, 1865. It is the motto of the Department of Veterans Affairs and the motivation behind this book.

The weapons and technology of today's armed forces have changed and may not be recognizable to the soldiers of even 50 years ago—but the value of service to our country will never change. Veterans and their families have borne extraordinary burdens in defense of America. As a nation we owe our veterans a debt of gratitude. The benefits we describe in the following chapters are well earned.

We wrote this book to meet the needs of all veterans—old and young. Just as this isn't your father's army—it's also not your father's VA. The bureaucracy is bigger, the forms have multiplied, the benefits have become more complicated. At the same time, the demand for these benefits has grown exponentially, as servicemembers return, often broken and in need of help, from current wars.

For Service to Your Country covers the wide range of legally mandated benefits, as well as the variety of opportunities that the Federal and state governments provide for veterans. Also included are a review of many programs that have been developed by private businesses to attract veterans and a list of those businesses that provide special discounts or gifts for former warriors and their families.

We've written this book to be a practical, step-by-step guide to *your* earned veterans' benefits. The VA, as well as many Veterans

Service Organizations (VSOs), have large websites that provide you with information. At times, these are confusing and require you to move from one link to another in search of information. Too often, these sites are written using technical language that is hard to decipher. But we know there is value to these sites and we've noted important websites for your use throughout this book.

For Service to Your Country is designed as a practical guide to securing your well-earned benefits. Mark it up, underline passages that apply to your case, and make notes in the margins. Take the book with you when you meet with representatives of VA or a Veterans Service Organization to discuss a problem or concern.

Acknowledgments

We are grateful for the assistance and support of many people. Many thanks to Richard Ember, editor extraordinaire at Kensington Publishing, whose vision for this book made it possible. Thanks too to Robert Diforio, our agent, for his wisdom and encouragement of this project.

Special thanks to Carole Johnson for her meticulous research contributions and to Dr. Elizabeth Rogers for her thoughtful assistance. For their insight, support, and encouragement, we are grateful to Ron Conley, Paul Morin, G. Michel Schlee, Steve Smithson, John Sommer, Robert Spanogle, Joseph B. Carr, Stephen Tuttle, and Stephen Versprille.

Our work and our lives are enriched by the love and support of our families. With heartfelt appreciation to Kimberly, Maria, and Sebastian Gaytan, Judy Gaytan; Maria and David Poore; and John, Charles, Rebecca, Sam, Jessica, Dan, and Maggie Borden.

Thank-you to the servicemen and -women who serve our country with honor. This book is for you.

CHAPTER 1

The VA and the Veteran

> *The willingness with which our young people are likely to serve in any war, no matter how justified, shall be directly proportional to how they perceive the veterans of earlier wars were treated and appreciated by their nation.*
>
> —George Washington

George Washington, our country's first President and a soldier himself, understood the critical role the treatment of veterans would play in the future defense of our nation. In fact, the Continental Congress of 1776 encouraged enlistment in the Revolutionary War by promising lifetime care for any soldier wounded or disabled.

An integral part of the bargain we make with our servicemen and -women is that when they have completed their service, either at the end of their tours of duty or because of illness or injury, they can count on America to honor its pledge to care for them, help to educate them, assist them in owning homes, and ultimately honor them in death. Treating veterans with respect, caring—if necessary for life—for our nation's wounded comrades-in-arms, providing incentives that enrich the post-military years of those who have served, is both an ethical and practical decision.

The concept that a nation owed something to the veterans of its armed forces is much older than our country. The Roman Empire gave land to its career soldiers who retired from service. Later there was precedent in English law that a nation had a responsibility to its soldiers. Our own obligation to veterans is evident even with the first Pilgrims. Those early colonists passed a law in 1636 that declared: "If any man shall be sent forth as a soldier and shall return maimed, he shall be maintained competently by the colony during his life."

The Foundation of American Veterans Benefits Is Set

Pensions for disabled veterans and their dependents was one of the laws passed by the first U.S. Congress in 1789. Steadily through the nineteenth century, there was a growing recognition that the Federal government must provide health care and pensions for veterans injured and disabled while in service. In 1811, the Federal government authorized the first domiciliary (residence) and medical facility for veterans. By 1818, the Secretary of War assumed the responsibility of administering veterans programs. The administration of this care shifted among Federal departments over the next century. At one point, the Bureau of Pensions was responsible; later, administration of these benefits was shifted to the Department of the Interior, with other agencies providing services to veterans. First the Marine Hospitals in 1798, and then the Public Health Service supplied medical examinations to veterans. The National Home for Disabled Volunteer Soldiers was founded in 1866.

The years following the Civil War were a critical period for the movement to provide care for veterans grievously wounded and dislocated during the conflict. Many states established veterans' homes, and during those years, medical care and hospital treatment were provided to veterans whether or not the injuries or disease were service based.

World War I Marks a New Era for Vets

But it is World War I, and the veterans who emerged from that global struggle, that marks the beginning of the modern veterans movement. What is evident over the past century is that it is always a battle of cost versus need. Moreover, it has been a constant clash of veterans versus bureaucracy. Ex-servicemen and -women have always needed to navigate through a confusing maze of rules, regulations, and paperwork. The result? Too often the veteran has had to fight two battles: first for his nation and then for his benefits.

In 1917, at the start of America's entry into the war, Congress authorized new benefits for veterans including disability compensation, life insurance for servicemen and veterans, and vocational rehabilitation for the disabled.

The Federal Board of Vocational Education (part of the Treasury Department) administered the vocational rehab provided for disabled veterans. Of interest is that the disability for which the veteran sought treatment could be one incurred while in service, or existed previously but was increased or aggravated by service. The Bureau of War Risk Insurance handled other veteran affairs.

During the 1920s, veterans' benefits were administered by three different Federal agencies: the Veterans Bureau, the Bureau of Pensions of the Interior Department, and the National Home for Disabled Volunteer Soldiers. In 1930, Congress authorized President Herbert Hoover to "consolidate and coordinate Government activities affecting war veterans." The Veterans Administration was established in answer to this law and the three component agencies became bureaus under the VA (note at that time it's the Veterans *Administration,* it's not until 1989 that it becomes the Department of Veterans *Affairs*). While the Federal government had provided benefits for veterans throughout its history, 1930 is considered the founding date of the VA and the modern veteran era.

The Bonus Army Marches on Washington

This interwar period is critical because the political power of veterans as a group becomes clear with the "Bonus Army" of 1932. Let's put it in context. Veterans were seeking immediate payment of the cash "bonus" that had been promised to them in 1924 by the Adjusted Service Certificate Law. That bonus was originally to be paid in 1945. But it's the height of the Great Depression, unemployment is rampant, and veterans insist they need the bonus immediately in order to survive and provide for their families. The result? A march on Washington by World War I veterans, a political move that would be repeated over the years by veterans and other groups seeking the attention of Congress and the public at large.

The Bonus Army (also known as the Bonus March or Bonus Expeditionary Force) was a group of 31,000 World War I veterans (with their families and other affiliated groups). They marched on Washington, D.C., in June 1932 and set up a camp in Anacostia, across the river from the Federal city. The Bonus Army demanded passage of the Patman Bonus Bill, which would move forward the date the bonus would be paid. President Hoover opposed the bill, and although it passed in the House of Representatives, it was blocked by the Senate.

The standoff between veterans and the very government they had served finally ended tragically in late July when Federal troops cleared the camps. Hundreds of veterans were injured, several were killed. But that image of America's own veterans, servicemen who had survived the horrors of World War I and now beset by American troops, was incredibly powerful. It set the stage for the Veterans Administration, but also forced elected officials to recognize the political power of veterans. Herbert Hoover's open opposition to the Bonus Bill and the rout of American veterans by U.S. troops helped defeat the Republican incumbent in November 1932.

While Franklin D. Roosevelt didn't want to pay the bonus early either, historians point out that he was more adept at skillfully handling the continuing veterans issue. When there was another march on Washington by veterans in 1933, Eleanor Roosevelt met with the group. A work program designed to give veterans jobs, building the Overseas Highway in Florida, was initially welcomed, but the Labor Day Hurricane of 1935 killed 259 veterans working on the highway. Public sentiment had shifted. The Federal government was seen as taking advantage of veterans, and Congress voted to enact the bonus in 1936. Roosevelt vetoed the bill, but it was an election year and Congress overrode the veto and prevailed.

The political power of veterans was established.

The G.I. Bill Transforms America

The VA grew exponentially at the end of World War II with the return of 16 million veterans. To offer new opportunities to these returning soldiers, the Servicemen's Readjustment Act of 1944, better known as the G.I. Bill, was signed by President Franklin D. Roosevelt just two weeks after D-day. It was, according to historian Stephen Ambrose, "the best piece of legislation ever passed by the U.S. Congress, and it made modern America." This historic piece of legislation was the result of the hard work of the American Legion. During organizational meetings held at the Mayflower Hotel in Washington, D.C., in 1943, past National Commander Harry W. Colmery of Topeka, Kansas, drafted—in longhand on hotel stationery—what would become the G.I. Bill. Ironically, this bill passed by a slim margin and didn't even get much attention at that time. Its long-term impact on American society was yet to be understood.

Besides providing health care for returning veterans, there were two landmark features of the G.I. Bill that transformed this nation, socially and economically. According to the historian Doris Kearns Goodwin, the education component of the G.I. Bill meant that "a whole generation of blue collar workers were enabled to go to college, become doctors, lawyers, and engineers, and that their children would grow up in a middle class family. . . . In 1940, the average GI was 26 years old and had an average of one year of high school as his only education, and now, suddenly, the college doors were open." In its first year, the VA processed more than 83,000 applications for educational benefits.

The historian Michael Beschloss believes that the G.I. Bill of 1944 "linked the idea of service to education. You serve the country; the government pays you back by allowing you educational opportunities you otherwise wouldn't have had, and that in turn helps to improve this society."

The low-cost VA housing loans created by the G.I. Bill transformed America from a nation of renters to a country of homeowners. The net effect of the bill was the creation of suburbs as the population moved out of the rental apartments in the cities and into the new communities being developed with affordable housing. There were 13 million homes built in the 1950s, 11 million of which were built with VA loans. These new communities forced the creation of a new interstate highway system, which helped fuel the decay of many inner cities.

By 1947, World War II veterans and their families made up one-fourth of the U.S. population.

Health Care for Veterans Is Guaranteed

The history of VA medical care seems to repeat itself through the years. The news stories of 1933 seem sadly familiar to our current veterans. To cut government costs in 1933, the VA reviewed more than a million cases to insure "veterans' relief" payments were justified. VA hospital and domiciliary workloads dropped 23 and 40 percent respectively because new laws limited eligibility for VA medical care.

Providing medical care for our nation's ex–servicemembers is undoubtedly expensive, but it is necessary and honorable. In 1930, the Veterans Administration operated 48 hospitals and 54 regional offices. The demand for medical care by returning World War II veterans meant that by 1948, the VA operated 125 hospitals with 102,200 beds. But demand then, as today, outpaced availability of services. At the end of 1948, 20, 700 veterans deemed eligible for VA medical care awaited hospital admission.

Today, medical care for veterans is still rationed. Although there are 154 VA medical centers in the VA system, and the VHA treats more than 5 million patients each year, the average wait time for treatment at a VA medical center can be several months. (Entering the system is different from waiting to be seen. Enrolling is not delayed. A veteran enrolls without delay but, once in the system, the wait time for an appointment can be up to a year at some facilities.)

For two years following separation from active duty, if you are a veteran who served in combat locations during active military service (after November 11, 1998), you are eligible for free health care service for conditions potentially related to combat service. Legislation is currently before Congress that seeks to extend that period to five years following separation from active duty. At the end of that time, however, you will be assigned to a priority group. Depending on your disability rating and service-connected eligibility, you may no longer be able to access the VA health care system.

VA has experienced unprecedented growth in the medical system workload since the beginning of the Global War on Terrorism (GWOT). According to VA, the number of patients treated at VA medical centers increased by 22 percent from 4.1 million in 2001 to more than 5.3 million in 2005.

Most veterans must enroll with VA in order to receive VA health care benefits. As of October 2005, 7.7 million veterans were enrolled in the VA health care system. Once enrolled with VA, veterans are placed in priority groups based on service connection, extent of injury or illness, and income level. Depending on the individual situation, the veteran could possibly be shut out of the VA health care system regardless of his service in the military.

Veterans who do not have to enroll include those with a service-connected disability of 50 percent or more, veterans who were discharged from the military within one year but have not yet been rated for a VA disability benefit, and veterans seeking care for only a service-connected disability.

Korean War Veterans Win Benefits

In anticipation of the needs of returning servicemembers, Congress crafted legislation that would help in the transition from military to civilian life. Korean War veterans secured World War II–era G.I. Bill–like benefits with the passage of the Veterans' Readjustment Act of 1952 or the Korean Conflict G.I. Bill. This new G.I. Bill provided unemployment insurance, job placement assistance, and transition benefits similar, but not equal, to those provided to World War II veterans. The Korean Conflict G.I. Bill provided only 36 months of education benefits compared to the 48 months provided to World War II veterans under the original G.I. Bill. Also, instead of making tuition payments to the colleges, Korean War veterans received a subsistence check that was intended to pay for their college tuition.

In December 1950 Congress passed the Vocational Rehabilitation Act of 1950 to help Korean War veterans find employment after losing their pre-war jobs due to disabilities caused by war. According to VA, some 2.4 million Korean War–era veterans received education and training under the Korean Conflict G.I. Bill.

Vietnam War Veterans Push for Change

Unlike World War II veterans, the servicemembers who returned home after tours of duty in Vietnam were not met with parades and welcoming arms. The nation was divided over the war and veterans bore the brunt of the anger. There was a lack of public and institutional support for Vietnam-era veterans. The returning combatants also faced benefits that, in comparison, were far smaller than those provided to World War II veterans. Transitional benefits in areas such as education, home loan, and job assistance did not meet the actual needs of this new era of veteran.

Society had changed dramatically since the return of the World War II veteran, but the benefits of the Vietnam-era veteran did not reflect societal changes. Although benefits were provided to Vietnam veterans, they fell short of the actual needs of the transitioning veteran. The Vietnam Era Veterans' Readjustment Assistance Act of 1974 finally provided those veterans with the benefits they had earned.

Vietnam-era veterans, feeling distant from the government and society, shunned VA hospitals. In 1979, to provide readjustment counseling services to these veterans, the VA developed Vietnam Veteran Outreach Centers, now known as Vet Centers. These centers, staffed primarily by veterans, continue to provide counseling, especially for those suffering from Post-traumatic Stress Disorder (PTSD). They are still used, and are often preferred, by returning combatants from Iraq and Afghanistan.

The VA faced another health care crisis as thousands of Vietnam-era veterans began suffering from a variety of illnesses and symptoms. For over a decade their complaints were met with confusion and resistance. Only later did the VA relate these symptoms to exposure to Agent Orange during the war. The VA developed a health care registry to track and research the effects of this toxic exposure. Now veterans from Gulf War I and Gulf War II have also developed mysterious symptoms and illnesses. New health registries have been developed for those servicemembers.

The lessons learned through the monitoring of Agent Orange exposure have enabled VA to more proactively identify symptoms and illnesses attributed to chemical and biological exposures during combat. The health registries help to identify veterans who may manifest symptoms and develop illnesses long after their exposure to toxic agents. Once identified as resulting from exposure, VA has an obligation to treat veterans who are suffering as a result of exposure to chemical and biological agents during service.

The Role of African American Veterans

But it's important to remember that as valuable as the G.I. Bill was in transforming post-war America economically, segregation was also still part of the American landscape. President Harry S. Truman signed Executive Order 9981 in 1948 integrating the military and mandating equality of treatment and opportunity, but the country was still racially divided. Although VA loans made homeownership a possibility, affordable communities like Levittown on Long Island were closed to African American veterans.

It was not until 1963 that the VA enforced an equal housing order by placing a special emphasis on securing nondiscrimination certification from GI homebuilders. Many colleges were segregated, so even with the GI education benefits, admission was still denied to African American veterans. It was not until 1953 that all VA hospitals, including those in the South, were fully integrated.

The Role of Women Veterans

Since the founding of this great nation, women have aided in the protection of freedom and liberty. Whether providing comfort and care for the wounded or disguising themselves as men so they could actually serve in uniform, women have been a part of the U.S. military since the Revolutionary and Civil wars.

With the establishment of the Army and Navy Nurse Corps in the early 1900s, women were formally allowed to serve in the U.S. military. After the onset of World War I, women gained an active role in the Navy and Marine Corps. While the Army was still seeking authorization to recruit and enlist women, the Navy and Marine Corps were already adding women to the active-duty roles. As a result of Japan's attack on Pearl Harbor, the Women's Army Auxiliary Corps (WAAC) became a reality through congressional action.

The modern-day military from Vietnam to the Global War on Terrorism has seen the full integration of women in the U.S. military. Women who have honorably served are eligible for the same veterans benefits as their male counterparts. In fact, VA provides specialized health care for women veterans in the fields of osteoporosis screening, menopausal care, gynecological services, as well as mental health services.

The New VA Emerges

This is no longer your father's—or grandfathers—VA. The needs of the twenty-first-century veteran continue to change and the services and programs offered through VA continue to evolve as well.

In 1989, the Veterans Administration became the Department of Veterans Affairs, a cabinet-level department. It is the second largest Federal agency, after the Department of Defense. The VA comprises the Veterans Benefits Administration (VBA), the Veterans Health Administration (VHA), and the National Cemetery Administration (NCA).

The Veterans Benefits Administration is responsible for the administration of benefits provided by the department to veterans and dependents, including compensation, pension, education, home loan guaranty, vocational rehabilitation, and life insurance.

The Veterans Health Administration is the largest integrated health system in the country. It includes more than 1,400 health care delivery locations including hospitals, community-based outpatient clinics, nursing homes, domiciliaries, and readjustment counseling centers.

The VHA also provides unparalleled training in its facilities for students of medical schools nationwide. The VHA is the nation's largest provider of graduate medical education and a major contributor to medical and scientific research that benefits all Americans, not just veterans seeking care at VA facilities. Medical training offered through VHA for civilian medical students in practical applications as well as research have led to groundbreaking advances in medicine over the years.

The National Cemetery Administration oversees the operations of 125 national cemeteries worldwide that provide dignified burial services for military veterans and eligible family members. The NCA also issues headstones, markers, and Presidential Memorial certificates for eligible deceased veterans, as well as administering Federal grants to states that establish state veterans' cemeteries.

The VA and Veterans Work with Congress

The Secretary of the Department of Veterans Affairs (VA) works closely with Congress to ensure VA is capable of meeting the nation's obligation to provide health care and benefits to all eligible veterans.

The House Committee on Veterans' Affairs was authorized by enactment of Public Law 601, 79th Congress, to consist of 27 members. That number has changed over the years, and there are currently 30 members of the House Committee on Veterans' Affairs. The committee also has subcommittees: the Subcommittee on Disability Assistance and Memorial Affairs, Subcommittee on Economic Opportunity, Subcommittee on Health, and the Subcommittee on Oversight and Investigations.

The House Committee on Veterans Affairs is the authorizing committee for the Department of Veterans Affairs. The committee recommends legislation creating and improving existing laws relating to veterans' health care and benefits. The committee also has oversight responsibility, to ensure VA is indeed providing benefits to eligible veterans in a timely manner and that veterans are properly recognized.

If a veteran experiences problems with accessing health care or benefits through VA they can turn to their congressional representatives for assistance. Senators and Congressmen have staff dedicated to veterans' issues who can usually cut through some of the bureaucratic red tape that hinders access to VA benefits. It is important for veterans to play an active role in the political process by registering to vote and by sharing their concerns with their elected officials.

In Conclusion

From its founding, America has been committed to supporting those who have risked their lives in defense of their country. As the number of veterans has grown, and as a broad range of benefits has been authorized, so, too, has the bureaucracy expanded to administer them. We'll discuss the agency and the VA benefits it governs in the chapters ahead.

CHAPTER 2

In Times of War and Peace

Who Is Eligible for VA Benefits

The conditions under which a servicemember leaves the armed forces will determine his or her eligibility for veterans benefits. Anything less than an honorable discharge will impact eligibility. This chapter reviews the various categories of discharge and offers guidance for appealing a less than honorable discharge. We will also review other criteria for benefits eligibility.

Former prisoners of war (POWs) have earned special benefits. Nearly a third of the Americans held prisoner in the last five conflicts are now living. The physical hardships and psychological stress endured by POWs have lifelong ramifications. This chapter will detail the eligibility requirements to be considered a POW and the additional benefits earned.

Your Military Discharge Papers Are the Key

Every servicemember who is discharged from active duty receives a *DD Form 214*, a military discharge certificate. This document is essential for all former servicemembers applying for benefits. Keep the original in a safe place and make copies to attach to your applications for benefits.

Actually there are eight copies of the DD Form 214. You automatically receive copy 1 when you separate, and have the option of receiving—or not receiving—copy 4. This is important because only on copy 4 does one find the character of service and reason for discharge. This means that only by looking at copy 4 can anyone determine under what circumstances you separated from the service, which may be of importance to future employers.

The DD Form 214 is a complete summary of your military service. Employers will often request an applicant's DD Form 214 and may or may not hire an individual based on the information within. The DD-214 includes:

- Total time in service
- Dates of entry and separation
- Dates of rank
- Documentation of foreign service, ribbons, medals, and badges awarded
- Military education completed

and as we will discuss in this chapter,

- Characterization of service
- Reason for discharge

Both the *character of service* and *reason for discharge* items play a role in determining your eligibility for veterans benefits. Ideally, you paid careful attention to your discharge status *before* you left the service. If, however, you now believe there is an error in the type of discharge you received or that the decision was inequitable or improper, we'll review your options for reconsideration.

The character of your discharge is how it is described on your discharge papers:

- Honorable
- General (under honorable conditions)
- Under other than honorable conditions
- Uncharacterized (entry-level separation)
- Bad conduct
- Dishonorable

The first four are considered administrative separations. A bad conduct discharge and a dishonorable discharge are considered punitive discharges and can only result from a special or general court-martial.

If You Received an Honorable Discharge

This is the gold standard. As long as the individual benefit criteria are met, it opens the door to all veterans benefits.

An honorable characterization is issued when the servicemember has met the standards of acceptable conduct and performance of duty for military personnel. You may not necessarily have completed your term of service to receive an honorable discharge, as long as your separation is not due to misconduct. For example, if you incurred an injury or illness and can't perform your assigned duties, you may receive an honorable discharge even if you have not completed your term of service. An *Honorable Discharge Certificate (DD Form 256)* is awarded along with the standard copy of the discharge form, DD Form 214.

If You Received a General Discharge (Under Honorable Conditions)

This characterization is issued to a servicemember when his or her service has been honest and faithful but is marred by significant negative aspects of conduct or performance of military duty. For example, a servicemember who performs his duties satisfactorily but has an ongoing pattern of minor misconduct during his off-hours that is burdensome to his command. Servicemembers with this classification of discharge will not normally be able to reenlist in any branch of the U.S. military.

A general Discharge, even "under honorable conditions," is not an honorable Discharge. A servicemember with this characterization of service is eligible for most VA benefits provided the individual benefit criteria is met. The major exception is the Montgomery GI Bill education benefits.

There is a common misconception that less than honorable discharges are automatically upgraded to "honorable" discharges after six months. *This is absolutely untrue.* You are *eligible* to appeal for an honorable discharge after six months, but there are no guarantees and in fact, the chances of being granted an upgrade are slim. We'll discuss how to file an appeal for an upgrade, however, after reviewing the other types of discharges.

If You Received an Under Other Than Honorable Conditions Discharge

This characterization of service is given to a servicemember when the reason for separation is based on behavior for one or more acts that are a significant departure from the conduct expected of members of the military services. These violations are punishable under the punitive articles of the Uniform Code of Justice and subject to trial by court-martial. Examples include failure to follow a lawful order, missing movement, extended unauthorized absence, desertion, and assault.

It is generally believed that an under other than honorable conditions discharge will render an individual ineligible for all VA benefits. This is not always so. The Department of Veterans Affairs can make its own determination as to whether the misconduct should warrant denial of any or all VA benefits. The determination is only for VA benefits and does not change the character of service. The VA will not grant any benefits if it determines that the reason for the discharge was due to the following offenses: (1) desertion; (2) sentence by general court-martial; (3) conscientious objector who refuses to perform military duties, wear the uniform, or comply with lawful orders of competent military authorities; (4) willful or persistent misconduct; (5) offense (s) involving moral turpitude; (6) mutiny or spying; (7) homosexual acts involving aggravating circumstances; (8) alien requesting release during a period of hostilities, or (9) absence without leave for 180 days or more without compelling reasons.

Former servicemembers seeking this form of relief should apply for VA benefits. Then, if benefits are denied, they should request that an administrative board review the discharge for possible benefits. The VA does not provide a special form, so the request should be in a letter format addressed to the VA regional office that denied the benefits.

If You Received a Bad Conduct Discharge

A bad conduct discharge is awarded only by an approved sentence of a general or a special court-martial, and is usually part of a sentence that includes confinement. The servicemember doesn't receive the bad conduct discharge until he or she completes his or her incarceration and the appeals process. The servicemember is ineligible for veterans benefits.

If You Received a Dishonorable Discharge

This is the most severe type of discharge that can be awarded. A servicemember receives a dishonorable discharge only as part of a sentence imposed by a general court-martial for offenses like rape, murder, or desertion. All veterans benefits are forfeited. This characterization will likely affect post-service employment, as well, as most employers are reluctant to hire individuals who have dishonorable discharges.

Uncharacterized (entry-level separation)

This type of separation is given to a servicemember who has less than 180 days of military service or when discharge action was initiated prior to 180 days of service. The individual's service is not characterized as good or bad. A servicemember who receives an uncharacterized (entry-level separation) is not eligible for veterans benefits unless injury or illness was incurred as a result of service.

Administrative separations are usually initiated by the unit commander to correct unacceptable behavior before starting discharge procedures. Once discharge proceedings are begun, a certain procedure must be followed. (If these steps are not followed, you may have reason for appeal.)

- The commanding officer must put in writing why he or she is initiating discharge and the reasons for this category of separation.
- The servicemember must be advised that he or she can seek counsel and present statement on his or her own behalf.
- The servicemember must sign an acknowledgment that he or she received and understands the discharge memorandum.
- The servicemember must sign a document that acknowledges the type of discharge being issued.

The Reason for Discharge Makes a Difference

The second element of your separation is the reason for discharge. This explains why you have left the service. You want to be sure, if possible, that the reason given for your discharge reflects well on your character and military service. If not, as you will see later in this chapter, you may want to appeal the reason given for discharge.

The most common reasons given for discharge are

- Expiration of term of service
- Disability, dependency, or hardship
- Pregnancy/parenthood
- Physical or mental conditions that interfere with military service
- Convenience of the government
- Misconduct

If You Want to Appeal a Discharge

Former servicemembers can and should apply for a correction if they believe that their character of service, reason for discharge, or any other aspect of their service record is in error or unjust.

Congress has authorized two administrative boards to consider these issues: the *Military Discharge Review Boards* and the *Boards for Correction of Military Records.* While the purpose of each of the boards is to correct service records, their composition and authority, as well as the criteria for applying, are different. The following provides some basic guidance on what each board can consider and how to apply.

The Military Discharge Review Boards (MDRB) have authority to review the discharge or dismissal of any former servicemember, not sentenced by a general court-martial, who applies within 15 years from the date of discharge.

Their jurisdiction is limited to review of the character of service and reason for discharge. More specifically, the MDRB has authority to review the following characterization of service:

- Uncharacterized (entry-level separation)
- General (under honorable conditions)
- Under other than honorable conditions
- Bad conduct discharges issued by special court-martial

The MDRB can also correct all administrative narrative reasons, except physical disability.

The MDRB do not have authority to

- Downgrade any discharge or dismissal being reviewed
- Review discharges issued by general court-martial
- Change reenlistment codes or SPD codes
- Reinstate former servicemembers to active duty
- Change physical disability separations

Application for Review of Discharge or Dismissal from the Armed Forces of the United States (DD Form 293) is the proper form to use in applying to the MDRB. It is available on the Web, at VA offices, and through veterans service organizations.

The Board for Correction of Military Records (BCMR) has authority to correct any error or injustice in the service record of active duty or discharged members with the following stipulations:

- All other administrative remedies have been exhausted.
- The application is filed within three years of the date of discovery of an error or injustice.

All other administrative remedies include MDRB review, if applicable, for less than honorable discharges, and National Personnel Records Center (NPRC) and service department reviews for awards and decorations. The BCMR will waive the three-year rule if it is found in the interest of justice.

Application for Correction of Military Record Under the Provisions of Title 10, U.S. Code, Section 1552 (DD Form 149) is the proper form to use in applying to the BCMR. It is available on the Web, at VA offices, and through Veterans Service Organizations.

This information provides you with the basics for applying. However, many filing procedures and issues presented for consideration can become quite complicated, and both the MDRB and the BCMR are prevented, under law, from providing former servicemembers any assistance with their petition. A few of the major Veterans Service Organizations have representatives that specialize in this area. It is in your best interest to contact one of them if you need assistance. The cost of the service is paid for by their members and is free to you.

Appeals are difficult and do not often succeed. You might appeal over a relatively minor typo on the DD Form 214, or a more grievous charge such as abuse of command influence. Overall grants (e.g., the veteran's appeal is granted) for both active duty and separated personnel at the BCMR are in the 30 percent to 40 percent range. Discharge reviews at the MDRB are in the 5 percent to 10 percent range. Exact numbers are hard to get.

Clemency is the only way to have a bad conduct discharge upgraded. You must apply for it. Both MDRB and BCMR have authority to grant clemency. The most common reason for granting clemency is by documenting outstanding post-service conduct. If the board determines that the circumstances, in total, warrant relief, they may grant it.

You can also appeal for a change to the reason assigned for discharge. For example, you may believe that there is a serious stigma associated with personality disorder as the reason for discharge and seek a different description.

Prisoner of War Status Confers Additional Benefits

As a veteran, you are entitled to certain benefits and services. If you are also a former prisoner of war, you are eligible for additional benefits including medical care in VA hospitals and disability compensation for injuries and disease *presumed* to be caused by your internment. Some states offer additional benefits, large and small, to former POWs. For example, California extends to qualified disabled war veterans or prisoners of war a pass for a onetime fee of $3.50, which entitles the holder to the use of all basic state park system–operated facilities, at no further charge. Check Appendix H for a complete list of the Department of Veterans Affairs for each state.

Remember: These benefits are not charity. You have *earned* them and should take full advantage of benefits and services to which you are entitled. You should pursue this claim both for yourself, but also for your spouse. The compensation will pass on to him/her.

Congress defines a prisoner of war as a person who, while serving on active military, naval, or air service, was forcibly detained by an enemy government or a hostile force, during a period of war or in situations comparable to war. For some presumed conditions, there is a requirement that the POW was interned for at least 30 days. However, the individual would still be considered a POW if he or she were held for less time. Nearly a third of the Americans held prisoner in the last five conflicts are now living. The physical hardships and psychological stress endured by POWs have lifelong ramifications.

According to the Department of Veterans Affairs, 142,246 Americans were captured and interned during World War I, World War II, the Korean War, the Vietnam War, the Gulf War, the Somalia and Kosovo conflicts, and Operation Iraqi Freedom. As you can see, POW status is conferred on servicemembers held captive by enemy government not only when war has been formally declared, such as World War I and World War II, but also in "situations comparable to war," such as Kosovo, Somalia, and the current Global War on Terrorism. However, you are not considered a POW if you were held hostage by a terrorist or detained by a government with which the United States is not engaged actively in armed conflict. If you have been interned during your service, but have questions as to your status, consult with a Veterans Service Organization to clarify your rights.

POW coordinators are assigned to each VA regional office and medical center. Veterans Service Organizations, both the general ones and those specifically for former prisoners of war, train service officers to advocate for veterans and specifically, to assist former POWs with their claims. Appendix G includes a complete list of Veterans Service Organizations and requirements for membership.

Medical Evaluation of Former POWs

If you are a former POW, you are enrolled in Priority Group 3 and receive special priority for VA health care even if your illness is not formally associated with your service. You are also exempt from co-payments for inpatient and outpatient medical care and medications, but are responsible for the same co-pay rules for extended care. As of August 2006, 16,884 former POWs were listed as receiving compensation benefits from the VA, with 13,000 rated at 100 percent disabled.

Usually, proving that your injury or disease is service connected is a critical element of the VA compensation process. Detailed medical records are required to establish the connection between service and injury.

But the VA recognizes that military medical records do not cover the period of captivity for former POWs so it has developed the concept of *presumptive basis.* This means the VA assumes that the disease or injury in the present is a result of captivity or internment in the past if any of the following disabilities are found at *any time* after service at a compensable level (at least 10 percent disabling). Remember: Symptoms may show up years after captivity, but may still be considered related to captivity.

For POWs detained for 30 days or more, the conditions that meet the eligibility requirements for presumptive basis include vitamin deficiency diseases such as beriberi and pellagra, chronic dysentery, helminthiasis, malnutrition, miscellaneous nutritional deficiencies, residuals of frostbite, post-traumatic osteoarthritis, peripheral neuropathy, irritable bowel syndrome, peptic ulcer disease, or ischemic heart disease (if there was localized edema during captivity). Several diseases are presumptively associated with captivity and do not require meeting the 30-day captivity limit: psychosis, any anxiety state, dysthymic disorders, cold injury, post-traumatic arthritis, strokes, and common heart diseases.

Although there is a "presumptive basis" of connection between disability and captivity, the VA retains the right to determine the level of disability. The amount of disability compensation you receive is based on your disability rating by the VA Rating Board. Your compensation may be increased or affected by the following factors.

- If you are rated 30 percent or more disabled, you qualify for additional allowance for your dependents.

- If you are rated 100 percent disabled, your dependents may also qualify for educational assistance.
- If you were rated 100 percent disabled for 10 years prior to your death (or if you die as the result of service-connected disabilities), your spouse is eligible for dependency and indemnity compensation.

The length of your captivity also affects your eligibility for other benefits. For example, if you were held for more than 90 days, you are eligible for any needed dental treatment. If you were held for less than 90 days, you are eligible only for service-connected, noncompensable (e.g., not compensated for) dental conditions.

Presenting a Claim

Use a service officer from a Veterans Service Organization to help you file a claim *VA Form 21–526 Veterans Application for Compensation and/or Pension* for POW benefits. There is no charge for assistance, which you undoubtedly will need for this complicated form. The claim must clearly demonstrate how some of the 20-plus POW presumptives apply to your case. Even if your captivity took place more than 25 years ago, the circumstances of your imprisonment may be affecting your health today. For example, most prisoners of war are physically abused and oftentimes beaten. The injuries may heal, but lasting disabling effects may not develop until years later such as post-traumatic osteoarthritis.

In Conclusion

Establishing eligibility for veterans benefits is the critical first step. The type of military discharge you receive will determine the benefits for which you are eligible. If you are a former prisoner of war, you are entitled to additional benefits. Make sure your discharge papers are in order, and keep them in a safe place.

CHAPTER 3

In Triplicate, Please

Singer Pearl Bailey once said, "What the world really needs is more love and less paperwork."

Clearly the Department of Veterans Affairs never got the message. As every military vet can testify, whatever you need from the VA, paperwork is involved (even if it's the virtual kind). Proving eligibility for Federal, state, and private programs requires documentation. Applying for benefits entails completing forms that are often confusing. Appendix A details a complete listing of all VA forms.

Some paperwork has actually become "paperless." You will be able to complete certain forms online (although you may be required, in order for the form to be processed, to print out a signature verification form and mail/fax it in). But you will want to maintain a record of all applications, even if you've completed the electronic "paperwork," in a well-maintained home filing system.

This chapter will help you organize the documents you need to prove eligibility; provide you with an attack plan for filling out the endless forms (which can seem daunting); offer you smart filing systems so you can always produce the information you need; and even take you step-by-step through the process of replacing military documentation.

Tackling a VA Form

Filling out forms was part of military service. It's also part of your life as a veteran. Job and school applications, taxes, home purchases, mortgage applications—paperwork is part of our daily lives. Confronted with a three-page form that seems deliberately difficult to understand is frustrating. Here are some steps to simplify the most complex document.

Rule Number One: Don't Be Afraid to Ask for Help

An important sign of maturity is knowing when you need help and asking for it. Don't let pride or misinformation stand in the way of getting the benefits you've earned. Ask help from a Veterans Service Organization, the regional VA office, a fellow vet, teacher, religious leader, friend, or relative. Just be careful that the person you ask is honest enough to admit when they don't understand something either.

Make a Trial Run

If it's a complex form, make a photocopy of the blank document and fill it out. If there is an essay, write it out, edit, rewrite as necessary. When you are satisfied with your answers, neatly copy them into the form you will submit.

Take Your Time

When you have to complete a form, don't rush. Think before you write. Read through it carefully before you fill it out. If it is a complex and important document, set aside time without interruption to work through it step-by-step.

Answer One Question at a Time

Don't be overwhelmed by the length of a form, the number of questions asked, or the amount of information required. Look over the form, make note of what data you will need in order to complete it, and assemble the necessary documents before you begin. You want to have everything at hand before starting.

Remember: Legibility and Neatness Count

It's not that you get extra credit for presenting a pristine form, but you want to be sure that the person who evaluates your application can clearly read your answers.

Don't Make Up Answers

Use the correct names and dates in your applications. If necessary, check reference sites online, in a dictionary, or veterans sites. If a word or question stumps you, check a dictionary for a definition—or ask for help (see rule number one).

Proofread and Then Proofread Again

Take your time and double-check your form before submitting it.

Important Documents/Forms You Will Need

Almost all VA benefits require proof of your military discharge, DD Form 214. You received this form when you separated from the service. Your discharge status (honorable, general, dishonorable, etc.) will impact the benefits you and your heirs may use. In chapter 2, we reviewed exactly what each type of discharge means and the appeals process should you want to attempt to change your discharge status.

But for the topics covered in this chapter, it is important that you have your discharge papers—and that you keep the original in a safe place and make multiple copies. You will never be required to submit the original; a photocopy is fully admissible for eligibility purposes.

Should you lose the original DD Form 214, you can apply to replace it (see below for more information). But it requires more paperwork and time. Keep the original in a safe, waterproof, fireproof place.

You will also want to keep in a safe place the originals of the following documents. You will need them for certain VA benefits. Make photocopies of each.

- Birth certificate
- Passport
- Marriage license
- Divorce papers
- Will
- Medical care directives
- Letter of last instructions/funeral plans
- Social Security card

Do I need a safe-deposit box?

Everyone has important documents that need to be kept in a safe place. These are the documents (and valuables) that must be protected in case of theft, fire, or natural disaster. Your will, the deed to your home, stock certificates, insurance policies, bonds, and your military discharge papers should all be kept in a fireproof, floodproof place. A safe-deposit box in a bank is a good idea. If you also store investments in the box—or information relating to investments—that generate taxable income, the rental fees may be tax deductible.

Make a list of all the items you place in your safe-deposit box and keep the list in your filing cabinet in a folder titled Important Documents.

If you don't want to rent your own box, consider asking your parents or a close relative to keep your military discharge papers and other important documentation in theirs.

Let's Get Organized

Kate Kelly, author of *Organize Yourself* and eight other organizing books, offers solid advice on developing a filing system that always puts the paperwork you need at your fingertips.

She points out that people tend to make four common mistakes when filing:

1. By not establishing a logical system, they can't remember where they've filed something.
2. If they establish a workable system, they don't keep up with it so filing becomes a huge chore (and gets ignored).
3. If they filed it once, they feel like they have to keep it forever—which is not necessarily true.
4. They file information readily available on the Internet, which just takes up space.

Kelly suggests that you need a filing system that is simple, easy to understand, and easily accessible to anyone. Let's start.

Contacts

You want to create a file of veteran-related contacts. If you already have an address book, create a separate section that will include all your VA and VA-related contacts.

- Ask for the business card of each person with whom you meet or get the contact details: name, title, address (postal and e-mail), telephone number and extension.
- Add in a brief explanation of job duties. You'll want to annotate the contact details because sometimes it's hard to remember exactly who does what when the file grows larger.
- Don't strive to be fancy: index cards in a file box are fine or you can create a file on your computer if you prefer.

Portable Files

This system is to organize the documents and correspondence you need to take with you when you meet with VA officials, VSO reps, doctors, educational administrators, and so forth.

This is a low-tech, simple, inexpensive method that lets you organize and carry all the information. You will need:

- Three-ring binder
- Folders with pockets
- Plastic tabs for labels

In the three-ring binder, put *copies* of the files you will need to take with you to various appointments. *Do not take the originals.*

Create labels that describe the material you will file in each folder. For example: VA medical information with names and contact info of doctors; applications to education programs and copies of VA benefits forms completed; correspondence and forms for appeals of VA benefits denied.

The basic rule is to create labels that will simplify your filing system and be easily understood for anyone trying to access your files.

Make duplicate copies of all correspondence: one for your file cabinet, one for the portable file. If you remove a file from a folder, make a note of the date and where you are taking it.

Set aside time to file paperwork each week, otherwise, it gets too overwhelming.

Create a Home Filing System

If you build yourself a good home filing system, you'll be able to locate important documents quickly. Here's what you need to know to create a home filing system that works for you.

The Hardware

This is the basic equipment you will need for a home filing system.

- Invest in a good, sturdy file cabinet. It can be used or new, one-, two-, or four-drawer, depending on the number of files you have. Allow room to grow. Put the cabinet near the place in your home where you will do your paperwork. You want to be able to easily access the files while you work.
- File folders and labels
- Waterproof pens
- An explanatory key to the files so that others can access the information if you are not available

The System

Kate Kelly recommends developing personalized, but easily understood filing categories. Here are some suggestions:

- Automobile
- Cash receipts (receipts for major purchases like appliances, jewelry, television)
- Credit records (for each credit card you have) including account numbers and name, address, and phone number to contact in case card is stolen or lost
- Employment
- Financial planning
- Guarantees and warranties—including instruction manuals
- Housing
- Important documents—copies of military discharge papers, birth certificates, passports, marriage license, divorce papers, will, information on location of original documents (If documents are in a safe-deposit box, note location of box *and* safe-deposit box key.)

- Insurance—copies of all policies
- Medical history records—for every member of family (Use a separate file folder for each family member and include history of family illnesses. For veteran, note dates of symptoms for possible documentation of service-related illness.)
- VA-related issues

Devise a Process That Works

Set aside time to think about the personal filing system you want to create for your papers. Go through all your paperwork and carefully file it according to the categories you have created. Ask yourself for each piece: Do I really need to save it? Can I get the information elsewhere? In what category does it belong?

If you have difficulty deciding on the category, cross-reference it in two files. Just put a reference slip in one file indicating the location of the information. Don't rely on your memory to keep track of files. Make a notation so you can easily access necessary documents.

The secret to a successful filing system is to keep up with the paperwork. Don't let it pile up. You can drown in paperwork, but more important, especially for VA-related issues, you must be able to easily and quickly access pertinent information.

If You Need to Replace Lost Documents

If you are a military veteran, you can get duplicates of your military records from the National Personnel Records Center, Military Personnel Records: NPRC (MPR). Next of kin of military veterans can also request these records. Next of kin is defined as surviving spouse who has not remarried, father, mother, son, daughter, sister, or brother.

There are several ways to request the information. The simplest method is to complete a request form online via E-vetrecs, www.archives.gov/veterans/evetrecs/.

Let's go page-by-page (screen-by-screen) through the questionnaire. Once you've completed it, you will have to print out a signature verification form, sign and date it, and submit it via U.S. mail or fax, in order to get the documentation you are requesting. The National Personnel Records Center cannot release documentation without a signature. You must submit the signature verification form within 20 days of filling out the online form, or the data is discarded.

Step 1

Privacy Act of 1974 Compliance Information and Paperwork Reduction Act Public Burden Statement.

PRESS CONTINUE BUTTON.

Step 2

Are you the veteran or next of kin of deceased veteran? If next of kin, what is your relationship (un-remarried surviving spouse, mother, father, son, daughter, sister, brother)?

Are you seeking information about former military service or current military service?

PRESS CONTINUE BUTTON.

Step 3 (a series of questions to answer)

What was the veteran's branch of service? (Army, Army Air Corps, Army Air Force, Air Force, Marine Corps, Navy, Coast Guard, Philippine Commonwealth Army, Philippine Guerillas, Philippine Scouts) If you served in more than one branch, you must complete a separate request for each branch.

What was the veteran's service component? (Active, Reserve, National Guard)

Was the veteran an officer or enlisted?

Select the most appropriate category for your request. Even if more than one applies: Benefits, Employment, Medical, Retirement, Military Awards/Decorations, Correction of Records, Personal Military History, Genealogy, Decline to Disclose. Depending on which category you select, on the right side of the screen, you will see what type of information the National Personnel Records Center will send you. In italics, you'll find what NPRC will answer for each category.

If you select:

BENEFITS

Based on the selections you have made, we will provide you with a Report of Separation.

A Report of Separation generally is needed for the following:

- *Home Loans*
- *Veteran Organizations Membership*
- *Social Security*
- *Burial/Flag*
- *Education*
- *Homeless Veteran Services*

EMPLOYMENT

You will be asked to answer whether you need Service Verification or Other.

If you select *OTHER:* Indicate in the "Comments" section in step 3 the specific documents or information you need.

MEDICAL

You will be asked to answer if you are requesting outpatient treatment records, inpatient treatment records, or mental health clinic records. You may request all three kinds of medical records in the "Comments" section of step 3. If you select OUTPATIENT TREATment records, you will be asked to choose whether you want records from when you were in service or after retirement from service.

If you choose in service medical records: *This treatment consists of physical examinations, sick call/clinic visits, immunizations, and so forth, and is filed in the veteran's service health record. We will provide a copy of the veteran's last physical examination report (performed at the time of separation/retirement from service). If you are seeking medical records for a specific injury or illness, please explain the nature of that injury/illness in the "Comments" section of step 3.*

If you choose after retirement from service: *In the Comments section of step 3 please provide the name or number and location of the hospital where the veteran was last treated and the last year of treatment.*

If you choose inpatient treatment records: *These are records of treatment created during a period of hospitalization. In the "Comments" section of step 3 please provide the name or number and location of the hospital and the year the veteran was hospitalized.*

If you choose mental health clinic records: *In the "Comments" section of step 3 please provide the name or number and location of the treatment facility and the month/year of treatment.*

RETIREMENT

You will be asked to answer if you are referencing Social Security Administration (SSA), Federal Civil Service Retirement, Other.

If you answer SSA, you will go to a new screen that will ask you to select the choice that best describes the veteran's status and year of discharge: Active Duty Only Prior to 1968; Active Duty Only After 1968; Active Duty Training Prior to 1968; Active Duty Training After 1968; Don't know.

If you answer active duty only prior to 1968, you will see: *Based on the selections you have made, we will provide you with a Report of Separation.*

If you answer active duty only after 1968, you will see that SSA has all military service earnings information. You do not need to verify with documents or information. You don't need to request duplicate documentation for this purpose and *you will exit this questionnaire.*

If you answer ACTIVE DUTY TRAINING PRIOR TO 1968, you will see: *Based on the selections you have made, we will provide you with a statement of your active-duty training dates.*

If you answer ACTIVE DUTY TRAINING AFTER 1968, you will see: *SSA has all military service earnings information.* You do not need to verify with documents or information. You don't need to request duplicate documentation for this purpose and *you will exit this questionnaire.*

If you answer DON'T KNOW, you will see: *Based on the selections you have made, we will provide you with a Report of Separation.*

MILITARY AWARDS/DECORATION

Submit requests for Navy, Marine Corps, and Coast Guard awards by mail to:

Bureau of Naval Personnel
Retired Records Section
Room 5409
Attn: PERS-313E
9700 Page Avenue
Saint Louis, MO 63132-5100

You will then exit this questionnaire.

Submit requests for replacement of Army or Air Force awards by clicking on the CONTINUE button. *Indicate in the "Comments" section of step 3 the specific awards to which the veteran is entitled that you wish to replace.*

CORRECTION OF RECORDS

You will be asked to answer whether it's Clerical Error or Board Action.

If you select CLERICAL ERROR, you will see: *We are authorized to make minor corrections on the Report of Separation, if the record contains substantiating documentation.*

Examples include:

- *Misspelled name*
- *Incorrect birth date*
- *Transposed digits in service number or SSN*

Please indicate in the "Comments" section in step 3 the specific correction required. You may send copies of official documents supporting the requested correction with your signature verification page.

If you select BOARD ACTION, you will see: *You will need to complete DD Form 293 or DD Form 149, as appropriate.*

Plus you will be asked to select one of the following: DISCHARGE UPGRADE: *If your discharge date is within the last 15 years, please complete and send DD Form 293 to the address listed on page 2 of the form. If your discharge date is more than 15 years ago, please complete and send DD Form 149 to the address listed on page 2 of the form.* OTHER RECORD CORRECTION: *Complete and send DD Form 149 to the address listed on page 2 of the form.*

You will then exit this online questionnaire.

PERSONAL MILITARY HISTORY

Based on the selections you have made, we will provide you with a Report of Separation.

If you require documents other than a Report of Separation, please indicate in the "Comments" section in step 3 the specific documents or information you need.

GENEALOGY

Based on the selections you have made, we will provide you with a Report of Separation.

If you require documents other than a Report of Separation, please indicate in the "Comments" section in step 3 the specific documents or information you need.

DECLINE TO DISCLOSE

We ask for the information to help us provide the best possible response and it will in no way be used to deny your request. If you wish to change your response, please do so now.

Based on the selections you have made, we will provide you with a Report of Separation. Please indicate in the "Comments" section in step 3 other documents required.

RECORD LOCATOR INFORMATION

You will need your military service information to complete this section. Besides your name (the one used during service), address, Social Security number, and date and place of birth, you will be asked for your service number and approximate date of separation from service.

If you don't have some of the information, complete what you do have. It will then take you to the next screen, which asks what documentation you are requesting. If it's a Separation Document, you may choose to get an *undeleted* version which includes such sensitive items as the character of separation, authority for separation, reason for separation, reenlistment eligibility code, separation (SPD/SPN) code, and dates of time lost. An undeleted version is ordinarily required to determine eligibility for benefits.

If you choose a deleted version, the following information will be deleted from the copy sent: authority for separation, reason for separation, reenlistment eligibility code, separation (SPD/SPN) code, and for separations after June 30, 1979, character of separation and dates of time lost. Since this section includes the character of your separation, if it reveals a less than honorable or more severe discharge, you may prefer this edited version.

This page also has a box to add other documents you are requesting.

On the next page, you will give your contact information.

PRESS CONTINUE BUTTON.

The final screen allows you to review the information you've submitted. Once you press CONTINUE, you won't be able to go back and make any changes. You will then move to a signature verification page. Your request *will not be processed* until you either print out the Signature Verification form *or* write the Service Request Number (the bar code with numbers underneath on the right side of the screen) and the declaration statement on a blank sheet of paper. Sign, date, and mail to:

NPRC WEB
9700 Page Avenue
St. Louis, MO 63132-5100
Sign, date, and fax to:
314-801-9049

If you don't want to complete an online form, you can download a copy of Form 180 from the National Personnel Records Center website: www.archives.gov/st-louis/military-personnel/standard-form-180.html. You can also obtain a copy of Form 180 if you write to:

The National Personnel Records Center
9700 Page Avenue
St. Louis, MO 63132

Other sources of a copy of Form 180 include the Department of Defense, Federal Information centers, your local Veterans Affairs office, Veterans Service Organizations. Note that you can use a photocopy of the form to submit your request, but you must submit a separate form for each individual whose records are being requested.

You can also submit a request for military records without Form 180. But it is not a good idea since you must include enough information to identify the record from the more than 70 million on file. Include the following:

- The veteran's complete name used while in service
- Service number or Social Security number

- Branch of service
- Dates of service
- Date and place of birth (especially if the service number is not known)

1973 Fire Destroys Military Personnel Records

In 1973, a fire at the National Personnel Records Center destroyed approximately 16 to 18 million Official Military Personnel Files. What was lost?

- Eighty percent of records of Army personnel who were discharged November 1, 1912, to January 1, 1960
- Seventy-five percent of records of Air Force personnel discharged September 25, 1947, to January 1, 1964 (with names alphabetically after Hubbard, James E.)

No duplicate copies of the records that were destroyed in the fire were maintained, nor was a microfilm copy ever produced. There were no indexes created prior to the fire. In addition, millions of documents had been lent to the Department of Veterans Affairs before the fire occurred. Therefore, a complete listing of the records that were lost is not available.

The NPRC does use alternate sources to re-create basic service information to respond to requests. A primary source of alternate data is a collection of 19 million final pay vouchers. These records provide name, service number, dates of service, and character of service. These are the most critical service data elements needed for the reconstruction process. With these and other organizational records (enlistment ledgers, service number indexes, etc.), NPRC personnel can usually verify military service and provide a Certification of Military Service. This certification can be used for any purpose for which the original discharge document was used, including the application for veterans benefits.

To reconstruct Medical-Related Alternate Records, NPRC, Military Personnel Records (MPR) uses several sources. In 1988, a collection of computer tapes containing 10 million hospital/treatment facility admission records was transferred to NPRC (MPR). These records, originally created by the U.S. Army Surgeon General's Office (SGO), were discovered by the National Academy of Sciences and offered to the National Archives for use by NPRC (MPR). The source records existed in a computer code format and required extensive analysis to interpret the code into English. Between 1988 and 1990, NPRC (MPR) was able to salvage 7.8 million records of individual admissions for use as a major supplement to other smaller sources of medical information.

The subjects of the records were active-duty Army and Army Air Corps personnel in service between 1942 and 1945. In addition, active-duty Army personnel who served between 1950 and 1954 and a limited number of Marine Corps, Navy, Air Force, and military cadet personnel for the same period (about 5 percent of the 1950–1954 file) are included.

The admissions records are not specific or detailed medical documents, but summarized information indexed by military service number. They contain limited medical treatment information, but diagnosis, type of operation, and dates/places of treatment or hospitalization are frequently included. Although no names are shown, patients are identified by military service number and certain personal data including age, race, sex, and place of birth. The reconstructed records were created using data sampling techniques for statistical purposes. Therefore, the listings are not complete and many admissions were skipped during the sampling process. Nevertheless, the information is useful as proof to support certain benefit claims.

To access any of this reconstructed data, you must supply NPRC (MPR) as much information from old personal records as possible. Once you have submitted a request, if NPRC (MPR) doesn't have enough information to act, you may be asked to complete NA Form 13075, Questionnaire About Military Service and/or NA Form 13055, Request for Information Needed to Reconstruct Medical Data.

Patience Required for Documentation Request

It's hurry-up-and-wait once your request is submitted. You may submit more than one request per envelope or fax, but you need a separate form/request for each individual whose records are being requested.

Address to:

National Personnel Records Center
Military Personnel Records
9700 Page Avenue
St. Louis, MO 63132-5100
Fax: 314-801-9195

Currently, NPRC (MPR) has a pending workload of 45,000 requests, and receives 4,000 requests per day! NPRC (MPR) says it is able to fulfill requests for separation documents in about 10 days (in 92 percent of cases). But reconstructing information that was lost in the 1973 fire takes much longer (six months or more).

In Conclusion

One of the keys to success in life is being organized. It's also one of the most important factors in dealing with a huge bureaucracy—and that's certainly the case with the VA. You need to be able to put your hand on your documents and correspondence, even if the person at the other end of the line can't find their copies. Keep on top of the paperwork when you file a claim.

CHAPTER 4

Advocates for Vets

There is strength in numbers. A lone voice can be easily ignored. But joined together with others who have been in the literal and figurative foxhole with you, you will be noticed. Your cause will be heard.

There are strong practical and emotional reasons to join one or more Veterans Service Organizations (VSOs). In addition to a variety of membership perks, it's important to remember that these groups are strong advocates for the men and women who have served their country. They are your representatives. They lobby Federal and state legislatures on your behalf to ensure adequate funding for veterans benefits and health care. They are the leaders who speak out on behalf of veterans of wars past, present, and future.

Consider Different Types of Organizations

There are hundreds of different Veterans Service Organizations. Some are all-inclusive, like American Veterans (AMVETS), while others are limited to those who have served during wartime, like the American Legion. Others represent specific religious groups of veterans, for example, Catholic War Veterans, USA. and Jewish War Veterans, USA. Still others recruit members who share a race or ethnicity, such as National Association for Black Veterans, or Italian-American War Veterans of the USA. For some, the focus is on veterans of a certain war, like Veterans of World War I of the USA, and Vietnam Veterans of America. There are groups for dependents of veterans, for example, American Gold Star Wives and Gold Star Mothers. And there are organizations for veterans who are disabled during their service such as Disabled American Veterans and Paralyzed Veterans of America.

Without question, there is a group, probably several groups, that will meet your interests and needs.

Chartered Organizations

The VSOs below are "chartered," which means they are "Organizations Chartered by Congress and/or Recognized by VA for Claim Representation." These organizations have staff (volunteer and/or paid) to assist veterans in pursuit of benefits denied.

Air Force Sergeants Association
American Defenders of Bataan and Corregidor
American Ex–Prisoners of War
American GI Forum of the United States
American Gold Star Mothers, Inc.
American Legion
American Red Cross
American War Mothers
AMVETS
Armed Forces Services Corporation
Army and Navy Union, USA, Inc.
Blinded Veterans Association
Blue Star Mothers of America, Inc.
Catholic War Veterans, USA, Inc.
Congressional Medal of Honor Society of the United States of America
Disabled American Veterans
Fleet Reserve Association
Gold Star Wives of America, Inc.
Italian American War Veterans of the USA

Jewish War Veterans of the USA
Legion of Valor of the USA, Inc.
Marine Corps League
Military Chaplains Association of the United States of America
Military Order of the Purple Heart of the USA, Inc.
Military Order of the World Wars
National Amputation Foundation, Inc.
National Association for Black Veterans, Inc.
National Association of County Veterans Service Officers, Inc.
National Association of State Directors of Veterans Affairs (NASDVA)
National Veterans Legal Services Program
Navy Club of the United States of America
Navy Mutual Aid Association
Non Commissioned Officers Association
Paralyzed Veterans of America
Pearl Harbor Survivors Association, Inc.
Polish Legion of American Veterans, USA
The Retired Enlisted Association
Swords to Plowshares: Veterans Rights Organization
United Spinal Association
US Submarine Veterans of World War II
Veterans Assistance Foundation, Inc.
Veterans of Foreign Wars of the United States
Veterans of the Vietnam War, Inc./Vets. Coalition
Veterans of World War I of the USA, Inc.
Vietnam Veterans of America
Women's Army Corps Veterans Association

Non-Chartered Organizations

These Veteran Service Organizations are *not* chartered or recognized by Congress and/or Recognized by VA for Claim Representation. Membership in these groups is also beneficial in ensuring that veterans benefits are secured and protected. The larger the membership, the stronger the voice of advocacy.

African American Veterans and Families
Air Force Association
Air Force Women Officers Association
Air Warrior Courage Foundation, Inc.
All Faith Consortium
Alliance of Women Veterans
Americal Division Veterans Association
American Coalition for Filipino Veterans
American Merchant Marine Veterans
American Military Retirees Association
American Military Society
American Retiree Association
American Veterans Alliance, Inc.
American Veterans for Equal Rights, Inc.
American Volunteer Reserve
American World War II Orphans Network (AWON)
Arab American War Veterans, Inc.
Army Aviation Association of America
Asian American Veterans Association
Association of the 199th Light Infantry Brigade
Association of Ex-POW of the Korean War, Inc.
Association of Military Surgeons (AMSUS)
Association for Service Disabled Veterans
Association of the US Army, USA
Association of Veterans Education Certifying Ofc.
Blinded American Veterans Foundation
Bureau of Maine Veterans Services
BVL Fund—Bowlers Serving America's Veterans
The Center for Internee Rights, Inc.
China Burma India Veterans Association, Inc.
The Chosin Few

Cold War Veterans Association
Combined National Veterans Association of America
Congressional Black Caucus Veterans Braintrust
CWO&WO Association US Coast Guard
Daughters of Union Veterans of the Civil War
Destroyer Escort Sailors Association
Eighth Air Force Historical Society
Enlisted Association of the National Guard of the US
Florida Department of Veterans Affairs
The Forty & Eight
Help Hospitalized Veterans
Hispanic War Veterans of America
Homeless & Disabled Veterans
Japanese American Veterans Association
Japanese American Veterans Counsel
Korea Veterans of America
Korean Defense Veterans of America
Korean Ex–Prisoners of War
Korean War Veterans Association of the USA, Inc.
LSM-LSMR Association
Marine Corps Reserve Association
Military Justice Clinic, Inc.
Military Officers Association of America
NAM-POWS, Inc.
National 4th Infantry (IVY) Division Association
National Academy for Veterans Service Officers
National Alliance for the Mentally Ill
National American Indian Veterans
National Association of American Veterans, Inc.
National Association of Atomic Veterans
National Association of Black Military Women (NABMW)
National Association of Concerned Veterans
National Association of Fleet Tug Sailors, Inc.
National Association of Radiation Survivors

National Association for Society of Military Widows
National Association of State Veterans Homes
National Association of State Women Veterans Coordinators
National Association for Uniformed Services
National Association of Veterans Program Administrators
National Coalition for Homeless Veterans
National Congress of Puerto Rican Veterans, Inc.
National Guard Association of the United States
National Gulf War Resource Center, Inc.
National League of Families of American Prisoners and Missing in Southeast Asia
National Military Family Association
National Order of Battlefield Commissions
National Society Daughters of the American Revolution
National Society of New England Women
National Veterans Business Development Corporation
National Veterans Foundation
The National Veterans Organization of America
National Vietnam Veterans Coalition
Naval Enlisted Reserve Association
Naval Reserve Association
Navy League of the United States
Navy Nurse Corps Association
Navy Seabee Veterans of America
New Era Veterans, Inc. (NY & PA Registered)
OSS-101 Veterans Association
P-38 National Association
The Red River Valley Fighter Pilot
Reserve Officers Association of the United States
The 2nd Airborne Ranger Association, Inc.
SHAEF/Etousa Veterans Association
Society of Military Widows
TLC Brotherhood, Inc.

Tragedy Assistance Program for Survivors, Inc.
United Armed Forces Association
United States Army Warrant Officers Association
United States Federation of Korea Veterans Org.
United States Merchant Marine Veterans of World War I
United States Merchant Marine Veterans of World War II
United States Navy Cruiser Sailors Association
United States Navy Veterans Association
United States Submarine Veterans, Inc.
United States Volunteers
USCG Chief Petty Officers Association
Veterans of America
Veterans of the Battle of the Bulge
Veterans Leadership Program of Western PA
Veterans and Military Families for Progress
Veterans United for a Strong America
Veterans' Widows/ers International Network, Inc.
Vietnam Veterans Institute
Vietnam Veterans Memorial Fund
Vietnam Women's Memorial Foundation, Inc.
WAVES National
Women Airforce Service Pilots of World War II
Women in Military Service for America Memorial
The Women Marines Association
Women's Overseas Service League

VSOs Serve as Legislative Advocates

The camaraderie of a Veterans Service Organization is always welcome. Being surrounded by others who have shared similar experiences can be comforting. There are extra membership perks in many of these organizations. But one of the strongest reasons for joining one or more VSOs is that they represent you before Congress and state legislatures. They are your voices in Washington, D.C., and in state capitols. When the issue of veterans rights and benefits is being debated, VSOs take the lead to make sure that you and your family will not be shortchanged.

The national staffs of these organizations keep a close watch on all legislation and budgets that will affect vets. They advocate for veterans at each step of the legislative process. These efforts begin before any specific bill is introduced in Congress. At the start of each session of Congress, VSOs formally present their legislative goals to the House and Senate committees on Veterans' Affairs.

Let's take a piece of legislation step-by-step through Congress—and indicate when and where VSOs are involved.

1. At a VSO national convention, members pass an organizational resolution endorsing increases in a GI Bill benefit.
2. The national staff of the VSO edit the resolution if needed to put it into the technical language needed for a bill to be introduced in Congress.
3. The VSO staff works with the staff of the House and Senate Veterans' Affairs Committees to get the legislation drafted and introduced in Congress. The VSO staff also coordinates efforts with other members of Congress who have shown a strong interest in that particular issue or in veterans affairs in general. Sometimes members of Congress will approach a VSO offering to sponsor or cosponsor a certain piece of legislation. The congressional staff will work with the VSO staff in ensuring the legislation adequately addresses the issue.
4. Once the bill is introduced in either the House of Representatives or the Senate, it is referred to the standing Veterans' Affairs Committee or Veterans' Affairs Subcommittee with jurisdiction over the issue. Generally all veterans legislation is referred to these committees. Some legislation, like Mandatory Funding for VA health care will

require consideration in more than just the Veterans Affairs committees.

5. Once the bill is referred to the relevant committee or subcommittee (the Senate Veterans Affairs Committee does not have any subcommittees) VSO staff urges the chairman of the House committee or subcommittee and of the Senate committee to schedule hearings on the bill and work closely with the professional staff of the congressional committees.
6. The key to a successful lobbying effort is the combined strength of the VSO staff efforts on Capitol Hill coupled with the grassroots efforts of the volunteer side of the organization. VSO members write letters and send e-mails to members of Congress. Also, it is extremely helpful to actually take the time to visit the state office of individual members of Congress to discuss legislation.
7. Once a hearing has been scheduled by the committee or subcommittee of either the House or Senate, representatives of several veterans organizations are called as witnesses to testify on the legislation. Staff of the organization or one of the national officers then actually delivers testimony at a congressional hearing in the committee or subcommittee.
8. Once the full committee has approved the bill, it is "ordered reported" to the floor of the House for full member consideration. A similar track for this legislation is followed in the Senate. Once both houses of Congress have passed their versions of the legislation, it may be referred to an informal conference between the professional staffs of the two Veterans' Affairs committees (under the direction of the committee chairs) to iron out any minor differences. When there are major differences in the House and Senate versions of a bill, a formal conference of the members of Congress would be required.
9. After the final passage of a bill by Congress, the next step

is consideration by the President and hopefully his signature, which makes that bill a law.

Step Up as a Citizen Lobbyist

As a member of any Veterans Service Organization, you may be asked to be part of a grassroots effort in behalf of a piece of legislation. While members of Congress work closely with advocacy groups like the American Legion, the Veterans of Foreign Wars, and the Disabled Veterans, they also pay close attention to their constituents. After all, it's their constituents who vote on re-election of these legislators. Your letter, e-mail, or phone call to your Representative or Senator (or state legislator) could be the key to the passage of a bill that benefits all veterans. Step up when asked to support Veterans' Affairs legislation. If we as veterans do not join the fight to secure and protect the benefits that each of us earned through our service to this country, then we cannot expect Congress to do what is right.

Similar legislative advocacy takes place on the state level. Many state legislatures have committees on Veterans' Affairs. Veterans Service Organizations, on the national and local level, monitor and lobby on behalf of state legislation as well.

Veteran Service Officers Can Help You

Besides advocacy, this is one of the most important benefits many VSOs offer. They have trained staff who can help you file claims and appeals for VA benefits denied (see chapter 7) free of charge. The paperwork is complicated and must be completed carefully in order to be processed. There are deadlines to be met and legal language to be understood. The VA encourages veterans to work with an accredited Veterans Service Officer when filing a claim. Veterans Service Organizations do not require membership in order to access their service officers.

How to lobby effectively

When you join a grassroots lobbying effort, keep these tips in mind.

1. Write a personal letter rather than signing a form letter or petition. Members of the Federal and state legislatures appreciate the time and effort it takes to compose a personal appeal. You can use the material a VSO sends you (even a proposed letter), but put your letter on your own stationery and in your own words.
2. Never be abusive or antagonistic. Whether in a letter, on the phone, or in person, your goal is to persuade. You can't do that if you're angry or aggressive. Practice what you want to say and keep it short, simple, and to the point.
3. Follow up any appointment with a personal note, thanking the staff members for their time, summarizing the discussion of the meeting, and reiterating exactly what you hope the legislator will do (for example, vote on behalf of—or against—a certain bill).

"We've Been There—We're Here for You Now"

One of the important benefits of belonging to a VSO is the opportunity to give back to those servicemembers who are currently serving. As a veteran, you know the importance of a helping hand, for yourself while on duty, for your family who is coping while you are away. All VSOs have opportunities and programs to support our troops and their families. Get involved. From financial assistance to volunteers to help with household chores, VSOs offer a wide variety of programs to provide direct assistance swiftly to active-duty, Guard, and reserve servicemembers, as well as veterans and their families.

Some veterans organizations also volunteer to provide final honors for those veterans who have passed away. Many state departments and local posts field Honor Guard units that volunteer time to train and actually assist in the delivery of honors at military funerals. This program serves to ensure that deceased veterans receive the honor and respect they deserve as veterans of this country. For many families, this final honor is a lasting memory of their loved one's military service.

Additionally, VSO volunteers plant small U.S. flags at the gravesites of deceased veterans on Memorial Day, as well as Veterans Day each year.

VSOs Offer Other Benefits

Many VSOs offer their members a variety of other helpful benefits. For example, some VSOs offer dental insurance or eye care discounts to their members. Others may also offer health insurance (including short-term recovery insurance). Some organizations offer prescription drug plans—which may provide prescription drugs at a cheaper price than your employer's health care plan. Compare to see which is more cost effective. Some offer discounts on travel, hotels, car rentals, computers, cell phones, even discounts on satellite dish service for your television! Some organizations have programs to facilitate moving, selling or buying a home, and even special mortgage rates for their members.

In Conclusion

Becoming a member of a Veterans Service Organization allows each of us to continue to serve our country as volunteer protectors of the benefits and services afforded the brave men and women of our military who have served before us, with us, and who are wearing the uniform today. Together, we can continue the proud tradition of the generations who came before us in service to this country, and working together, ensure that America's veterans continue to receive the thanks of a grateful nation.

CHAPTER 5

Health Care for Veterans

The February 2007 news stories about the treatment of outpatients at Walter Reed Army Medical Center were shocking, heartbreaking, and frustrating. The appalling conditions of outpatient rooms and the neglect, delay, and bureaucratic snafus heaped on the most vulnerable of America's valiant servicemembers were inexcusable. As you know, these patients were still active-duty servicemen and -women, many suffering devastating injuries of body and mind, and under the care of the Department of Defense (DOD).

The medical system run by the Department of Veterans Affairs is separate from the DOD health care system. But both bureaucracies are facing the same overwhelming burdens: too many patients, too many forms, too little manpower, and too little preparation to cope. The VA system is struggling to deal with an unprecedented volume of injured veterans from the Iraq/Afghanistan conflicts, in addition to an aging Vietnam War generation of vets. There are 2.5 million veterans with service-connected disabilities being treated by the VA medical system. Although 5 million veterans are eligible for care, 3 of the 5 million have access to other forms of private insurance or Medicare but opt to use the VA system. Larry Korb, a senior fellow at the Center for American Progress who served as assistant secretary of defense under President Ronald Reagan, points out, "The VA care is excellent—the problem is getting [access to] it."

The tales of waiting six months to a year for basic services are legendary, and unfortunately true. The medical care within VA hospitals is exceptional, but the path to treatment can be tortuous, riddled with paper hurdles, lost records, and compounded by a bloated, inefficient bureaucracy.

This chapter is designed to help you determine your eligibility for VA health care, the services available, and the resources and methods to use to successfully appeal VA decisions.

The VA health care system can be a difficult, frustrating maze to navigate. You must document every step along the way so that if roadblocks appear, if paperwork disappears, if answers seem contradictory—you are prepared to do battle.

Why the System Is Struggling More Than Ever

The VA bureaucracy has always been huge; the paperwork has always been overwhelming. But there has been a sea change in the past few years that has strained the system almost to the breaking point. Here's why.

The wars in Iraq and Afghanistan have lasted longer than originally expected, resulting in the number of injured servicemembers to be far higher than anticipated (more than 24,000). Ironically, not only is the number greater than projected, but more grievously injured servicemembers are surviving. Body armor and expert battle-

Stay connected

It's critically important, especially with health care issues, that you connect with other veterans, through organized Veterans Service Organizations (see Appendix G), Veterans Centers, as well as through informal local connections. Networking with other vets will often give you the information and news on medical conditions resulting from service that you will need to get compensation and/or treatment. As Paul L. Hastings wrote in the *News and Record*, "The government is not going to proactively seek out any of us to say it owes us anything. The veterans will need to rely on other veterans to uncover their potential rights and dues."

field medicine have combined to achieve a startling 90-plus percent survival rate of injured servicemembers. Contrast that number to the survival rate of Vietnam-era servicemembers of only 76 percent. Go back to the American Civil War and you'll find that most injured servicemembers died.

But survival of the initial injury does not mean complete recovery. Quite the opposite. Current combat injuries have been devastating, and many veterans will require long-term care. According to the Department of Defense, two-thirds of all injuries in Iraq are from bombs, and of that number, 28 percent of the injured have suffered brain trauma.

Moreover, beyond the observable brain trauma, there are the mental and emotional tolls that come from surviving a combat zone. As Sgt. Jesse A. Downey, himself in injured servicemember at Womack Army Medical Center, explained in an interview with the *News and Observer* (Raleigh, NC), "There's no unwounded soldiers in combat. Even if a soldier didn't get hit by an [improvised bomb] or shot at, the things you see and the things you go through over there . . . it's something that's etched in your mind." The demand for psychological care has stretched already limited resources.

Furthermore, the system needs to service increasing numbers of Vietnam-era vets, who with age are facing greater medical needs. Factor in that this group is also increasingly at risk for psychological troubles as the images and news reports of the current war rekindle old traumas from the war of the '60s.

DOD Issues Disability Rating

Again, it's important to remember that the Department of Defense and the Department of Veterans Affairs are separate bureaucracies. The decisions by DOD do not impact the medical decisions of the VA. Theoretically, the DOD is supposed to use the Veterans Affairs Schedule for Rating Disabilities as the standard for assigning a rating, but some Pentagon directives state the VA schedule is only a guide.

Army, Navy, Air Force? The ratings controversy

An investigative report by *US News and World Report* found that since 2000, "fewer veterans have received ratings of 30 percent or more since America went to war in Afghanistan and Iraq. . . . As of 2006, for example, 87,000 disabled retirees were on the list of those exceeding the 30 percent threshold; in 2000, there were 102,000 recipients. Last year, only 1,077 of 19,902 servicemembers made it over the 30 percent threshold." This is important because if an injured veteran's disability rating is 20 percent or less, then the servicemember is sent home with a severance check; over 30 percent and he is eligible for full retirement pay, plus a host of other benefits.

Furthermore, there is a huge discrepancy among the military services. Although most of the wounded are from the Army and Marine Corps, those services have granted far fewer full disability benefits than the Air Force.

- Number of disabled Air Force Servicemembers rated 30 percent or more disabled: 26.3 percent
- Number of disabled Army Servicemembers rated 30 percent or more disabled: 4.3 percent
- Number of disabled Marines rated 30 percent or more disabled: 2.7 percent.

The DOD rating is issued before discharge, which also complicates the issue. So many servicemembers anxious to get home are reluctant to fight their ratings, even if those ratings clearly are unjust.

Veterans advocates argue that the law is clear: the DOD is required to use the VA schedule. Furthermore, a Government Accountability Office (GAO) report (March 2006) revealed that each branch of service interprets the schedule differently. For example, while rating an amputee's disability is fairly straightforward—the schedule automatically grants the injured servicemember an over 30 percent disabled rating, there is wide variation in ratings for mental disorders. Ratings for servicemembers suffering from Post-

Traumatic Stress Disorder (PTSD) vary widely both within each branch of service and among them.

Let's review how a servicemember who has been injured or become ill moves from DOD to VA care. There are several steps along the way, with an opportunity to appeal the DOD decision on fitness for duty and disability percentage.

✦ *The role of the Medical Evaluation Board.* If a servicemember is still on active service when he becomes injured or ill, he is referred to a Medical Evaluation Board (MEB). The MEB determines whether a medical condition interferes significantly with the member's ability to carry out the duties of his rank and rate. If the MEB determines that there is a significant interference, then the case is referred to an informal Physical Evaluation Board (PEB).

✦ *Physical Evaluation Board makes critical decision.* The informal PEB will determine if the servicemember is fit or unfit for duty. If it is determined that a servicemember is unfit for duty then the informal PEB can recommend discharge with severance pay or a disability retirement. The informal PEB will also assign a disability percentage.

2 *To appeal a PEB decision.* If a servicemember is dissatisfied with the determination that he is unfit for service or believes that the disability percentage assigned is not high enough, he may appeal to the formal PEB. The formal PEB will conduct a hearing where additional medical evidence and witnesses will be called to testify. The formal PEB will make a determination of fitness for duty and disability level based upon the hearing. It's important to remember: *VSO representatives are available free of cost to assist servicemembers in preparing their case for the PEBs.*

DOD Disability Rating Affects Payout

If the PEB decides that a servicemember has a disability that renders him or her unfit for duty, the next step is to determine the *DOD* disability rating. This evaluation can determine how much the disability is expected to impact his or her daily existence, ability to earn a living, and life expectancy. A disability rating can range from 0 percent to 100 percent. Depending on the severity of the disability rating, the servicemember can receive severance pay or disability pay.

- *Severance pay.* If the servicemember receives a rating of 0 percent, 10 percent, or 20 percent and has at least six months of active-duty service, but less than 20 years of active-duty service, that servicemember is entitled to severance pay. The amount of severance pay allotted is not related to the percentage of disability. Severance pay is calculated as the sum of two months' basic pay multiplied by the number of combined years of active service and inactive-duty training (but not more than 12 years).
- *Disability pay.* A servicemember who receives a disability of 30 percent or more, or a servicemember who has 20 or more years of active-duty service (regardless of his or her disability ranking), is either permanently or temporarily retired from service. If the servicemember has a 30 percent disability ranking or higher, he or she is entitled to whatever percentage of base pay the disability rating entitles him or her to receive.

Veterans Affairs Processing Is Separate

It's important for all servicemembers to realize that the Department of Veterans Affairs (VA) has its own disability process independent of the Armed Forces. Servicemembers are evaluated by the VA for a rating *after* separation.

To Summarize

If you have served *less than 20 years,* the severity of the *DOD disability rating* will affect whether or not you receive *military retirement pay, life insurance, health insurance,* and *access to military commissaries.*

The *VA disability rating* will determine how much *disability pay* you receive and in which *priority group* you will be placed, which affects your *access to care.*

Who Is Eligible for Medical Benefits?

The VA offers a full range of outpatient and inpatient services to all enrolled veterans—but not all vets who are enrolled in the system can actually access care. The key to being able to use these benefits is in which *priority group* you are assigned. The VA has developed this ranking system in order to control the number of veterans who use the health care system. Once you are enrolled, you can receive health care at any VA facility in the country.

The casualties from the wars in Iraq and Afghanistan have taxed the limits of the DOD health care system, and are also taxing the VA system. Veterans with service-connected disabilities and those below the low-income threshold are given priority for care.

The criteria for eligibility for most veterans' health care benefits is based solely on active military service in the Army, Navy, Air Force, Marines, or Coast Guard (or in the Merchant Marines during World War II) *and* a discharge under other than dishonorable conditions. Reservists and National Guard members who were called to active duty by a Federal Executive Order (for example, to serve in Iraq or Afghanistan) may qualify for VA health care benefits.

Returning servicemembers, including *Reservists* and *National Guard* members who served on *active duty* in a *theater of combat* operations, have *special eligibility* for *hospital care, medical ser-*

vices, and *nursing home care* for *two years following discharge* from active duty. Legislation has been introduced in Congress that seeks to increase this to *five* years.

You are not required to enroll if:

1. You are a veteran with a service-connected disability of 50 percent or more.
2. You are a veteran, *within 12 months of discharge,* seeking care for a disability the military determined was incurred or aggravated in the line of duty, but which the VA has not yet rated.
3. You are a veteran seeking care for a service-connected disability *only.*

If you are in one of those three groups, completing the paperwork for enrollment is not required in order to seek care, but *is strongly advised.*

Your Priority Group Affects Your Access to Care

You are assigned to a priority group based on the VA evaluation of your medical condition, your service experience (if you were a POW or were awarded the Purple Heart), and your income level. Following are the eight groups.

PRIORITY 1

- Veterans with service-connected disabilities rated 50 percent or more disabling, or
- Veterans determined by VA to be unemployable due to service-connected conditions

PRIORITY 2

- Veterans with service-connected disabilities rated 30 percent or 40 percent disabling

Priority 3

- Veterans with service-connected disabilities rated 10 percent or 20 percent disabling
- Veterans who are former POWs
- Veterans awarded the Purple Heart
- Veterans whose discharge was for a disability that began in the line of duty
- Veterans who are disabled because of VA treatment or participation in VA vocational rehabilitation program

Priority 4

- Veterans who are receiving aid and attendance or household benefits (on pension) from VA
- Veterans who have been determined by VA to be catastrophically disabled

Priority 5

- Veterans receiving VA pension benefits
- Veterans who are eligible for Medicaid programs
- Veterans with income and assets below VA Means Test Thresholds

Priority 6

- Veterans with 0 percent service-connected conditions, but receiving VA compensation
- Veterans seeking care only for disorders relating to Ionizing Radiation and Project 112/SHAD
- Veterans seeking care for Agent Orange exposure during service in Vietnam
- Veterans seeking care for Gulf War illness or for conditions related to exposure to environmental contaminants during service in the Persian Gulf War
- Veterans of World War I or the Mexican Border War
- Veterans who served in combat in a war after the Gulf War or during a period of hostility after November 11, 1988

PRIORITY 7

- Veterans who agree to pay specified co-pay with income and/or net worth above VA Income Threshold and income below the Geographic Means Test Threshold
- *Subpriority a:* Non-compensable 0 percent service-connected veterans who were enrolled in VA Health Care System on a specified date and who have remained enrolled since that date.
- *Subpriority c:* Non-service-connected veterans who were enrolled in VA Health Care System on a specified date and who have remained enrolled since that date.

PRIORITY 8

- Veterans who agree to pay a specified co-pay with income and/or net worth above VA Means Test Threshold and the Geographic Means Test Threshold
- *Subpriority a:* Non-compensable 0 percent service-connected veterans enrolled as of January 16, 2003, and who have remained enrolled since that date.
- *Subpriority c:* Non-service-connected veterans enrolled as of January 16, 2003, and who have remained enrolled since that date.
- As of *January 17, 2003,* the VA *no longer* enrolls new veterans in *priority group 8.*

If you have private health insurance

You may use the VA health services even if you have private health insurance. However, if you apply for VA medical care, you are required to provide full information on your health insurance coverage including coverage from your spouse. You will not be responsible for the remaining balance of the VA bill not paid or covered by your private insurance. Any payment received can be used to offset, dollar for dollar, any VA co-pays you may have.

Who Gets Preference?

You will receive priority in scheduling hospital or outpatient medical appointments if you are a vet who is 50 percent or more disabled from service-connected conditions, unemployable due to a service-connected condition, or receiving care for a service-connected disability.

For two years following separation from active duty, if you are a vet who served in combat locations during active military service (after November 11, 1998) you are eligible for free health care service for conditions potentially related to combat service.

Your Income May Affect Priority Group Assignment

If you are not receiving VA disability compensation or pension, then your gross annual household income and net worth will be one determinant of your priority group. You must prove that your gross annual household income is below the financial threshold (it's adjusted annually) for your geographic area. You will have to provide information on *all* income including Social Security, retirement pay, unemployment insurance, interest and dividends, workers' compensation, black lung benefits, and any other income. The market value of property that is not your primary residence, stocks, bonds, notes, individual retirement accounts, bank deposits, cash, savings accounts—all of these assets are included in determining your net worth.

This financial assessment will also determine if you must contribute a co-pay for services.

Co-Pay Requirements

INPATIENT CARE. If you are in Priority Group 7 (your income is above the means threshold and below the VA's geographically based income threshold), then you are responsible for paying:

- 20 percent of the Medicare deductible for the first 90 days of inpatient care during any 365-day period. Note, it's not a calendar year (January 1–December 31), but starts with the first inpatient care and covers the next 365 days.
- 10 percent of the Medicare deductible for each additional 90 days of inpatient care
- $2/day for hospital care

If you are a nonservice-connected veteran or a non-compensable, zero percent service-connected veteran with a gross annual household income above the VA national and geographic income threshold, you must pay:

- The full Medicare deductible for the first 90 days of care during any 365-day period
- For each additional 90 days, one-half of the Medicare deductible
- $10 per day for hospital care

EXTENDED CARE. Veterans have a co-pay for extended care, but the amount is based on each veteran's financial situation and is determined at the time of application for extended care services.

MEDICATION. You will be charged $8 for each 30-day (or less) supply of medication provided by the VA unless it's treatment for a service-connected condition.

No Co-Pays Required

There is no co-pay for:

- Publicly announced VA health fairs
- Outpatient visits that are for preventive screening and or immunizations (for example, flu shots, blood pressure screening, tests for breast cancer and cervical cancer)

- Education programs, for example on the risks and benefits of prostate cancer screening
- Smoking cessation programs
- Laboratory, flat film radiology, and electrocardiograms

You May Be Reimbursed for Travel

You may be eligible for reimbursement of your travel expenses as you seek care from the VA. There is a deductible of $3 for each one-way trip (up to a maximum per month of $18). Reimbursement is 11 cents a mile, except when you are called for a repeat Compensation and Pension exam, when you will be reimbursed at the rate of 17 cents a mile.

If you meet one of these criteria, then you are eligible for travel reimbursement:

- Veterans whose service-connected disabilities are rated 30 percent or higher
- Veterans traveling for treatment of a service-connected condition
- Veterans who receive a VA pension
- Veterans traveling for a scheduled compensation or pension exam
- Veterans whose gross household income doesn't exceed the maximum annual VA pension (Please note that this category relates your gross household income to the VA pension, not to the VA national and geographic income thresholds.)
- Veterans whose medical condition requires a special mode of transportation, for example, a shuttle for wheelchairs, if they are unable to cover the cost of the special transportation on their own and travel is pre-authorized

In case of emergency, if a delay would endanger life or health, you do not need to get advance authorization.

In case of emergency

Some medical emergencies, such as a heart attack, require that you go to the nearest emergency facility for treatment even if it's not a VA hospital. In those cases, the VA may reimburse or pay for that medical care. But in general, if you are an enrolled veteran, you must proceed to the nearest VA medical facility for care.

VA Health Registries Monitor Toxic Exposure

In the course of your military service, you may have been exposed to toxic substances that have long-term effects on your health. The VA has established health registries for veterans exposed to environmental toxins. These programs offer free medical examinations, laboratory and other diagnostic tests, and provide health information for vets who are suffering a variety of ailments that may have resulted from exposure. In order to be included in the registry, you will need to be examined by a VA doctor. The only requirement for inclusion in a VA health registry is that your time of service and possible exposure to a toxic substance coincides with the registry's parameters. For example, a Vietnam veteran would not apply for the Gulf War Registry.

If you believe you are eligible to participate in a VA health registry, it's to your benefit to enroll. It will help with the continuing study of the illnesses associated with exposure, as well as facilitate, in the long term, the presumption of service-connection to illnesses. Visit the website www.va.gov/environagents for more information.

Here is a list of the current VA health registries.

- *Gulf War Registry.* For veterans who served in the Gulf War and Operation Iraqi Freedom (OIF)
- *Depleted Uranium Registries.* There are two different registries for veterans possibly exposed to depleted uranium:

(1) veterans who served in the Gulf War including Operation Iraqi Freedom; (2) veterans who served elsewhere including Bosnia and Afghanistan.

- *Agent Orange Registry.* Veterans who were exposed to dioxin (Agent Orange) or other toxic substances in herbicides during the Vietnam War, while serving in Korea in 1968 or 1969, or as a result of resting, transporting, or spraying herbicides for military purposes.
- *Ionizing Radiation Registry.* Veterans who were possibly exposed to atomic radiation serving in official military duties at the gaseous diffusion plants in Paducah, KY; Portsmouth, OH; or the K-25 area at Oak Ridge, TN; for at least 250 days before February 1, 1992, or in Longshot, Milrow, or Cannikin underground nuclear tests at Amchitka Island, Alaska, before January 1, 1974. Veterans who were treated with nasopharyngeal (NP) radium during military service. Veterans who were present during the detonation of an atomic device; who served during the occupation of Hiroshima and Nagasaki from August 6, 1945, through July 1, 1946; who were prisoners of war in Japan during World War II.

VA Provides Dental Care

The VA provides outpatient dental treatment including diagnostic, surgical, restorative, and preventive care. The following veterans are eligible to receive dental care:

- Veterans with service-connected, compensable dental conditions, e.g., those dental conditions that will be considered when calculating a veteran's pension
- Former POWs
- Veterans with service-connected, non-compensable dental conditions as a result of combat wounds or service injuries
- Veterans with non-service-connected dental conditions that

the VA determines to be aggravating a service-connected medical problem

- Veterans with service-connected conditions rated permanently and totally disabled or 100 percent by reason of being unemployable (For example, mental health determinations often lead to 100 percent disability ratings due to unemployability.)
- Veterans in a VA vocational rehabilitation program
- Certain homeless veterans who are enrolled in VA-sponsored rehabilitation programs
- Veterans with non-service-connected dental conditions who receive dental treatment while an inpatient in a VA facility
- Veterans requiring treatment for dental conditions that medical authorities determine are complicating a medical condition currently being treated

VA Offers Outpatient Pharmacy Services

Some veterans are eligible for free outpatient pharmacy services; most will be charged a co-pay for both prescription and over-the-counter drugs.

Those eligible for free outpatient prescription services include

- Veterans with a service-connected disability of 50 percent or more
- Veterans receiving medications for service-connected conditions
- Veterans whose annual income does not exceed the maximum annual rate of the VA pension
- Veterans enrolled in Priority Group 6 who receive medication for service-connected conditions
- Veterans receiving medication for conditions related to sexual trauma while serving on active duty

- Certain veterans receiving medication for treatment of the head or neck
- Veterans receiving medication for a VA-approved research project (They receive the medication for the project free, but all other medication falls under the general rules of coverage for prescription drugs.)
- Former POWs

Other veterans are charged a co-pay of $8 for each 30-day or less supply of medication and any over-the-counter medication dispensed by a VA pharmacy. You are not charged for medications injected during the course of treatment or for the medical supplies like syringes and alcohol wipes. You may find it less expensive to purchase over-the-counter medications at your local pharmacy rather than make the co-pay.

If you are enrolled in Priority Groups 2 through 6, the maximum co-pay for calendar year 2007 is $960. The maximum charge is reviewed annually.

VA Mental Health Care Services Are Overextended

The injuries of war are not all physical. Some of the worst damage is psychological. "The hallmark of this war [Iraq] is going to be psy-

Rural veterans gain access to VA health care

Those veterans seeking VA health care in rural areas either travel to the nearest VA health care facility or military treatment facility that is capable of treating veterans, or VA arranges contracted care for the treatment of service-connected disabilities. VA will authorize a veteran to receive treatment from an outside care provider if the condition is service connected and a VA or DOD facility is not located within a reasonable distance.

chological injury," says Stephen Robinson, director of government relations for Veterans for America. The psychological trauma grows exponentially as already traumatized troops are sent back for additional tours of duty. A study in the *New England Journal of Medicine* found that nearly 17 percent of servicemembers who have returned from Iraq show signs of major depression, generalized anxiety, or PTSD. A report in the *Journal of American Medicine* put the number of servicemembers at risk even higher for psychological trauma. In addition, veterans of the Vietnam War are increasingly at risk of a recurrence of PTSD as the images of current battles trigger flashbacks. Max Cleland, former Senator from Georgia who lost three limbs in Vietnam, announced in August 2006 that he was suffering from, and receiving treatment for, PTSD.

The Defense Department Task Force on Mental Health found that 38 percent of soldiers and 31 percent of Marines report mental health issues (from post-combat stress to severe brain injuries). The DOD believes that number will worsen as troops return for multiple deployments. The Task Force found that National Guard members were at even higher risk—nearly 50 percent of Guard members reported mental health issues after deployment.

Multiple deployments to Iraq have become routine for servicemembers, and the effects have been devastating on their mental health. The Pentagon reports that mental health problems, suicides, and family problems are higher for troops who have experienced multiple deployments to Iraq.

Sadly, despite the mushrooming problem, a 2004 report from the Government Accountability Office found that six of the seven VA medical facilities "may not be able to meet" the demands for care of vets suffering from PTSD.

An investigative report in *US News and World Report* (October 9, 2006) found "The number of veterans from all wars receiving disability payments for PTSD, about 216,000 last year [2005], has grown seven times as fast as the number receiving benefits from disabilities in general."

There are still a significant number of veterans suffering from mental health problems who must wait for care. Even Secretary of Veterans Affairs James Nicholson admits that at least 15 percent of new mental health patients must wait more than 30 days for care.

Like a physical injury, psychological trauma often worsens when left untreated. These problems are treatable—but you must seek help. Don't let paperwork, delays, and neglect stop you from getting the help you need—and are entitled to have.

Here are your options if you are seeking care for mental health issues.

The VA offers counseling services, both on an inpatient and outpatient basis.

To help with the readjustment from military to civilian life, there are readjustment-counseling services through 207 community-based Vet Centers located in all 50 states, the District of Columbia, Guam, Puerto Rico, and the U.S. Virgin Islands.

You are eligible if you served on active duty in a combat theater during the Vietnam War, the Gulf War, or the campaigns in Lebanon, Grenada, Panama, Somalia, Bosnia, Kosovo, Afghanistan, Iraq, and the Global War on Terror.

The services are broad. There are individual, group, and family counseling, and treatment is offered for substance abuse, PTSD, and any other military-related issue that affects functioning within your family, work, school, or other area of everyday life. Bereavement counseling is available for all family members including spouses, children, parents, and siblings of servicemembers who die while on active duty.

Many veterans seek help, through local *Veterans Centers.* While Vet Centers are part of the VA, they are much smaller, require considerably less paperwork, and services are generally faster. You can generally see a counselor within one week. See Appendix C for a listing, by state, of Veterans Centers. Many vets prefer these centers as it gives them an opportunity to talk to other vets who understand, very clearly, the problems they are facing.

Currently, there are serious delays in securing appointments for mental health services at Veterans Affairs Medical Centers. Tragically, there have been veterans who have committed suicide while waiting for care. Don't let that happen to you. If you can't get the immediate help you need at a VA facility, and are facing a mental health crisis, go immediately to the emergency room of your community hospital.

VA Dispenses Special Services for the Disabled Veteran

In chapters 2 and 6, we discuss service-connected pensions. In addition to financial support for service-connected disabilities, the VA also offers health services for disabled vets.

If you are receiving VA care for any condition, you are eligible for VA prosthetic appliances; equipment and services such as home respiratory therapy; artificial limbs, orthopedic braces, therapeutic shoes, wheelchairs, powered mobility like motorized scooters, crutches, canes, walkers, and other medical equipment and supplies.

The VA will provide necessary hearing aids and eyeglasses if you are in one of these groups:

You receive increased pension based on the need for regular aid and attendance

You are permanently housebound

You receive compensation for a service-connected disability

You are a former POW

If you are a blind veteran, you are eligible for services at a VA medical center, admission to a VA blind rehabilitation center, and the following additional services:

- A total health and benefits review
- Adjustment to blindness training
- Home improvement and structural alterations

- Specially adapted housing and adaptations to existing housing.
- Automobile grant
- Low-vision aids and training in their use
- Electronic and mechanical aids for the blind, including adaptive computers and computer-assisted devices such as reading machines and electronic travel aids
- Guide dogs, including cost of training the veteran to use the dog
- Talking books, tapes, and Braille literature

VA Provides Vocational Rehabilitation Programs

If you are receiving VA health care, you may also be eligible for vocational assistance and therapeutic work opportunities. These programs are designed to combine treatment *and* rehabilitation services so that you can live and work in your community. Your VA compensation or pension benefits *cannot* be denied, discontinued, or reduced if you participate in one of these programs.

Incentive Therapy

This program is available at 70 VA Medical Centers. It is primarily for seriously disabled veterans for whom employment is unlikely (at least for the foreseeable future) and provides prevocational skills development. Participants receive a token payment for providing services such as office support, housekeeping, filing, and so forth.

Compensated Work Therapy (CWT)

This program is available at 141 VA Medical Centers. It is designed to give veterans an individualized vocational assessment, rehabilitation planning, and work experience. The goal is a job in the community. The program works closely with community-based organizations, employers, and state and Federal agencies to establish work experiences, supported employment opportunities, job placement, and follow-up services.

Compensated Work Therapy/Transitional Residence

The program provides work-based, residential treatment in a stable living environment. It is designed for veterans who are disabled and need help making the transition to independent living and who require assistance regaining the skills needed to sustain independent living. It differs from other VA residential bed programs because the participants use their earnings to contribute to the cost of their residences and are responsible for planning, purchasing, and preparing their own meals. This program offers rehabilitation services including home, financial, and life skills management.

Health Care Information Just for Women Veterans

There is a VA Center for Women Veterans. The website is www1.va.gov/womenvet. Here are some numbers that put the issue into perspective.

- Today there are more than 1.7 million women veterans, which is about 7.2 percent of the total veteran population. That number is expected to rise steadily, with an anticipated 1.9 million women veterans by 2020. In contrast, the number of male veterans is projected to decline from 27.6 million in 1980 to 16.2 million by 2020.
- Fifty-six percent of women veterans who use VA are less than 45 years of age.

- Sixty-two percent of women veterans are less than 45 years of age.
- Women make up about 10.26 percent of the 22.8 million veterans who use VA for health care.
- Women using the VA are generally younger than men, better educated, and less likely to be married.
- Women make up 14.8 percent of the active-duty military force and approximately 22.8 percent of the reserve force.
- By 2010, women are expected to represent more than 14 percent of the total veteran population.

While there are significantly more men than women on active duty, and therefore more male veterans than females, veteran population estimates tell an interesting story. The population of female veterans has actually increased over the last decade (in contrast to the population of male veterans, which has declined) because:

- There are an increasing number of women who enter—and eventually exit—active service.
- There is a more favorable survival rate of women to men at any given age.
- There is a younger age distribution of women veterans to male veterans, which translates into more women with lower mortality rates.

Women veterans are entitled to the same VA benefits (education, home ownership, death benefits, etc.) as male vets. But women veterans also have a unique group of physical and mental health issues that must be addressed. Each VA hospital has a *Women Veterans Coordinator*, who is responsible for coordinating the care of female vets. To apply for VA health care, you must complete *VA Form 10-10EZ*.

There are 130 women's clinics in the VA system, and eight Women Veterans' Comprehensive Health Care Centers (see Appendix D). Contact the Women Veterans Coordinator in your local VA hospital to see what services are available there.

Sexism and Sexual Harassment

Sadly, sexual harassment and sexist attitudes toward women are an alarming reality in today's workforce. Women in the armed forces continue to face issues of sexism. In the military, an astonishing 55–90 percent of women veterans reported experiencing sexual harassment while on active duty. Approximated 13–20 percent of women vets reported being assaulted or raped while on active duty.

The effects of this maltreatment can be long term and devastating. The stress you endure from coping with sexual harassment or trauma can lead to emotional and physical health problems such as depression, anxiety, sleep difficulties, headaches, sexual dysfunction, and stomach problems. The effects of rape may include chronic pelvic pain, stomach problems, low self-esteem, eating disorders, hypertension, respiratory problems, apprehension to becoming pregnant, and other relationship problems. Women who have been raped are at higher risk for abuse and maltreatment later in life.

These traumatic experiences can also lead to Post-Traumatic Stress Disorder. Symptoms include nightmares, flashbacks, intrusive thoughts, sleep disturbances, hypervigilance, memory impairment, depression, anger, numbing, guilt, shame, foreshortened sense of the future, and isolation.

The VA operates both inpatient and outpatient programs to deal with women vets who suffered rape or sexual assault. Contact your VA Women Veterans Coordinator for a referral for dealing with past experiences of sexism or to help you out of a current abusive relationship. There are four stress disorder treatment teams, and a women veterans' division at the VA National Center for Post-Traumatic Stress Disorder in Boston.

If you have been diagnosed with Post-Traumatic Stress Disorder as a result of a sexual assault or sexual harassment while on active

Was your discharge from the service affected by a report of sexism and sexual assault?

Do you believe that your less than honorable discharge was payback for reporting an incident (s) of sexual assault or sexual harassment? Were you treated as the criminal instead of the victim? Contact a service officer in one of the veteran groups (for example, the American Legion) to help you upgrade your discharge.

duty, or as a result of war zone stress, you may be eligible for a VA service-connected disability.

To prove your claim, you can offer in evidence:

- Military records and awards
- Private civilian records
- Treatment records for a physical injury from the assault, but not reported
- Civilian police reports
- Reports from Crisis Centers
- Testimonial statements from friends (civilian and military), family, coworkers, clergy
- Personal diary or journal
- Request for changes in military assignment
- Increase in sick leave or leave slips
- Change in military performance evaluations
- Increased use of prescription and over-the-counter medications
- Substance abuse and/or other compulsive behavior
- Request for a pregnancy test
- Request for HIV tests or counseling for sexually transmitted diseases
- Counseling statements in personnel file
- Breakup of marriage or relationship

- Reports to Children's Protective Services (in cases of domestic violence)

Substance Abuse

Both men and women sometimes use alcohol and/or drugs to cope with stress, depression, and anxiety. The VA has inpatient and outpatient substance abuse treatment programs for women. There is a Women's Addictive Disorder Unit at the VA Medical Center in Cleveland, Ohio. Any female veteran can be referred to it.

Sexually Transmitted Diseases

The VA offers both men and women testing and treatment for sexually transmitted diseases, including hepatitis and HIV/AIDS.

Environmental Health Hazards

Health registries for exposure to toxic materials (Agent Orange, depleted uranium, etc.) are also important for female veterans. Servicemembers who served in combat zones are at risk for a variety of illnesses related to environmental exposure. The VA has conducted studies of the personal health of female veterans, as well as research on birth defects of children born of vets exposed to these toxins. If you are a female veteran who thinks she may have been exposed, contact your local VA hospital for an Agent Orange or Persian Gulf Registry exam.

Gynecological Care and Female-Related Cancers

The VA offers free screening for breast (mammograms) and cervical cancers (pap smears) to all female veterans who are enrolled and eligible for care at VA. This excludes Priority Group 8. VA will not deliver babies at their Medical Centers, even to enrolled female veterans, because the Department of Veterans Affairs has no authority to provide care to newborns. VAMCs will assist veterans in accessing community resources.

Should a pregnant veteran be totally and permanently disabled from a service-connected disability, after delivery, if the child is not eligible for care under TRICARE, then the newborn infant could receive care under the Civilian Health and Medical Program of VA (CHAMPVA) (see chapter 12).

VA Delivers Long-Term/Rehabilitative Care

The VA offers domiciliary care for vets who meet eligibility requirements. These programs are designed to fulfill the needs of a vet who requires some medical care, like changing bandages, assistance with administering medication, assistance in eating, or who is at risk of falling, but can't get that attention at home (it's unavailable or unsuitable). Domiciliary care is only for individuals who require some medical care, but don't need acute hospitalization or skilled nursing services.

Eligibility is limited to veterans whose annual gross household income does not exceed the maximum annual rate of VA pension or to veterans the Secretary of Veterans Affairs determines have no adequate means of support, for example, indigent veterans who meet the income threshold. The co-payments for extended care services apply to domiciliary care.

VA Provides Nursing Home Care

There are three different VA programs of nursing home care. Each one has its own set of eligibility and admission requirements.

VA-Owned and -Operated Nursing Homes

These homes are typically for short-term skilled care, such as rehabilitation time for a hip replacement, or any condition that requires rehabilitative care to return to full functioning, or for vets who have a 70 percent or greater service-connected disability.

State Veterans Nursing Homes Owned and Operated by the States

These nursing homes are a cooperative venture between the VA and the states. States can get Federal money for construction of nursing homes for vets. The VA, the state, and the veteran share the per diem costs. The state legislatures set the per diem. State veterans homes accept *all* veterans in need of short- and long-term nursing home care. However, specialized services for physical therapy, spinal cord rehabilitation, Alzheimer's unit, dementia unit, may not be available at all state nursing homes.

Community Nursing Home Program

Every VA medical center has contracts with non-VA nursing homes in their local communities. This permits veterans who need this type of care to remain in their own communities, close to family and friends.

In general, to enter any nursing home, a resident must be medically stable (that is, not acutely ill and requiring hospitalization); has condition (s) that requires inpatient nursing home care; and is judged by a medical provider to need nursing home care. There may also be specific eligibility requirements by each state or community nursing home program. Some co-pay may be required (this is determined by completing VA Form 10-10EZ).

Other Long-Term Care Available

Nursing homes are not the only type of long-term care available. The VA, either through its own facilities or via contracts with community-based agencies, offers adult day health care, inpatient or outpatient respite care, inpatient or outpatient geriatric evaluation and management, hospice and palliative care, and home-based primary care. Some co-pay may be required.

In Conclusion

The VA health care service is generally regarded as providing excellent medical care, once a veteran can enter the system. But veterans confront lengthy delays in accessing the care because of the heavy demands placed on it by the rapidly growing number of ex-servicemembers who are returning from war in need of medical attention. You must know what services are available near you (see Appendix B) and be persistent in trying to get the help you need.

CHAPTER 6

Disability and Rehabilitation

The toll of service can be severe. Becoming classified as disabled, at the appropriate level of impairment, entails a series of steps. Getting needed rehabilitation can be a frustrating ordeal. The disability rating a veteran receives will determine his or her eligibility for lifetime benefits.

This chapter explains how to access the rehabilitation services offered by the Department of Veterans Affairs. It will include the VA definitions and categories for disabilities and treatment and reentry programs available.

The VA Rating System

As we discussed in chapter 5, the VA rating system for disabilities is distinct from the rating that is given to injured servicemembers by the Department of Defense. Once you are discharged, you will be re-evaluated and rated by the VA.

This is the breakdown of costs for compensating disabled veterans.

- Approximately 2.7 million veterans are currently receiving disability compensation benefits, an increase of approximately 400,000 since 2003. This equates to about $34.5 billion in disability benefits paid to veterans and their survivors in fiscal year (FY) 2006.

- The VA reported that its 57 Veterans Benefits Administration (VBA) regional offices issued more than 774,000 disability determinations in FY 2006. This represents an increase of about 11,000 decisions from the previous fiscal year.
- The VA received 806,382 rating claims in FY 2006 and expects to receive approximately 811,000 in FY 2007. A majority of these claims involves multiple issues that are legally and medically complex and time consuming to adjudicate.
- Approximately 494,000 veterans are receiving 100 percent service-connected disability compensation or a total compensation rating based on individual unemployability.

The current VA disability ratings system was included in The War Risk Insurance Act of 1917 that called for the creation of the first disability ratings schedule. The schedule underwent major revisions in 1921, 1925, 1933, and 1945. It has not been updated since then, but the Dole/Shalala Commission is recommending a complete overhaul of the VA Disability Compensation System.

The purpose of the VA disability program is to compensate veterans for the loss in earning capacity in civilian occupations that result from injuries or conditions incurred or aggravated during military service. In FY 2006, the VA paid about $ 34.5 billion to veterans and their survivors. For more than 50 years, the number of veterans on disability rolls remained fairly constant. But with the huge improvements in medical care in the field, the number of injured soldiers who survive has grown, hence an increase in the number of veterans now receiving disability compensation.

How much disability compensation a veteran receives is based on the "percentage evaluation," more commonly known as the disability rating, he receives. The *Schedule for Ratings Disabilities* contains medical criteria and assigns a rating to a broad assortment of injuries and illnesses, both physical and mental.

The medical criteria consist of a list of diagnoses organized by body system and a number of levels of medical severity for each di-

What are the primary disabilities covered?

An increasing number of servicemembers are returning from active duty in Iraq and Afghanistan suffering from severe brain trauma. Even more come home suffering from Post-Traumatic Stress Disorder (PTSD). This means a growing number of veterans on the disability rolls (now about 20 percent) are receiving disability compensation for psychiatric and neurological conditions. The remainder are being compensated for physical disabilities.

agnosis. How much a veteran receives in compensation is based on the disability rating for his or her specific condition. Congress reviews and adjusts the compensation rates annually based on cost of living adjustment (COLA). The law requires the VA to revise the Schedule for Ratings Disabilities periodically.

Here's the problem. According to a GAO report, "The disability ratings in VA's current schedule are still primarily based on physicians' and lawyers' judgments made in 1945 about the effect service-connected conditions had on the average individual's ability to perform jobs requiring manual or physical labor." But today's marketplace is no longer primarily reliant on manual labor. Disabilities that would have prohibited a veteran from a full-time, productive job in 1945 are no longer the same impediment owing to medical advances and the invention of sophisticated prostheses, assistive technology, and computers.

For example, a veteran who lost the use of his nonpredominant hand is generally awarded a disability rating of 60 percent. The loss of a dominant hand would result in a disability rating of 70 percent. That is supposed to reflect the loss in the veteran's earning capacity. But in fact, losing a hand, studies show, results in a reduction of earning capacity of only about 40 percent. Conversely, a GAO study showed that "veterans who had a disability rating of 70 percent for pronounced psychotic conditions were found, on average, to have experienced a reduction in earnings closer to 80 percent."

Furthermore, the compensation is based on average impairment in earning capacity associated with the level of severity. So again referring to the example above, a veteran who loses his dominant hand as a result of military service is assigned a 70 percent disability rating, because the VA presumes this kind of loss means a 70 percent loss in earning capacity, *on average*, among veterans with this kind of injury. Therefore, all veterans who lose their dominant hands should receive a 70 percent disability rating, whether or not this injury actually reduces their earning capacity by this amount or not.

Finally, with the passage in 1990 of the Americans with Disabilities Act, which supports the full participation of people with disabilities in society, there is the expectation that being disabled does not preclude you from a full and meaningful career. Employers are prohibited from discriminating against qualified individuals who are disabled. Employers are required to make reasonable workplace accommodations for the disabled. Society's attitude toward the disabled has undergone many changes since the Schedule of Disability Ratings was first developed in the 1920s.

A veteran's disability rating should take into account all injuries and illnesses, so that if the vet is suffering from the loss of his leg *and* PTSD, then his disability rating would include compensation for both. Furthermore, disability ratings can change over time as an injury or illness worsens or new symptoms appear.

Additional Compensation Awards

Under certain circumstances, the VA will provide additional monthly compensation above the amount awarded under the Disability Ratings Schedule.

Although the VA's disability compensation is to deal with the ex-servicemember's loss of earning capacity, the program also provides for additional monthly compensation for loss of "physical integrity." That means the VA compensates veterans for tissue loss, loss of body parts (including procreative organs), or any disease or injury that makes an individual less functionally whole.

The VA can also choose to bestow veterans "extra-schedular" awards when the VA determines that the severity of the veteran's condition is not adequately covered by the ratings schedule. This type of award permits the veteran to receive a higher rating than the schedule would give for the specific condition. Technically, the VA has the discretion to give a 100 percent disability rating to a veteran it considers to be unemployable because of special circumstances, even if the veteran's condition warrants only a 60 percent rating according to the Schedule for Ratings Disabilities. For example, consider the case of a veteran who is rated 70 percent disabled for a mental disorder, but actually is unable to work at all because of this mental disability. Even though the veteran doesn't meet all of the 100 percent schedular requirements for a mental disorder, VA could bestow an extra-schedular award.

VA regulations also permit compensation for "social inadaptability" or "social impairment." This compensation is focused on the *professional*, not personal, life. It's intended to adjust for the loss of a veteran's earning capacity because, as a result of service-connected injury or illness, the veteran has abnormal conduct, judgment, or emotional reactions that affect his or her working ability.

Rehabilitation for Veterans

In addition to providing veterans with compensation for service-connected disabilities, the VA has other programs for disabled vets. VA Medical Centers can provide physical and occupational therapy for disabled veterans to help them achieve the fullest physical recovery. Mental health services can offer ongoing therapy. The VA does a good job of sending patients to the facilities that provide the best specialized care.

The VA also offers broader rehabilitation services. The Vocational Rehabilitation and Employment Service (VR&E) has two main goals:

- To help veterans with service-connected disabilities prepare for, find, and keep suitable jobs
- To improve the lives of veterans with service-connected disabilities so severe that they cannot immediately work. The goal for these veterans is to help them live as independently as possible.

Who Is Eligible for VR&E?

There are several steps a veteran must take in order to use the services of VR&E. First to receive an evaluation, a veteran must:

- Have received a discharge that is other than dishonorable
- Have at least a 10 percent service-connected disability
- Submit an application, VA Form 28-1900 for VR&E services

You have 12 years of eligibility for VR&E services, although the period can be extended if the Vocational Rehabilitation Counselor (VRC) determines that a veteran has a *Serious Employment Handicap.* The period begins either on:

- The date of separation from active military service *or*
- The date the veteran was first notified by the VA of his service-connected disability rating

Once you have established eligibility, you must meet with a Vocational Rehabilitation Counselor to determine if you are *entitled* to receive services. The VRC must do an extensive evaluation, which includes

- An assessment of your interests, aptitudes, and abilities
- An assessment of whether your service-connected disability

will impair your ability to find and hold a job using the skills you already have

- An investigation of your vocational interests and discussion/development of your goals

If the VRC determines that you have an employment handicap based on the results of the evaluation, and you meet the eligibility qualifications, then you may receive VR&E services.

If You Are Entitled to VR&E Services

To achieve your rehabilitation goals, you will work with a VRC to develop an individualized rehabilitation plan. It should be a written outline of the services, resources, and criteria that will be used to achieve (and measure) successful rehabilitation. You will be asked to sign the plan, as does the VRC. It is reviewed annually and changes can be made to the plan if necessary.

To develop a viable rehabilitation plan takes a comprehensive and honest evaluation of your current physical and mental health, your job skills, the current job market, training requirements in order to develop new skills if necessary or adapt the skills you have, and identification of the resources needed to achieve rehabilitation.

Working with the VRC, you will choose one of the following Five Tracks of Services:

1. Reemployment (with a former employer)
2. Rapid employment services for new employment, a fast-track employment program
3. Self-employment
4. Employment through long-term services, a longer program offered through VR&E
5. Independent living services (for veterans with service-connected disabilities so severe that they cannot immediately work. The goal for these veterans is to help them live as independently as possible.)

Your VRC or case manager will help you implement the plan by coordinating the necessary services such as tutorial assistance, training in job-seeking skills, medical and dental referrals, adjustment counseling, and payment of training allowances (if applicable).

If You Are Not Entitled to Services

If after an evaluation, the VA determines that you are not entitled to VR&E services, a VRC should help you locate other resources for rehabilitation and employment needs. This may include state vocational rehabilitation programs; Department of Labor employment programs for disabled veterans; state, federal, or local agencies for employment or small business development; helpful Internet websites; and information about financial aid.

Note: You can *appeal* an entitlement decision through the standard *appellate procedures* (see chapter 7). It's best to use a *Veterans Service Officer* for the appeal.

For Veterans Who Require an Independent Living Program

If you are a veteran whose service-connected disabilities are so severe that you cannot, at least immediately, pursue an employment goal, you may be eligible for the VA Independent Living Program (ILP).

The first steps toward entering the ILP are similar to all veterans seeking help from VR&E. You must complete VA Form 28-1900 for Vocational and Rehabilitation Services and undergo a comprehensive evaluation with a Vocational Rehabilitation Counselor. The VRC will determine your entitlement to services and whether an ILP program is appropriate.

The goals of this program are to help a severely disabled veteran live as independently as possible, as well as participate in family and community life. An ILP also hopes to increase the veteran's potential for employment. A VRC will work with the veteran to develop an individualized Independent Living Program plan.

To achieve these goals, ILP services may include

- Assistive technology
- Specialized medical, health, and/or rehabilitation services
- Services to address any personal and family adjustment issues
- Independent skills living
- Contact with community-based support services

Two Job Websites of Special Interest for Disabled Veterans

You can find employment information and jobs targeted for veterans with service-connected disabilities at two VA sites.

- www.VetSuccess.gov. In addition to information on VR&E, at this site you can find information about vocational counseling services. VetSuccess partners with employers looking to hire vets. Veterans can access a veterans-only module and create a personal account (password protected). You can store your resume, documents, and prospective employer contacts in this account. If you choose, you can enable prospective employers to view your resume from this site.

- /www1.va.gov/vetind/. This is the Compensated Work Therapy/Veterans Industries (VI/CWT) site. It is part of the VA's vocational rehabilitation program. VI/CWT matches work-ready veterans to competitive jobs and then supports them for continued success. VI/CWT also works with businesses and industry to promote employment opportunities for veterans with physical and mental disabilities. There are 162 VI/CWT locations around the nation and on this web site you can find one close to you.

In order to assist in continued employment success, VI/CWT staff will provide disabled veterans with:

- State-of-the-art vocation rehabilitation services
- Job matching and employment supports
- Case management, worksite and job analysis
- Consultation regarding assistive technology, accommodation, and guidance regarding Americans with Disabilities Act (ADA) regulation compliance

VI/CWT also provides industries with a work-ready, prescreened applicant pool of disabled veterans. Only disabled veterans who are eligible for VR&E services can use these services.

In Conclusion

VA provides a range of rehabilitation services for veterans with service-connected disabilities. The goal is to help disabled veterans prepare, find, and keep jobs. For those veterans who are so severely disabled that employment is unlikely, the goal is to help them live as independently as possible. VA also compensates veterans who have service-connected disabilities. Compensation and rehabilitation are both benefits a disabled veteran has earned.

CHAPTER 7

The Appeals Process

You have the right to appeal any decision of a claim for veterans benefits. Just be forewarned. It's a lengthy, frustrating process taking many months, and even years, to complete. In a recent study, Harvard professor Linda J. Bilmes found that it took up to 177 days for the VA to process an initial claim for benefits and that the average appeal takes 657 days (which means that some appeals take less time, but also many take more time).

Some statistics will help put this process in perspective. In May 2007, there were 638,000 claims pending in the VA's 58 Regional Offices. More than 400,000 were disability claims. Of the total claims, more than 28 percent had been pending for more than 180 days. Remember, these are the original applications for benefits—not appeals of VA decisions.

Now consider the next group of statistics. At this same time, there were approximately 159,000 appeals pending in the VA Regional Offices. There were about 32,000 appeals at the Board of Veterans' Appeals in Washington, D.C., and about 16,000 cases remanded and pending at the Appeals Management Center.

With the rapidly growing number of injured veterans returning from the wars in Iraq and Afghanistan, the number of claims filed for disabilities has increased exponentially. At the same time, there has also been a huge increase in denials of benefits, first by the VA and then denial of appeals by the Board of Veterans' Appeals (BVA).

The statistics are troubling:

YEAR	NUMBER OF BENEFITS CLAIMS DENIED BY THE BVA
2004	9,299
2005	13,033
2006	18,107

The United States Court of Appeals for Veterans Claims (CAVC), the Federal court that hears veterans' disability appeals (once they have gone through the VA appeal process), is facing its highest caseload ever. In the first half of fiscal year 2007, 2,542 appeals were filed with the court. In contrast, for the entire previous year, there were 3,729 appeals filed. This growing backlog of appeals is a result of the increased number of claims and the rising number of veterans unhappy with the VA rejection of their claims or the level of benefits allowed.

Who Handles the Appeal?

The appeals process involves lots of paperwork and you must develop a logical, clear, well-documented argument in response to the VA's decision(s). All VA decisions will be couched in legal language and are based on the laws about veterans benefits found in the United States Code (U.S.C.) and the Code of Federal Regulations (C.F.R.).

You will want to obtain representation to help you with your appeal. While you are legally permitted to represent yourself, about 90 percent of all appellants do get representation. About 85 percent of them use a representative from a Veterans Service Organization (VSO), such as the American Legion or Disabled American Veterans (see Appendix G for a list of VSOs). These representatives are trained in the legal code that regulates VA benefits and have experience navigating the appeals process. VSOs don't charge for representation and don't even require you to be a member. Your local VA office can provide a list of approved veterans appeal representatives in your area.

You can also contact your state or county governments. Some have trained personnel in their veterans departments who will help you with the appeals process.

You have the right to hire a lawyer to represent you. A new law, PL 109–461, Section 101, now permits attorneys to represent veterans for a fee after a Notice of Disagreement (NOD) has been filed.

If you have been turned down by the Board of Veterans' Appeals, you can go to the Court of Appeals for Veterans' Claims. The Veterans Consortium Pro Bono Program offers *free* legal representation for veterans appealing to the Court (www.vetsprobono.org/). A veteran can also hire his own lawyer to represent him before the court. Unless the lawyer agrees to represent you for free, you will be charged for representation. If the fee is a percentage of the benefit received, the VA limits those fees to 20 percent of the benefit granted if the final decision is in favor of the veteran.

Aside from paid attorney representation, veterans can have an appeals representative from a VSO represent them for free before the CAVC.

Before you begin the appeal:

- Ask friends and fellow vets for recommendations of VSO representatives.
- Make an appointment with a VSO representative to discuss your case.
- Ask the representative how long he or she has worked in this field.
- Ask the representative if he or she has handled this type of appeal before.
- While there are deadlines for filing an appeal, generally you have up to one year to file. If you are not comfortable with a particular representative, you have time to look elsewhere. It is absolutely essential that you have confidence in the individual representing you.

Referral to VSO representatives is usually based on word of mouth or loyalty to the VSO. Members of the American Legion most often prefer having a Legion representative, members of Disabled American Veterans (DAV) enlist the help of DAV, and so on. Veterans who are not members of VSOs usually go with one of the top two VSOs in terms of the number of cases handled. DAV is first and the American Legion is second in terms of cases represented. A veteran who receives a favorable outcome due to a VSO representative's good work is likely to tell other veterans, and so the word spreads within the community. Good representatives evolve through experience and hard work and are very dedicated to what they do.

It is important to realize that Veterans Service Officers often correct problems prior to the decision being disseminated. Much of what the service officer does is behind the scenes without the veteran being aware of all that transpires.

To authorize someone to represent you, you must complete *VA Form 21-22* to authorize a VSO, or *VA Form 22a* to authorize an attorney or recognized agent (an individual such as a representative from a State Veterans Affairs Office).

Three Critical Points to Remember

In this chapter we will review the appeals process, from start to finish. Remember:

- It's absolutely vital that you keep copies of every piece of correspondence, both to and from the VA, as well as any with other experts you consult. Keep a detailed record (date, time, as well as complete notes on what was said) of any phone calls and always get the name of the person to whom you spoke. Keep the file in a safe, fireproof box so that you have ready access to your materials.
- Always notify your local VA office of any change in your address, home and work telephone numbers.

- Keep a record of your claim number easily available. State it in any conversation (should you call) with the VA, as well as mark it on any correspondence with the VA.

Let's Go Step-by-Step Through the Appeals Process

After your separation from the service, you enter the VA system. *All decisions about eligibility for benefits are from the VA—not the Department of Defense.* For each claim for a benefit, you will receive written notice of the VA determination of your eligibility (for example, priority group assignment, disability rating, etc.). This decision may come from a VA regional Office (RO), VA medical facility, or other local VA office. You may appeal any VA decision, but must follow the rules for appeal, being sure to meet each deadline. Let's start.

Who's in Charge: The Board of Veterans' Appeals

The Board of Veterans' Appeals (BVA) is part of the Department of Veterans Affairs. There are about 60 veterans law judges (VLJ) and a large staff of attorneys. The BVA has four decision teams set up by geographical region. The chairman is appointed by the President (by advice of the Secretary of Veterans Affairs) and the VLJs are appointed by the Secretary. To a degree these are political appointments, but the VLJs do not change with a change in administration. The VLJs make the decisions on each appeal. The BVA has a staff of lawyers, referred to as Counsel or Associate Counsel, and they review the facts of each appeal and make recommendations to the VLJ.

What Can Be Appealed

You can appeal any determination by a VA Regional Office of a claim for benefits, and some determinations by VA medical facilities, such as eligibility for medical treatment (for example, your priority group assignment).

You can decide to accept part of a VA determination and appeal another section of the decision, and you can appeal the level of benefit granted. For example, if a veteran does not agree with the percentage rating for any disability, he or she can appeal. Or let's say that a veteran receives a 10 percent rating for loss of limb, but he believes it should be a higher percentage rating, he can appeal the decision. You can include the medical opinions of outside doctors to support your case. VSO reps also research prior decisions that have set precedents and cite them in their claims when relevant.

However, you can't appeal (1) decisions concerning the need for medical care or (2) the type of medical treatment needed.

The First Deadline

You have up to *one year* from the date that your local VA office mails you its initial determination of your claim. So, make sure the VA has your current address because *the clock is ticking once that letter is mailed.* Unless you can prove that there was a "clear and unmistakable error" (CUE) by the VA, when the year has passed the VA decision is considered final. Proving a "clear and unmistaken error" is extremely difficult, and only about 3 out of every 20 cases filed late for a CUE are accepted for review.

The First Step

Once you receive the initial determination of your claim and decide to challenge it, you must send a letter to the same local VA Regional Office that issued the decision, called a *Notice of Disagreement* (NOD), that states:

1. You disagree with the local VA office's claim determination, and
2. You want to appeal it

There is no special form required at this point (eventually you will complete VA Form 9 that details your rationale for appeal). You are simply putting the VA on notice that you are appealing the decision. Send the letter by registered mail with return receipt requested so you will have a record of delivery confirmation.

In your NOD, you must be specific about the issue or issues you are appealing. For example, if you have filed a claim for a knee disability and a heart condition, but only disagree with the VA determination on the heart condition, make that clear in your NOD. Here's an example of what a NOD should say: "I disagree with the rating decision, dated June 1, 2006, denying service connection for right ear hearing loss and tinnitus."

The VA will establish a *claims folder* for your case that includes all correspondence and reports. The claims folder remains in your local VA office until and unless you request a BVA hearing. It is the basis for adding your case to the Board of Veterans' Appeals *docket* (schedule). Appeals are assigned a docket number/date once the Form 9 is filed. The BVA reviews appeals based on the order in which they are added to the docket.

Next Step: Statement of the Case

Once the local VA Regional Office receives your NOD, it is possible that the staff may decide to review your case, change its original decision, and grant your claim. This doesn't happen often.

If you move

You normally file a Notice of Disagreement with the same local regional VA office that issued the determination. That is where your claims file (also called a claims folder) is housed. If you move, you should request, in writing, that the claims file also be moved to a local VA office close to your current residence and all appeals should be directed to the new RO.

When it does, in most cases it is usually because the claimant submitted additional evidence with the NOD or informed the VA of the existence of additional evidence. Upon receipt of the new evidence, the VA may grant the claim, or may grant one part of the claim but continue the denial of other issues in the claim. Each issue on appeal receives its own separate decision. Since Decision Review Officers (DRO) have "difference of opinion" authority to change a denial of benefits, most decisions that are overturned after an NOD usually are a result of a DRO review and not the traditional appeals process.

But assuming that doesn't happen, the next step is for the local VA Regional Office to mail you a *Statement of the Case* (SOC) and a blank VA Form 9 that you will need to complete in order to proceed with the appeal. The SOC summarizes the evidence and laws on which the VA decided your case. You (or your representative) will have to prove why this reasoning is incorrect.

Next Deadline: Substantive Appeal Due 60 Days Later (with some exceptions)

Once your local VA Regional Office sends you the SOC, the clock starts ticking again. You have 60 days from the date when the local VA office mails you the SOC (*not* the date you receive the SOC), to file a *Substantive Appeal.* You do that by completing VA Form 9 (included in the packet that had the SOC). Although you may complete this form by yourself, it would be wise to get help from a VSO or from your State Veterans Office (see Appendix H for a list of all State Veterans Offices).

In completing VA Form 9, you have three objectives:

1. State clearly the benefit(s) you want.
2. Identify, point-by-point, the mistakes the VA made in denying your claim(s).
3. Add in any evidence that supports your case by proving the SOC is wrong.

Do not use inflammatory language. Keep your claim straightforward, civil, logical, and stated in clear, point-by-point language. You may be justifiably angry or confused by the VA's decision to deny your claim, but keep your eyes focused on your long-term goal. Clearly present the evidence to prove your claim was unjustly denied.

In VA Form 9, include evidence that supports your argument of the wrongful VA determination. Be specific: for example, include records from your doctor (recent medical treatment or evaluations), as well as waivers granted due to physical inability to perform functions at work. Your appeals representative will help you complete the form and advise you of the support documentation that will strengthen your case.

Send VA Form 9 back to your local VA office—again by registered mail, return receipt requested, so you have proof of delivery.

You can also request an extension of the 60-day period for filing a Substantive Appeal (as well as for responding to a Supplemental Statement of the Case [SSOC], see next page). You will need to show "good cause" for the extension and should document your reason for the extension request. For example, if you have been hospitalized and can't meet the deadline for filing, your written request should include a statement from your doctor documenting your recent hospital stay. Generally these requests for an extension are routinely granted the first time.

Shorter Deadlines Set for Certain Appeals

There's a different clock used for *simultaneously contested claims.* These are rare appeal cases in which two parties are both claiming entitlement to fight the denial of a claim or for status, and where one party will be accepted and one will be rejected. For example, two people may both claim entitlement to the full proceeds of a veteran's life insurance policy, or a veteran's spouse and ex-spouse may both try to get Dependency and Indemnity Compensation (DIC).

Exception to the 60-days rule

Once the SOC has been mailed, the rule is that you have 60 days in which to file your appeal. But here's the exception.

You have one year to appeal following the mailing of the original determination of your claim. If there is still time left in your one-year window of opportunity to appeal beyond the 60 days, then you are entitled to use up the entire remaining days. Here's the VA formula:

Regional Office determination mailing date + 1 year

or

SOC + 60 days

For example: VA's notice of rating decision is 6/1/07 and veteran files an NOD on 7/1/07. VA issues an SOC on 8/1/07. The veteran has until 6/1/08 to file the Form 9. If the veteran waited until 5/1/08 to file the NOD and VA issued the SOC on 6/30/08, the veteran has 60 days to file the Form 9 (this is because the veteran filed the NOD prior to the expiration of the year, but since VA issued the SOC after the expiration the veteran is allowed 60 days to file the Form 9 since he or she got the NOD in before the year deadline).

Whichever date is later, that is the date the VA Form 9 must be received at the local VA office. But don't delay simply because you have more time. Remember: If you miss the deadline, the original determination is considered final.

In these types of cases, each party must file a NOD *within 60 days* from the date the local VA office mailed its determination of a claim, not the one-year clock for routine appeals. VA Form 9 must be filed within 30 days of the date that the local VA office mailed the Statement of the Case (SOC), not 60 days. If there is a SSOC, the parties must file within 30 days, not 60 days.

Deadlines for filing

	NOD	VA FORM 9	SSOC
Simultaneously Contested Claim	60 days	30 days	30 days
Regular Veterans Appeal	One year	60 days	60 days

New Evidence to Support Your Claim and a New Clock

You may submit new information and/or evidence to buttress your appeal (for example, a new medical diagnosis from a VA medical facility that supports your claim). The VA prefers copies of the doctor's treatment records, rather than just a statement from the physician.

The local VA offices will respond to this new information with a *Supplemental Statement of the Case* (SSOC), which starts a new clock ticking. If you are dissatisfied with the VA response to the new evidence, *you have 60 days from the date the SSOC was mailed to you*, to submit, in writing, your disagreement with the VA response.

The Paperwork's Complete: When Will Your Case Be Heard?

Once you have filed all the paperwork (VA Form 9), your case is placed on the BVA's docket. The schedule is based on "first come, first served." You are assigned a docket number that indicates when your case was received. The first two numbers are the year, and the remaining digits are the order in which the case was added to the list that year. For example: 07-00235, would mean that your case was the 235th case added to the BVA docket in 2007. The older the year and the lower the number for that year, the sooner your case will be reviewed.

Occasionally, when there are compelling circumstances, you can

If you change your mind on an issue on appeal

You are permitted to withdraw a portion of your appeal, while continuing with the remaining issues, without losing your "place" in the line of appeals cases to be decided (the docket).

If you don't want the BVA to examine an issue that is listed in either the SOC or the SSOC, you must put in writing on VA Form 9 that you are withdrawing your appeal on that specific issue. Be very clear which issue is being withdrawn—and which issues are still to be considered on appeal.

On the other hand, if you later decide to appeal a separate VA claims decision, you must repeat the process for that issue. For example, if you appeal a decision on your arm disability, but later receive a denial of benefits for treatment of PTSD, you would have to go through the appeals process for the PTSD decision separately. You can't incorporate the new issue into your earlier case.

petition to have your appeal decided sooner. You would file a *motion to advance on the docket,* but they are rarely granted (fewer than 3 out of every 20 requests are approved). This is reserved for dire circumstances when delay of a decision could be disastrous, for example, an imminent bankruptcy or foreclosure, a terminal illness, or an error by the VA that caused a significant delay in getting a case on the docket.

You will have to provide documentation of these circumstances (for example, the letter from the bank that notifies you of foreclosure on your home).

To file a motion to advance on the docket, send your request to:

Board of Veterans' Appeals (014)
Department of Veterans Affairs
810 Vermont Avenue, NW
Washington, DC 20420

Request a Personal Hearing of Your Case

You are entitled to—and should request—a personal hearing of your case. Although you are not required to have a hearing, it is in your best interest to seek a personal hearing rather than rely solely on making your case based on a reading of your claims file. You, your representative, and the VLJ who will decide your case will be present at the hearing. You will need to present testimony and evidence to support your case.

There are different types of BVA personal hearings. You may select the one that you believe best meets your needs: (1) BVA hearing in Washington, D.C.; (2) BVA Travel Board hearing; and (3) BVA Videoconference hearing. An alternate route outside the BVA appeal process would be to request a local Regional Office hearing (see box on page 109). That is *not* heard by the BVA.

Options 2 and 3 are held at the Regional Office in your home state and should be easier for you to attend, more convenient, and more affordable. But all three types of hearings allow the appellant to plead his or her appeal directly to the VLJ. Here are some additional specifics about each option.

BVA Hearing

The Board of Veterans' Appeals can hear your case either in Washington, D.C., or at your local Regional Office via a *travel board* hearing. The VA does not pay for your travel or lodging expenses should you choose to hold the hearing in Washington, D.C.

Check the box on VA Form 9 if you want a BVA hearing. You must note where you want to hold the hearing (locally or in Washington, D.C.). You can't have a hearing in both places. To request a local Regional Office hearing, do not use VA Form 9. Write directly to your RO for that type of hearing.

Some ROs are equipped to hold BVA hearings by *videoconference*. You report to your local RO, but the board member conducts the hearing in Washington, D.C., via closed-circuit television. You must check with your RO to see if it is equipped to conduct videoconference hearings.

Scheduling BVA hearings is more complicated than scheduling a local office hearing. The VA advises that a videoconferenced hearing is generally faster to schedule because it doesn't involve travel by board members.

Travel board hearings are dependent on the backlog of cases, the total number of requests for hearings in your area (the VA prefers to group several hearings at the same time), and the amount of time needed to review the cases to be heard. The travel board will only go to a particular geographic location when they have a group of cases to consider and travel funding available. Each case will have a separate hearing before the board.

Hearings held at the board offices in Washington, D.C., are scheduled close to the time when the BVA will consider the case, usually about three months before the case is reviewed for a final decision. Decisions are generally made by one VLJ unless the BVA grants a motion for reconsideration. Then the decision is made by a panel of three VLJs.

Depending on which hearing option you choose, your claims folder may move.

- Your claims folder will remain at your local VA Regional Office if you have requested a local office hearing.
- If you request a travel board hearing, then it remains at the local VA office until the hearing is completed and then is transferred to the board.
- If you request a videoconferenced BVA hearing or a hearing at the Washington, D.C., office, your claims folder remains at your local VA office until shortly before the hearing, when it's transferred to the BVA.

Local office hearing may be effective

This is also known as a Regional Office hearing, RO hearing, or a Hearing Officer hearing.

This type of hearing is held at a local VA office and the hearing officer is from the local office staff, NOT the Board of Veterans' Appeals. To arrange a local office hearing, contact your local VA office directly. These types of hearings tend to be held faster than BVA hearings. Choosing a Regional Office hearing does not eliminate your right to appeal to the BVA.

New Clock Ticking: The 90-Day Rule

If you have requested a BVA hearing, your local VA office will send you a letter when it has transferred your claims folder to Washington, D.C. Now you have a new deadline.

You have 90 days from the date when the letter informing you that your claims folder has been transferred to Washington, D.C., was mailed or until the board decides your case—*whichever comes first*—to add more evidence to your file, request a hearing, or select or change your representative.

Once the 90 days has elapsed, if you want to add anything more to your claims folder, you have to file a motion (a written request) with the item you want to add and a compelling reason for why the board should accept it (that's called "showing good cause"). A board member will review the motion and decide whether to accept or deny it.

Here's the key: you might not have the full 90 days. Remember, it's *either* 90 days *or* when the board decides the case (which could happen before 90 days). If you want to add more evidence to your file, act early.

Status of your appeal update

Your local VA office will notify you in writing when it transfers your file to Washington, D.C. Furthermore, the board will notify you in writing once it receives your file. So if you haven't received any written notices, contact your local VA office for updates on the status of your appeal.

Once the claims folder has been transferred and accepted by the Washington, D.C., office, call 202-565-5436 to check on the status of your case. Be sure to have your claims folder number ready before you call.

A Decision Is Made

Let's briefly review the steps before a decision is made on your case.

1. You filed a claim for a benefit.
2. The VA ruled on the claim and you disagree with the decision.
3. You filed a Notice of Disagreement (NOD).
4. The VA sent you a Statement of the Case (SOC) outlining the law and rationale for denying you the benefit.
5. You filed a VA Form 9 (Substantive Appeal) that laid out the reasons why the decision was incorrect and offered evidence/documentation supporting your position. You selected either a local Regional Office hearing or a BVA hearing (done locally by the travel board or by videoconference, or you traveled to the Washington, D.C., office).
6. If you have requested a BVA hearing, your case is assigned to a board member for review and the board member held a hearing.

When your docket number is reached, a decision will be made. The board member and a staff attorney will review your claims folder. They will review all the evidence, the transcript of the hearing (if you requested one), the statement from your representative (if you have one), and any other information in the folder. The staff attorney, if directed by the board member, may conduct additional research on the case. The staff attorney may also offer a recommendation to the board member—which the board member may choose to accept, reject, or amend. Only the board member has the legal authority to issue a decision. A decision is then issued in writing and mailed to you. Remember, it will be mailed to your home address so be sure that your claims folder has your current address.

If You Lose Your Appeal

It is hoped the board will agree with your appeal and grant your claim. But given the growing number of appeals to the United States Court of Appeals for Veterans Affairs, you must be prepared for a negative decision. You may decide to appeal that decision, or it's possible that your case will be remanded (sent back) to the local VA office or to the Appeals Management Center (AMC) for further study.

If Your Case Is Remanded

The majority of appeals that are remanded by the BVA are sent to the Appeals Management Center (AMC). The AMC was developed to shift the growing backlog of remanded cases from the Regional Offices. Here's what happens whether the case is sent to the AMC or to the RO. If the BVA decides to remand your case, also called "additional development," it means more work is needed on the case. This happens because there is new case law, as a result of changes in the law by Congress, or because of new rulings from the United States Court of Appeals for Veterans Claims. The BVA may also choose to remand your case if they believe you have not provided all the necessary information to make a decision or it's not in the form required. For example, the BVA prefers copies of your doctor's treatment records, not just a statement from your doctor.

If the case is remanded, the AMC or local VA office will review the file once more and may issue a new determination. They may also provide you with a new Supplemental Statement of the Case (SSOC), detailing the reasons, upon additional review, for their decision to reject your claim. You will then have 60 days to comment on this new SSOC.

At this point, your case is returned to the BVA, but on an expedited basis. You return to your original place on the docket and the BVA generally reviews the case shortly after receiving the updated info and issues a final decision.

If You Want to Appeal the Decision

You have several options if you want to appeal the BVA decision.

1. *Motion for Reconsideration.* This is a long shot. You may file a Motion for Reconsideration directly with the Board of Veterans' Appeals, but only if you can show that the board has made an obvious error of fact or law in its decision. Your VSO representative can help you with the motion. For example, if the servicemember's medical record (SMR) shows that the veteran was diagnosed with a chronic ulcer in service and the BVA in its decision states that the SMRs are negative for treatment or diagnosis of a chronic ulcer condition. The BVA decision is wrong because it's based on an obvious error of fact.

   A Motion for Reconsideration is not used if you simply disagree with the board's decision. You have other avenues of appeal for that. This motion is only used if you can show that the board made a mistake of law or fact *and* that the decision would have been different if the error had not been made.

2. *Reopening.* This venue is used if you have "new and material evidence" that you believe would affect the decision in

your case. Again, the bar is set high. The material must be new, not something that has already been included in the claims folder when the board made its decision. For example, the new evidence demonstrates an increase in disability because of impaired mobility, or a general increase in severity of the disability.

If you request that your case be re-opened, you must submit this material to your local VA office. It does not go to the BVA.

You would use this option only if you believe that the *new* evidence is so compelling that it would change the decision. Otherwise, you would choose another option to appeal.

3. *CUE Motion.* Again, this type of motion is a long shot. You file a CUE Motion when there is "clear and unmistakable error" in the board's decision. You must file a motion (a written request) directly to the BVA, asking it to review its decision based on CUE. This does not go to your local VA office. A CUE is very similar to a motion for reconsideration, but is even more restrictive and harder to prove.

   Unless you are an expert in veterans law, you should seek help for this motion. The law is complicated, and proving CUE is very difficult. Your motion must meet very specific requirements (see VBA's *Rules of Practice*) and must be prepared properly. You only get one shot with a CUE motion.

   If it's denied, you can't request a second review of the issues you raised in your first CUE motion. This type of motion is not filed just because you disagree with the VBA's decision. It's a legal claim based on the fact that you believe that the board's decision would have been different had it not made this error.

   You may file a CUE motion at any time; however, the

board will not rule on your CUE motion if you file a timely Notice of Appeal with the Court of Appeals for Veterans Claims.

Filing an Appeal to the Court

In most cases, if you decide to appeal a VBA decision, you will file a motion with the United States Court of Appeals for Veterans Claims (CAVC). You will receive a booklet, *Notice of Appellate Rights* with the VBA decision.

It's important to understand that the Court of Appeals for Veterans Claims is an appellate-level court. The appellant cannot add evidence to the record after the BVA decision and the CAVC will not decide factual questions or issues unless the BVA's factual determination is clearly wrong. This means that in most cases the CAVC will not overturn the BVA's factual interpretation of a case. The focus of the CAVC review is whether the BVA properly applied the law and court precedents. Because of this, most BVA decisions that are not upheld by the CAVC are remanded—and not reversed by the CAVC. Unfortunately, many veterans have the unrealistic expectation that the CAVC will reverse the BVA's decision. Although reversals do happen, they are very rare.

If that is your path, then you will start a new clock ticking. You have *120 days* from the date when the board's decision is mailed to file a Notice of Appeal with the United States Court of Appeals for Veterans Claims. This court is independent and *not* part of the Department of Veterans Affairs.

You (your representative or lawyer) must file the notice of appeal directly with the court:

United States Court of Appeals for Veterans Claims
625 Indiana Avenue, NW, Suite 900
Washington, DC 20004

You must also file a copy of the Notice of Appeal with the Veterans Affairs General Counsel:

Office of the General Counsel (027)
Department of Veterans Affairs
810 Vermont Avenue, NW
Washington, DC 20420

While you are required to file notice to the VA General Counsel, this filing does *not* preserve your right to appeal. Only your original Notice of Appeal filed with the court protects your right to appeal a BVA decision and serves as your official appeal filing.

The court holds oral arguments on some, but not all, cases. It is the court's decision whether or not to hold oral arguments. While a veteran has a right to go to the court pro se (without representation), it is not recommended. If the legal fee is a percentage of the benefit received, the VA limits those fees to 20 percent of the benefit granted if the final decision is in favor of the veteran. The fee agreement is subject to review by the Secretary of VA.

You Have Two Final Appeals Options

If the CAVC rules against him, the veteran can appeal that decision to the U.S. Court of Appeals for the Federal Circuit, and if denied,

If the veteran dies before a decision

If a veteran dies before the board issues a decision on his case, then generally the board dismisses the case without a decision. This does not affect the rights of his survivor(s) to file a claim for any benefits to which they are entitled.

to the Supreme Court. The likelihood of success at these levels is minimal.

In Conclusion

The veteran has a right to appeal a VA decision, but the road to success is long and filled with paperwork. Keep a careful file of all correspondence and appeal data. It's in your best interest to work with a representative from a Veterans Service Organization, whose services are free of charge to any veteran, not just members of the organization.

CHAPTER 8

With Honor and Respect

Death Benefits Including Burial, Cemetery Plot, Honors

You've served your country honorably. Where will you be buried, with what military honors, and who will cover your funeral expenses? In this chapter you will learn what you and your family need to know at this difficult time. The death benefits for a veteran include burial in a national cemetery, a grave marker, a flag, a funeral honor guard, and a Presidential Memorial Certificate for your survivors. There are also death benefits available for the spouse of a veteran.

Advance Planning = Peace of Mind

Too often families don't want to talk about funeral and burial wishes. But making clear your preferences in advance relieves some of the pressure that your survivors will face at a difficult time.

While you can't reserve a burial spot in advance in a national cemetery, you can make clear in writing exactly what you hope your survivors will do with your remains.

- Do you want a funeral or graveside services?
- Do you want to be buried or would you prefer to be cremated?
- Where do you want to be buried?
- Do you want a funeral honor guard?

Keep your preferences and the necessary papers in a safe place and be sure to tell your survivors where they can find them. In the midst of their grief, they shouldn't have to struggle with paperwork.

If you choose to be buried in a private cemetery or in a state veterans cemetery, you may still choose a government headstone or marker. Complete Form 40-1330, the application for a government marker, and place it with copies of your discharge papers so your family has all the necessary information in one place.

Federal and State Agencies That Administer Cemetery Systems

There are 140 national cemeteries. The VA administers 124 of them, the Army administers two (Arlington and Soldiers Home), and the Department of Interior maintains 14 national cemeteries. Since 1873, all honorably discharged veterans are eligible for burial in a national cemetery (see list of cemeteries in Appendix F). Currently 64 VA cemeteries (in 34 states) are able to provide the full range of service to America's veterans and their families. An additional 21 cemeteries provide burial for family members of veterans already interred there.

All states, except Alabama, Alaska, Florida, Mississippi, New Mexico, New York, Oregon, South Carolina, and West Virginia, have state veteran cemeteries (the one in Louisiana is not yet open, and the one in Oklahoma is now closed). Eligibility for burial in a state veterans cemetery is similar to the requirements for burial in a national cemetery, but there may also be pre-death residency requirements as well. (See Appendix F for a full listing of state veterans cemeteries and contact information.)

Who Is Eligible to Be Buried in a National Cemetery?

This benefit applies to many groups of individuals. As usual, there are Federal regulations that spell out the qualifications for each eligibility group. But in general, all veterans, except those with a dishonorable discharge, are entitled to burial in a national cemetery, a grave marker, and a flag. But depending on the circumstances of a veteran's death, he or she may also be entitled to other benefits.

Here are the groups that are eligible for burial in a national cemetery, with marker and flag:

1. *Members of the armed forces* (that includes Army, Navy, Air Force, Marine Corps, Coast Guard):
   - Any member of the armed forces of the United States who dies on active duty.
   - Any veteran who was discharged under conditions other than dishonorable. *As an enlisted person,* for service beginning after September 7, 1980, you must have served for a minimum of 24 continuous months or the full period for which you were called to active duty. *As an officer,* for service beginning after October 16, 1981, the same requirements as above.
   - Any citizen of the United States who served in a war in which the United States has or may be engaged, and served in the armed forces of any government allied with the United States during that war, and whose last active service was terminated honorably by death or otherwise, and who was a citizen of the United States at the time of entry into such service and at the time of death.

2. *Members of the Reserves.* Given the number of Reserve units currently being called up, it's important that these servicemembers understand their eligibility.
   - Reservists and National Guard members who, at the time of death, were entitled to retired pay under Chapter 1223, title 10, United States Code, or would have been entitled, except that they weren't under the age of 60. Any honorably discharged veteran of the Guard or Reserve who has performed at least 20 years of qualifying

service. A qualifying year is one in which you have accrued at least 50 "points" toward retirement.

- Members of the Reserves, and members of the Army National Guard or the Air National Guard, who die while hospitalized or undergoing treatment at government expense for injury or disease contracted or incurred while on active duty for training or inactive duty training, or undergoing such hospitalization or treatment.
- Members of the Reserve Officers' Training Corps (ROTC) of the Army, Navy, or Air Force who die under honorable conditions while attending an authorized training camp or an authorized cruise, while performing authorized travel to or from that camp or cruise, or while hospitalized or undergoing treatment at government expense for injury or disease contracted or incurred under honorable conditions while engaged in one of those activities.
- Members of Reserve components who, during a period of active duty for training, were disabled or died from a disease or injury incurred or aggravated in the line of duty or, during a period of inactive duty training, were disabled or died from an injury or certain cardiovascular disorders incurred or aggravated in the line of duty.

3. *Commissioned officers, National Oceanic and Atmospheric Administration* (NOAA), formerly called the Coast and Geodetic Survey and the Environmental Science Services Administration, with full-time duty on or after July 29, 1945. Though many of these veterans have died, many family members wish to add veterans headstones or markers after the death of the former servicemember.
   - If the individual served before July 29, 1945, he or she had to be assigned to an area of immediate military hazard as determined by the Secretary of Defense while in time of war, or in a national emergency (as declared by the Presi-

dent) *or* served in the Philippine Islands on December 7, 1941, and continuously in such islands thereafter.

4. *Public Health Service*
   - A Commissioned Officer of the Regular or Reserve Corps of the Public Health Service who served on full-time duty on or after July 29, 1945, and who was disabled or died from a disease or injury incurred or aggravated in the line of duty.
   - If service was prior to July 29, 1945, this benefit applies to a Commissioned Officer of the Regular or Reserve Corps of the Public Health Service in time of war, on detail for duty with the Army, Navy, Air Force, Marine Corps, or Coast Guard; or while the service was part of the military forces of the United States pursuant to Executive Order of the President.
   - A Commissioned Officer serving on inactive duty training whose death resulted from an injury incurred or aggravated in the line of duty.

5. *World War II Merchant Mariners*

   Merchant Mariners with oceangoing service during the period of armed conflict December 7, 1941, to December 31, 1946, are eligible, as are U.S. Merchant Mariners who served on blockships in support of Operation Mulberry during World War II.

6. *The Philippine Armed Forces*

   Certain Philippine veterans of World War II are eligible for these benefits. It requires that the Philippine veteran was a citizen of the United States or an alien legally admitted for permanent residence, who resided in the U.S. *at the time of their death* AND
   - Served before July 1, 1946, in the organized military forces of the Government of the Commonwealth of the

Philippines, while those forces were in the service of the U.S. armed forces (this includes organized guerrilla forces under commanders appointed, designated, or subsequently recognized by Commander in Chief, Southwest Pacific Area, or other competent authority in the U.S. Army, and who died on or after November 1, 2000, OR

- Enlisted between October 6, 1945, and June 30, 1947, with the armed forces of the United States with the consent of the Philippine government, and who died on or after December 16, 2003.

7. *Spouses and dependents*

Spouses and dependents of eligible veterans may be buried in a national cemetery. This group includes

- Surviving spouses even if the eligible veteran is *not* buried or memorialized in a national cemetery.
- Surviving spouses who subsequently remarried a non-veteran. The spouse's status is based on marriage to the deceased eligible vet.
- Children of an eligible veteran may be buried in a national cemetery if they meet one of these criteria: A minor child which is defined as one who is unmarried and under the age of 21 years of age or under the age of 23 if a full-time student at an approved educational institution *or* an adult child of any age who became permanently physically or mentally disabled and incapable of self-support before reaching the age of 21 or 23 if a full-time student at an approved educational institution (supporting documentation of disability must be provided).

Burial Benefits Payout Varies

If the death is service related, the VA pays up to $2,000 toward burial expenses. If the vet is buried in a VA national cemetery, some of the costs for transporting the remains may be reimbursed.

Does a less than honorable discharge eliminate all veteran death benefits?

A VA Regional Office will determine if a veteran with an undesirable, bad conduct, and any other discharge other than honorable, will qualify the veteran for these benefits.

If the death is not service related, the VA pays up to $300 toward burial and funeral expenses. There is also a $300 plot-interment allowance. Even if the death is not service related, if the veteran died in a VA hospital or in VA-approved home care, transport of the remains to the cemetery may be partially reimbursed.

The person who has paid for the veteran's burial or funeral may claim this reimbursement *provided* he has not already been reimbursed by another government agency or some other source such as the veteran's employer. For example, the families of Federal employees who die from an injury sustained in the line of duty (of their non-military job) may be paid a death gratuity of up to $10,000. Additionally, the family may receive up to $800 payable by the Department of Labor to a surviving spouse or children for funeral expenses of a Federal employee who died as a result of injuries sus-

Who is not eligible for burial in a national cemetery?

The following groups are not eligible to be buried in a national cemetery: former spouses of eligible vets whose marriages have ended by annulment or divorce rather than death; family members other than the surviving spouse and dependent children; individuals with dishonorable discharges; individuals who reported for the draft but were not inducted into the military; individuals convicted of a capital crime; individuals convicted of subversive activities; individuals whose only service is active duty for training or inactive duty training in the National Guard or Reserves.

tained in the line of duty. If they receive these monies, they are not eligible for reimbursement by the VA.

If You Choose to Be Buried in a National Cemetery

While you can't reserve a plot in a national cemetery, a licensed funeral home can readily make arrangements for burial when the need arises. While scheduling a burial can be made seven days a week, interment is only possible Monday through Fridays. Burial in a national cemetery also includes perpetual care of the gravesite at no cost to the family.

Your survivors will need to provide a copy of your discharge documents in order to prove your active military duty service and that your discharge was *not* under dishonorable conditions. The cemetery will need certain kinds of information. Help your survivors by collecting the following information in advance (they will need to add the date and place of death), and putting it together with your discharge papers.

- Your full name and military rank
- Branch of service
- Social Security number
- Service number
- VA claim number, if applicable
- Date and place of birth
- Date of retirement or last separation from active duty

There are no viewing facilities available at national cemeteries nor can funeral services be held there. A final committal service (right before interment) may be held, but not at graveside. These services are held in committal shelters at a distance from the grave. Burial follows.

If You Choose to Be Buried in a Private Cemetery

If you do not want to be buried in a national cemetery, you are still eligible for other burial benefits including a military honor guard, a flag, and a headstone/marker. Your family will need to provide eligibility information to the cemetery director.

Some private cemeteries may offer "free" gravesites to veterans. If you are making pre-burial arrangements, make sure you get in writing what the cemetery is offering and what is required. Leave those papers in a safe place, with the other information for your family.

If you expect your family to make the necessary arrangements, make sure they understand that *free* may come with some serious and expensive requirements attached to the offer. Some cemeteries offer a free gravesite to the veteran, but insist that an additional gravesite be purchased, and not necessarily adjacent to the veteran's plot. There may be restrictions on the type of headstone or marker that may be used to mark the grave; there may be a charge for setting the free government headstone or for the base that is used for the marker. In other words, the free gravesite may be more costly than burial in other private cemeteries. It would be nice to think that no one would take advantage of a family at a time like this—but unfortunately, that isn't always true.

Not sure if a deceased family member is an eligible vet?

Veterans are entitled to a proper, respectful burial. If you are unsure if a deceased adult is a veteran, you can verify their status by calling the VA toll-free benefits number: 1-800-827-1000, or contact your local VA Regional Office representative. This cannot be used for unidentified remains. Have at hand the following information: decedent's name and VA claim number (if known); decedent's Social Security number; date of birth; branch of military service; service number; service dates. Generally a decision on eligibility is made within three days.

If You Choose Burial at Sea

All veterans, not just those who served in the Navy or Coast Guard, are eligible for burial at sea (or to have their cremated remains scattered at sea). The Navy and Coast Guard provide this service. However, the family may not witness the burial. It is done at a time and place that is convenient for the military. There are specific requirements for embalming the body and for the casket that must be used. If this is your choice, contact www.militaryfuneralhonors.osd.mil

The Burial Flag on the Casket

Veterans are entitled to have their caskets draped with the United States flag. To apply for a flag, your family will complete VA Form 21-2008, Application for United States Flag for Burial Purposes. Your survivors may obtain a flag at any VA Regional Office or the U.S. Post Office. Generally, the funeral home director will help with this request.

Directions for how to display and fold the flag are included in Form 21–2008. These flags are not appropriate for outside use except on a very limited basis. They are made of cotton and can easily be damaged by the weather.

After interment services, the flag will be folded and presented to veteran's next of kin.

Even when parents are not the primary next of kin, they may also receive a flag and flag case.

Certain VA cemeteries have an Avenue of Flags. Families of veterans buried in those cemeteries may donate the burial flags to be flown on patriotic holidays.

Gravestones: VA-Approved Headstones and Markers

The VA provides a headstone (upright marble or upright granite) or marker (flat bronze, flat marble, or flat granite) at the graves of el-

Who is considered next of kin?

For a married veteran, it's his spouse. When there is no spouse, next of kin is considered in the following order:

- Sons or daughters in the order of seniority
- Oldest parent unless legal custody was granted to another person
- Blood or adoptive relative granted legal custody
- Brothers or sisters in order of seniority
- Oldest grandparent
- Other relative in accordance with the laws in the deceased's state of residence.

igible veterans. Also available are bronze niche markers used to mark the niches that hold the urns with cremated remains.

For deaths occuring *before* September 11, 2001, the VA may provide a headstone or marker only for graves that are not marked with a private headstone.

If you will be buried in a national cemetery, then the National Cemetery Administration will handle preparation of the marker. Upright headstones are standard in most national cemeteries, but in some, there are both upright stones as well as flat marker sections. Make sure you indicate your preference to your survivors.

If the veteran's eligible spouse or dependent children predecease him or her, a single gravesite and a single headstone or marker is provided. If the spouse and dependent children are buried in a private cemetery, they are *not* eligible for a government-furnished headstone or marker.

If both spouses are veterans, then two gravesites and two headstones may be provided if requested.

If you are *not* being buried in a national cemetery, then your next of kin or a representative such as the funeral home director, cemetery official, and veterans counselor must apply for a VA headstone, using VA Form 40-1330, Application for Standard Government

Headstone or Marker for Installation in a Private or State Veterans' Cemetery, and include a copy of the veteran's military discharge papers. The cemetery director can assist with the application.

If you are making arrangements before death, complete this form and put it with copies of your military discharge papers and other burial wishes for use in time of need.

There are limitations on the kind of inscription that is permitted on a government-furnished headstone or marker. The inscription must say, in this order, the legal name of the deceased, branch of service, and years of birth and death.

If there is space, the inscription can also include the veteran's rank, war service, military decorations, awards, and the month and day of birth and death. Personal inscriptions, such as "beloved son" or "loving husband, father, grandfather," can be included at the bottom of the headstone with VA approval and provided there is space and the personalized information is in good taste.

There are approved "emblems of belief" that may be included on the headstone. These include Christian, Buddhist, Jewish, Presbyterian Cross, Russian Orthodox Cross, Lutheran Cross, Episcopal Cross, Unitarian Church/Unitarian Universalist Association, United Methodist Church, Aaronic Order Church, Mormon (Angel Moroni), Native American Church of North America, Serbian Orthodox, Greek Cross, Bahai (9-pointed Star), Atheist, Muslim (Crescent

Still waiting for a headstone or marker?

If more than 30 days have passed since an application was submitted for a government headstone or marker, call the Applicant Assistance Office, 1-800-697-6947, to verify that the application was received. If it has and is being processed, check again at 60 days following the death of the veteran. At that time, if the headstone or marker has not been installed, contact the party responsible for accepting delivery of the headstone or marker (that may be the cemetery or funeral home).

and Star), Hindu, Konko-Kyo Faith, Community of Christ, Sufism Reoriented, Tenrikyo Church, Seicho-No-Ie, Church of World Messianity (Izunome), United Church of Religious Science, Christian Reformed Church, Eckankar, Christian Church, Christian & Missionary Alliance, United Church of Christ, Humanist Emblem of Spirit, Presbyterian Church (USA), Izumo Taishakyo Mission of Hawaii, Soka Gakkai International—USA, Sikh (khanda), Christian Scientist (Cross & Crown), Muslim (Islamic 5-Pointed Star).

Presidential Memorial Certificate

The veteran's next of kin will, upon request, receive a Presidential Memorial Certificate (PMC). It bears the current President's signature. Additional copies may also be requested for other family members.

Applications for a PMC must be made in person at any VA regional office or by U.S. mail addressed to:

Presidential Memorial Certificates (41A1C)
Department of Veterans Affairs
5109 Russell Road
Quantico, VA 22134-3903

No requests via e-mail will be accepted. Accompanying the request must be copies of the veteran's discharge papers and death certificate.

Military Honors at Funerals

The Department of Defense, not the VA, is responsible for providing military funeral honors under a program titled Honoring Those Who Served. The honors include folding and presenting the United States burial flag and playing "Taps." At least two or more uniformed military persons will be members of the funeral honors detail, one of whom will be from the veteran's service of the armed forces. The funeral home director can request military honors. If the veteran is being buried in a VA national cemetery, then the Department of Veterans Affairs (VA) National Cemetery Administration staff will coordinate the military honors. Again, make clear your wishes about military honors in your pre-burial planning list.

In Conclusion

A veteran has earned the right to a proper burial with honor and respect. Plan ahead for this difficult time. Indicate clearly your preferences and leave the information with the required VA forms so that your family can easily follow your wishes.

CHAPTER 9

Education Is the Key to the Future

Montgomery G.I. Bill

Millions of veterans have used the G.I. Bill of Rights to pay for their educations. Literally billions of dollars have been paid since the "Servicemen's Readjustment Act of 1944," better known as the G.I. Bill of Rights, was enacted. In this chapter, you will learn who is eligible for these benefits, what you will still need to pay, and the kinds of programs that qualify.

The History and Purpose of the Bill

World War I vets got $60 and a train ticket home after discharge. During the Great Depression, many of these veterans found it nearly impossible to make a decent living.

The G.I. Bill of 1944 was created to ensure that this country took good care of the veterans who served it. The bill provided education and training benefits, as well as loan guarantees for homes (see chapter 10).

A college education, previously out of reach for many Americans, could now be part of their futures. In 1947, veterans accounted for 49 percent of all college admissions! When the original G.I. Bill expired in 1956, almost half of the 16 million World War II veterans had taken advantage of the education and training programs.

In 1984, Congressman Gillespie V. "Sonny" Montgomery revamped the G.I. Bill. It is now known as the "Montgomery GI Bill

(MGIB)," and continues to provide VA home loan guarantees and funds for veterans to use for education and training.

Overview of the Program

The MGIB provides up to 36 months of education assistance to eligible veterans for college, technical or vocational courses, correspondence courses, apprenticeships, job training, flight training, high-tech training, licensing and certification tests, entrepreneurship training, and certain entrance examinations. In short, most legitimate education and training programs are covered.

The monthly benefit you receive, up to $1,000 per month, is based on several criteria: the type of training you take, the length of your service, your category (there are four categories), and if you have earned additional funds through "kickers" (supplemental bonuses through special military service).

When the G.I. Bill was first enacted, the money a vet received was enough to support him (and his family) while he went to school, even full-time. Today, $1,000 per month is usually not enough to pay for classes and living expenses. You will probably have to supplement your income, and if necessary, take loans, if you plan to be in school full-time. But it's a benefit you've earned through your service. Take full advantage of it.

What Kinds of Education Programs Can You Take?

There are a wide range of education programs that are eligible for MGIB.

Institutes of Higher Learning

This refers to college classes. You can attend four-year colleges or universities, two-year community colleges, and may pursue either an undergraduate or advanced degree.

PAYMENT. Issued monthly, paid in arrears, which means that you receive the March check in April. How much you are paid is based on the number of classes you attend. Full-time is defined as 12 hours or more; three-quarter time is 9 to 11 hours; half-time is 6 to 8 hours. For less than 6 hours, you are reimbursed at a rate not to exceed the tuition and fees charged for the courses. If you are in a graduate program, you are considered full-time if the institution considers you full-time, and are paid accordingly.

Non–College Degree Training

These are training programs, for example, barber/beautician school, truck-driving courses, EMT certification.

PAYMENT. Issued monthly, paid in arrears, which means that you receive the March check in April. How much you are paid is based on the number of clock hours you attend the training program each month.

Apprenticeship and On-the-Job Training

These are training programs where you work in the field such as apprenticeship to a union plumber or master craftsman, or a firefighter-training program.

PAYMENT. Issued monthly, paid in arrears, which means that you receive the March check in April. You can receive a salary from your employer, as well as VA benefits. You receive 85 percent of the full-time GI Bill rate for the first six months; 65 percent of the full-time GI Bill rate for the second six months; 45 percent of the full-time GI Bill rate for the remainder of the program.

Flight Training

You can pursue additional flight training *if* you already have a private pilot's license and valid medical certification before beginning training.

PAYMENT. Issued *after* the training is completed and the school submits information to the VA. You will be reimbursed for 60 percent of approved charges.

Independent Training, Distance Learning, and Internet Training

These are courses, taken online, and usually offered by colleges and universities. The institution provides the course materials and grades. If you're a self-starter and able to work without direct supervision, this may be a good alternative for you.

PAYMENT. Same rules and payment schedule as for institutes of higher learning (see above).

Correspondence Courses

These are similar to distance learning (see above), but generally you receive the lessons in the mail, and within a prescribed time limit you must complete the material and return it for a grade.

PAYMENT. The VA will reimburse you 55 percent of the approved costs for this type of course. Please note: the VA's "approved costs" may be less than the actual cost for the course. You will be paid quarterly after the lessons are completed.

National Testing Program

You can be reimbursed for the fees paid for national tests required for admission to undergraduate programs, such as the SAT or ACT; and tests required for admission to graduate programs, such as the GRE, LSAT, or GMAT. You can also be reimbursed for the fees paid for national tests that offer you course credit at institutions of higher learning, such as the College Level Exam Program (CLEP).

PAYMENT. The VA will reimburse you for the costs of these tests after you submit proof of payment.

Licensing and Certification

This is limited to those tests specifically approved for the GI Bill but includes final tests for career fields that issue certification of licensing in order to work; HVAC technician, medical technician, jet engine mechanic, and others. The VA pays only for the cost of the tests, not other fees connected with obtaining a license or certification such as final fees for issuing the actual license.

PAYMENT. The VA will reimburse up to $2,000 for these tests, after you submit proof of payment. You can be paid for the cost of the test even if you fail the test.

Entrepreneurship Training

The Veterans Corporation and the Small Business Development Center (SBCD) offer programs designed to help you start your own business or improve the business you already own. The VA will pay for these courses.

PAYMENT. The VA will reimburse you for the cost of entrepreneurship training but *only* for programs offered by SBCD or Veterans Corporation.

Work-Study Program

This is an extra way to earn money if you are a student attending school at least three-quarter-time or more. You may receive your education benefits *and* work at the school veterans' office, VA Regional Office, VA medical facilities, or at approved state employment offices.

PAYMENT. You will be paid at either the state or Federal minimum wage, whichever is greater.

Co-Op Training

This program combines classroom learning with on-the-job training. You may attend classes in the morning and work in a related job in the afternoon; or attend school at night and work during the day. Some programs are structured so that you attend classes one semester, then work full-time in the following semester.

PAYMENT. The advantage of co-op programs is that you receive your GI benefits at the full-time rate during the entire period.

Payment Schedule for Montgomery GI Bill

While always subject to change, the following payment schedule is effective since October 1, 2006. Even if the payments increase, this chart will give you a framework for how much you might expect if you return to school on the MGIB.

The following rates apply to those completing an enlistment of three years or more.

Institutional training

TRAINING TIME	MONTHLY RATE
Full-time	$1,075.00
3/4-time	$806.25
1/2-time	$537.50

TRAINING TIME	MONTHLY RATE
less than 1/2-time more than 1/4-time	$537.50*
1/4-time or less	$268.75*

*Tuition and Fees *only*. Payment cannot exceed the listed amount.

Apprenticeship and on-job training

TRAINING TIME	MONTHLY RATE
First six months of training	$913.75
Second six months of training	$698.75
Remaining pursuit of training	$483.75
Correspondence and Flight	Entitlement charged at the rate of one month for each $1,075.00 paid.
Cooperative	$1,075.00

The following rates apply to those completing an enlistment of less than three years.

Institutional training

TRAINING TIME	MONTHLY RATE
Full time	$873.00
3/4 time	$654.75
1/2 time	$436.50
less than 1/2 time more than 1/4 time	$436.50*
1/4 time or less	$218.25*

*Tuition and Fees *only*. Payment cannot exceed the listed amount.

Apprenticeship and on-job training

TRAINING PERIOD	MONTHLY RATE
First six months of training	$742.05
Second six months of training	$567.45
Remaining pursuit of training	$392.85
Correspondence and Flight	Entitlement charged at the rate of one month for each $873.00 paid.
Cooperative	$873.00

Here are the basic institutional rates for persons with remaining entitlement.

Institutional training

TRAINING TIME	MONTHLY RATE			
	No deps	One dep	Two deps	Each add dep
Full-time	$1,263.00	$1,299.00	$1,330.00	$16.00
3/4-time	$947.75	$974.25	$997.75	$12.00
1/2-time	$631.50	$649.50	$665.00	$8.50
Less than 1/2-time; more than 1/4-time	$631.50*			
1/4-time or less	$315.75*			

*Tuition and Fees *only*. Payment cannot exceed the listed amount.

Apprenticeship and on-job training

TRAINING PERIOD	MONTHLY RATE			
	No deps	One dep	Two deps	Each add dep
1st six months of pursuit of program	$1,030.20	$1,044.23	$1,056.55	$5.95
2nd six months	$765.38	$766.43	$785.53	$4.55
3rd six months	$514.35	$522.23	$528.30	$3.15
Remaining pursuit of program	$499.05	$506.48	$513.23	$3.15

Cooperative course

TRAINING PERIOD	MONTHLY RATE			
Oct. 1, 2006–Sept. 30, 2007	$1,263.00	$1,299.00	$1,330.00	$16.00
Correspondence	55% of the approved charges			
Flight	60% of the approved charges			

You May Be Eligible for Accelerated Payment

To encourage veterans to enter certain high-tech fields, the government offers an accelerated payment program. If you are enrolled in a high-tech program and intend to seek employment in a high-tech industry, you may qualify.

You will be paid a lump sum payment of 60 percent of tuition and fees for high-cost, high tech programs. However, if you don't have enough in your entitlement to cover 60 percent of your costs, you will only be paid based on what is left of your remaining entitlement.

The tuition and fees must be more than double the Montgomery

GI Bill benefits that you would otherwise receive for that semester (or term, quarter). For example, if your full-time rate is $732 for a four-month semester, your tuition and fees must be over $5,856 to qualify. Here's how it's calculated: 4 months × $732 = $2,928. But the costs have to be double that ($2,928 × 2 = $5,856) in order to qualify for the program.

These programs qualify for the accelerated payment program:

- Life sciences or physical sciences (not social sciences)
- All fields of engineering
- Mathematics
- Engineering and science technology
- Computer specialties
- Engineering, science, and computer management

You must also certify that you intend to seek employment in one of these industries:

- Biotechnology
- Life sciences technologies
- Opto-electronics
- Computers and telecommunications
- Electronics
- Computer-integrated manufacturing
- Material design
- Aerospace
- Weapons
- Nuclear technology

You must ask your school to include a request for accelerated payment to the VA when it sends in your enrollment information. Your request *must* include certification that you intend to seek employment in one of the industries listed above.

Let's be clear. Your entitlement is reduced by the amount you receive—you just receive it as a lump sum payment, rather than monthly. For example, if your full-time rate is $900, and you qualify for an accelerated payment of $3,600, then the VA will charge your entitlement as follows: $3,600 ÷ $900 = 4 months.

You may receive accelerated payment for non-technical courses (for example, English, history) if these courses are pre-requisites for your degree.

Two important points to remember:

- If you receive a "non-punitive grade" (a grade that will not count toward graduation requirements, for example, you receive a "W" for withdrawing from a class), you may have to repay *all* or part of your accelerated payment. At the very least, you will have to defend that grade and may be liable for repayment.
- You must certify that you intend to find employment in a high-tech industry, but if you fail to obtain a job, you do not have to repay the money. You may be required to demonstrate efforts, however, that you attempted to find high-tech employment.

For a list of approved high-tech programs, go to www.gibill.va.gov/pamphlets/acceleratedpayinfo.htm.

Choosing the Right Program/College

Your education benefit is limited in time (must be used within 10 years of separation from service) and dollar amount—so you want to use it wisely. But you must choose smartly because this is your future. Take the time to carefully figure out, before you enroll in any school or program, exactly what kind of career you want and what courses or training you will need to achieve your goals.

Even if you've never been a strong student before, you may be ready now for a more challenging program. You're older, more mature, more experienced—all traits that bode well for handling the responsibilities of school or a training program.

Are All Courses Eligible?

You'll have plenty of options when deciding which educational path you want to take, but make sure that any program you take is approved by your State Approving Agency (SAA). See Appendix I for a list of each state's agency. Your school/program may have designated a staff person to work with veterans. If so, start there to make sure the program you want to take is SAA-approved or call the VA at 1-888-442-4551.

The Federal VA does *not* approve courses, programs, or schools. It's up to each state to regulate the eligible courses and schools within their borders. The SAA must approve each program of education into which vets will enroll. If there is a branch or extension facility of the school, the SAA must approve those sites separately.

Your options are open—so explore possibilities you might have previously thought closed to you. You may choose to go to a local school or program—or travel out of state for a school that offers more precisely what you want for the career you've chosen.

You'll need to balance your career goals with financial realities. Your state may offer free or reduced tuition to returning veterans. That may make a difference in whether you choose an in-state school or enroll in an out-of-state program.

Who Is Eligible?

As with other benefits, it begins with the assumption that you received an honorable discharge. You must also have a high school diploma or a GED. For some benefits, you must also have 12 hours of college credit.

CATEGORY 1

- You entered active duty for the first time *after* June 30, 1985.
- You had your military pay reduced by $100 a month for the first 12 months.
- Service requirements:
  - You continuously served for three years OR
  - You continuously served for two years if that is what you first enlisted for OR
  - You continuously served for two years if you entered the Selected Reserve within a year of leaving active duty and then served four years (this was called the "2 by 4" program).

CATEGORY 2

- You entered active duty before January 1, 1977
- You served at least one day between October 19, 1984, and June 30, 1985, AND stayed on active duty through June 30, 1988, OR June 30, 1987 if you entered the Selective Reserve within one year of leaving active duty and served four years.
- On December 31, 1989, you had entitlement left from Vietnam-Era G.I. Bill.

CATEGORY 3

- You are not eligible under Category 1 or 2.
- Before separation, you had your military pay reduced by $1,200 as your contribution to MGIB.
- Service Requirements
  - You were on active duty on September 30, 1990, AND separated involuntarily after February 2, 1991, OR
  - Involuntarily separated on or after November 30, 1993, OR
  - Voluntarily separated under either the Voluntary Separation Incentive (VSI) or Special Separation Benefit (SSB) program.

CATEGORY 4

- You were on active duty on October 9, 1996, AND you had money remaining in a VEAP (Veterans Education Assistance Program) on that date AND you elected MGIB by October 9, 1997, OR
- You entered full-time National Guard duty under Title 32, USC, between July 1, 1985, and November 28, 1989, AND you elected MGIB during the period October 9, 1996, through July 8, 1997
- You had your military pay reduced by $100 a month for 12 months or made a $1,200 lump-sum contribution as your contribution to MGIB

Your Contribution to MGIB—and Return on Your Investment

When you joined the service, you were given the option of enrolling in the Montgomery GI Bill. Within the first two weeks of

What is VEAP?

The Veterans Assistance Program (VEAP) was an educational incentive program offered to active servicemembers between January 1, 1977, through June 30, 1985. The Army matched the servicemember's contributions on a $2 to $1 basis. You could contribute additional money to VEAP at a late date if you were on active duty, *even if your service periods were broken.*

You were required to use the benefit within 10 years of the last separation. Any remaining funds of *your* personal unused contributions are refunded (but not the matching government contributions). The refund is given by the Department of Veterans Affairs (DVA) to the servicemember at the address the DVA has on file. If you have moved, contact the DVA. Upon your death, any refund will be given to the surviving beneficiaries designated on the Servicemembers' Group Life Insurance (SGLI) election form, or to your estate if no SGLI form is on record.

service, you had to specifically enroll or disenroll. If you enrolled, you could make a single lump-sum payment ($1,200) or your pay was reduced by $100 for 12 months to cover your contribution of $1,200.

In return, you get $28,800 for 36 months of benefits for individuals with three-year or more enlistments. Individuals with two-year enlistments get $23,400. To receive this benefit, you must be enrolled in a qualified program and file paperwork to prove your eligibility in order to receive the funds, and you must use it within 10 years of your separation. In other words, you don't receive a lump-sum payment when you are discharged. You must pursue an education or training in order to use this benefit.

Use It or Lose It

You have 10 years from the date of your separation to use MGIB for education, training, certification, and so forth. You cannot get your contribution refunded. (Keep in mind that once you elected to enroll in MGIB, you couldn't stop or suspend the deductions during your service.)

There are only two circumstances in which the servicemember's contribution to MGIB is refunded.

- If the servicemember dies on active duty (or within one year of separation) *for a service-connected death,* then his beneficiaries will receive a payment equal to the amount deducted for MGIB.
- If service ends because of a defective or erroneous enlistment, the initial period of active duty doesn't count and contributions made during that period are refunded.

Term of Service and Eligibility for MGIB

Time in service is a critical component for MGIB eligibility. Time spent in the Selected Reserves, active duty for training, or a delayed entry program does *not* count toward fulfilling your minimum time-in-service requirement for MGIB.

- You've got to complete your initial enlistment. For two year enlistees, you have to complete the full 24 months (see below for exception). If you enlisted for a longer period (three, four, five, or six years), then you have to have completed at least 36 months.
- But if your separation from the service is for the "convenience of the government (COG)," then the 20/30 rule is applicable. That means that you have to have served at least 20 months of the 24 months if you were enlisted for two years; 30 months if you were enlisted for a longer tour.

There are other exceptions to the rule. If you are separated because of a service-connected disability, hardship, pre-existing medical condition, and/or a condition (not a disability) that interferes with duty, you are entitled to one month of benefits for every month of active duty served up to 36 months.

Another variation: You had enlisted for more than two years. You served more than 24 months, but less than 30 months. You may still be eligible for MGIB if, within one year of separation, you enlist in the Selected Reserves.

And yet one more way to qualify. According to Public Law 106–419, Veterans Benefits and Health Care Improvement Act of 2000, if you did not meet the time in service requirement for MGIB eligibility during your initial obligated period of active duty, you can become eligible during a later period of active duty. You can reestablish eligibility by completing 36 months of service with a fully honorable discharge.

Here are the only two circumstances in which you may combine two different periods of service:

- You were a service academy cadet with prior service and you failed to complete a course of education and then re-entered active duty.
- You were separated during the first 12 months of active duty because of hardship, a service-connected disability, a pre-existing medical condition, a condition that interfered with duty, or a disability that restricted activity that was necessary for your position, such as lifting or walking—and then you later re-entered active duty.

Bottom line: Check with the education center of your service branch to determine which rule applies to your situation.

Kickers Add Value

Each service can offer extra MGIB money, a kicker, for enlisting in certain critical jobs. It can be as much as $30,000. The technical name for these kickers are the Army College Fund, the Navy College Fund, and the Marine College Fund.

To be eligible for a kicker, you must have enrolled in the MGIB when you began active duty. You also have to have met the requirements for basic MGIB and earned a fully honorable discharge.

Kickers are recruitment incentives. The kicker must be written in the enlistment contract; verbal agreements are not honored. For example, if, upon enlisting in the Army, you were promised a kicker, you should have received DA Form 3296–66/67 (Army Incentive Enlistment Program) when you began active duty.

I was promised a kicker, but my records do not include one—what can I do?

You will have to provide the VA a copy of your own record of the kicker that was promised. *Do not send the original.* You may send in both a copy of DA Form 3286–66 along with your application for benefits (VA Form 22–1990). Without documentary evidence to support your claim for a kicker, it will be denied.

Active-Duty Education Program Affects VA Benefit

While the Tuition Assistance Top-Up Program is only for active-duty personnel, it does impact their regular MGIB benefits. The Montgomery GI Bill—Active Duty education program permits VA to pay a Tuition Assistance Top-Up benefit. The amount of the benefit can be equal to the difference between the total cost of a college course and the amount of tuition assistance that is paid by the military for the course.

To be eligible for the Top-Up benefit, the person must be approved for Federal tuition assistance by a military department and be eligible for MGIB-Active-Duty benefits. To be eligible for MGIB benefits, the person must be an MGIB—Active-Duty participant and must have served at least two full years on active duty.

The amount of the benefit is limited to the amount that the person would receive for the same course if regular MGIB benefits were being paid. In no case can the amount paid by the military combined with the amount paid by VA be more than the total cost of the course.

If a person receives the Top-Up benefit, his or her regular MGIB benefits will be reduced. The amount of entitlement charged for Top-Up payments is determined by dividing the amount of the payment by the claimant's full-time monthly rate.

How to Handle (Over-)Payments

When you enroll in school or a training program, the certifying official at the institution will submit the VACERT (VA certification paperwork) to the VA regional processing office. This triggers payment of your education benefit.

You must notify the certifying official of any change in your academic status, including if you withdraw from courses; reduce your training time; change your program objective; or are terminated by the school (through academic suspension or dismissal). The certifying official will then notify the VA. Should you erroneously continue to receive payments, you will be required to make a full restitution.

Overpayments (and underpayments) happen fairly frequently. Correcting mistakes always requires additional paperwork. Whatever the reason for the change in status, whether it's to your advantage or not, however legitimate, you need to make sure that you keep your own documentation. Remember: You will be required to pay back any overpayment.

But wait: you may be able to keep overpayments *if* there are *mitigating circumstances*. This is VA-speak that considers situations in which a veteran may be able to justify payment for courses that would normally be denied.

Mitigating circumstances are unanticipated and unavoidable events or situations, like illness or a change in employment status, which prevent you from completing a course with a creditable grade. You will be required to submit evidence to corroborate your claim—like a doctor's certificate or a letter from your employer. Mitigating circumstances cover a wide range of situations. For example, if you have unexpected difficulties with child care arrangements during class time, that may be considered a mitigating circumstance.

Mitigating circumstances are automatically granted for the first instance of withdrawal from classes up to a total of six semester hours. The school must report that you have withdrawn from the courses, but you need not repay the benefits already paid. On the other hand, you can't claim mitigating circumstances to keep the education payment if you withdraw from the class because you don't like the instructor or you were going to fail the class.

Make the Grade: Punitive and Non-Punitive Grades

The VA classifies grades as Punitive or Non-Punitive. What they are really referring to are categories of classes and the grades you receive.

A *punitive grade* is one that affects the credit hours earned or your grade point average (GPA). For example, those grades would be A, B, C, D, or F (or your institution's equivalents) because they affect whether you earn credit hours for courses and because they affect your overall GPA. The VA pays for punitive grades only.

In contrast, a *non-punitive grade* would be one that doesn't affect the credit hours earned or your GPA, for example, if you audited a course or you received an I (incomplete) in the course.

Can you repeat the same course and get paid for it twice? Again, it's those mitigating circumstances that make the difference. The VA won't pay for any course that isn't computed in the graduation requirements of the school, except. . . . If the punitive grade is removed from your transcript or no longer computed in your grade point average, it becomes a non-punitive grade (ineligible for payment). However, if you repeat the course because you need it for graduation, and you receive a passing grade, then if it's the school's public published policy to replace the prior punitive grade with a creditable passing grade, those are considered mitigating circumstances, and *no* overpayment has occurred.

But this applies only if you have failed courses that are required for graduation or if you have passed the courses but didn't achieve the minimum acceptable grade that your school requires for your major (for example, your school may require that you receive at least a C or better in all courses in your major).

Let's say you fail an elective. It's not in your major. Can you repeat the class, and have you received an overpayment for the class you failed? Again, it depends. Most colleges require a certain number of electives as part of the overall distribution requirements to graduate. If you have not completed the number of credit hours necessary for graduation, then you may repeat an elective you've failed. So, let's say that you fail an art appreciation class in your freshman year. It's not your major, and in your senior year, you have still not fulfilled all the elective requirements you need for graduation. You may repeat the art appreciation class and VA benefits may be paid for the course. However, if you don't need additional electives to meet degree requirements, then you may not be paid for this course.

But, here's yet another exception even to that rule. If you are in your final term, have completed all other requirements, and wish to take the class in order to round out the program to full-time—then the VA will authorize this payment.

Here's one more common variation that many vets face. Let's say you need additional classes because you need to raise your grade point average in order to graduate. For example, you already have taken 120 hours in coursework, the minimum required for graduation. But your institution requires a minimum 2.0 GPA in order to graduate and you currently have a 1.85 GPA. Under those circumstances, the VA will permit you to take additional classes beyond those normally needed for a degree in order to raise your overall GPA. Your certifying official, however, must submit a statement that guarantees that (1) the courses are being taken in order to remove the grade point deficiency, (2) that none of the courses are ones you've previously taken *unless* the repetition is required to satisfy an approved program, and (3) that you are making satisfactory progress under the school's standards.

Are you ready for college?

If you are concerned that you are not academically prepared to take college-level classes or training programs, consider enrolling in the Veterans Upward Bound (VUB) program. It's free, sponsored by the Department of Education, offered in locations around the country, and will help you refresh your academic skills.

You must be a veteran who is either low income and/or first-generation college (meaning neither of your parents has a four-year college degree). You have to have served at least 180 days of active Federal service and have a discharge that is other than dishonorable.

In addition to academic instruction in a wide variety of programs necessary for success in education beyond high school, tutorial and study skills assistance is also available. Further, you'll find assistance with applications to post-secondary schools and applying for financial aid.

Contact the Veterans Upward Bound program at www.veteransupwardbound.org/navubppinst.html.

Do Grades Matter?

You need to maintain your own standard of excellence. The grades you earn in a class, the effort you put into a training program—all these reflect on you and may determine your professional future.

But your education benefits are not dependent on maintaining a certain grade point average or receiving all outstanding certifications. You will need to prove that you are making satisfactory progress toward your educational goal in order to continue to receive your benefits. Whether you receive an A grade or a C is not considered.

There's a lot of leeway, but your benefits will be discontinued if you don't make "satisfactory progress" toward completion of your training or educational objective. Whether it's based on grades or proficiency level, you will have to meet your school's minimum requirements as you move toward completing the objective you set for yourself when you applied for educational benefits.

Starting Over When You're Not Making Progress

If you drop out of school or a training program—or are asked to leave—you may still be able to be recertified and use your benefits at a later date. To be reinstated, you will be required to develop a plan that demonstrates that you will now be able to resolve any academic (or personal) problems that affected your previous performance. You must show that things have changed and that you can complete your education or training.

If you return to the same institution—and the school's officials are willing to recertify you to the VA—they must indicate on the enrollment form that the problems you had have been discussed and resolved. The VA will accept a school's re-certification as evidence that the problems are resolved.

In order to re-certify you, however, the school may require proof that things have changed. For example, if you dropped out because you were having problems academically, found the work too hard, or changed your mind about the program you had selected, you may be required to attend your school's academic counseling program. Using these services demonstrates that you are making a sincere effort to resolve your issues. If there are no counseling services available at the school, you can attend the programs offered by the VA.

If other problems (personal-, family-, health-, work-related) were the cause of your failure to satisfactorily complete your classes/program, then you may be asked to demonstrate how the situation has changed. For example, if your work hours prevented you from attending classes, you may be required to submit a letter from your employer with a work schedule that will now allow you to attend school.

The school certifying official must show you—and submit to the VA—the minimum standards you must meet during the next enrollment/evaluation period.

In addition to the plan developed with the certifying official and submitted to the VA, you are required to make a specific request to the VA to have your educational assistance allowance resumed. Use VA Form 22–1995 or VA Form 22–5495.

If the VA requests more evidence to determine your eligibility for resumption of benefits, it may ask you to complete VA Form 22–8873, Supplemental Information for Change of Program or Reenrollment After Unsatisfactory Progress or Conduct. You will need to explain the cause of the problem, how it has been resolved, and the suitability of the program you now intend to pursue.

State Education Benefits Available to Veterans

You may also be eligible for additional educational benefits from your state. Appendix H lists the contact information for each state's Department of Veterans Affairs. Your MGIB education benefit is unaffected by any state benefits you earn. Various states offer different educational benefits in addition to the Federal educational benefits.

This chapter will not include a breakdown of the benefits for each state because they are constantly changing. Go to your state's Department of Veterans Affairs website to determine what your state offers.

The eligibility requirements for assistance, as well as the amount of the benefit, differs state by state. Even within the state, eligibility requirements may vary between programs.

Let's take Wisconsin as an example. Here are the benefits for the Wisconsin GI Bill.

1. Tuition and fees (100 percent) for eligible vets are waived for up to eight full-time semesters or 128 credits at any institution that is part of the University of Wisconsin or Wisconsin Technical College system. Unlike the Federal Montgomery GI Bill, there is no post-service time limitation on the benefit (whereas Federal benefits expire after 10 years).
2. Tuition and fees (100 percent) are waived for the spouse,

un-remarried surviving spouse, and child between the ages of 18 and 25 for a qualifying Wisconsin veteran who is currently rated by the Federal VA with a combined service-connected disability rating of 30 percent or greater; or died in the line of duty while on active, Reserve, or Guard duty; or died as the direct result of a service-connected disability, as determined by the Federal VA.

3. The Veterans Education (VetEd) grant program provides a reimbursement grant to reimburse tuition and fees to eligible vets who have not yet been awarded a bachelor's degree following successful course completion at an eligible U.W. technical college, or approved private institution of higher learning. You must have applied and been using the Federal benefits in order to be eligible for VetEd.
4. Vets may qualify for a low-interest-rate personal loan, with up to 10 years to repay, to be used for the education of the vet, spouse, or children.

Other states offer no specific educational benefits for veterans. Some offer no benefits for vets, but do offer scholarships or tuition waivers to the surviving children and spouse of servicemembers killed in the line of duty or who died as a result of injuries incurred in the line of duty. Again, check your state's Department of Veterans Affairs for details.

More and more states are providing additional educational benefits for vets. Make sure that you take advantage of the assistance you have earned for service to your country.

In Conclusion

The education benefits you've earned for your service can play a vital role in your future. First, take the time to figure out *what* you want to do, and then apply for the MGIB benefits you need to pay for the education and training required to achieve your goals.

CHAPTER 10

Home Ownership

Home Sweet Home with a VA Loan

Buying a home? A VA Guaranteed Home Loan is one of the benefits of service to your country. Since 1944, the VA has guaranteed over 18.2 million loans totaling more than $980 billion. The VA makes about 29 million loans each year, and the average loan amount is $178,000.

If you are a *qualified* veteran, and we'll cover in this chapter what you need to qualify, you may secure a VA loan for the purchase of your primary residence.

How the Loan Program Works

The VA doesn't directly lend you the money for a mortgage (except for Native Americans on trust land or to supplement a grant to get a specially adapted home for certain eligible vets). You apply to a lender (banks, savings and loans, mortgage companies). The difference is the loan is backed up by the Federal government. The VA guarantees a certain amount of the loan to the lender, usually about 25 percent. That means the institution can offer these loans, at competitive rates with *no down payment* to even those borrowers with bad credit, because unlike conventional mortgages, there is little or no risk involved to the institution. The Federal government has guaranteed that if the borrower doesn't repay the loan, the government will.

In 2005, the VA effectively raised the amount that a veteran could borrow for a home to $417,000 (and even higher in areas with

Choose your lender carefully

If possible, choose a lender that has "automatic basis" status. This means the lender can make the credit decision on the loan *without* VA approval. Although a VA appraisal is still required, you save time because there's no need to await VA approval. Not all lenders have the authority to process loans on an automatic basis—ask before beginning the loan application process. Lenders approved to participate in the VA's Lender Appraisal Processing Program (LAPP) can usually expedite the processing of VA appraisals.

a high cost of living like Alaska, Hawaii, Guam, and the U.S. Virgin Islands). How does the VA decide on the limit? The limit is tied to the standard loan that lenders sell to Freddie Mac (Federal Home Loan Mortgage Corporation, a government-sponsored company that acts as a secondary mortgage market investor to buy and sell loans). The maximum VA guarantee is 25 percent of the current Freddie Mac conforming loan for a single-family residence. The guaranteed amount can rise or fall, depending on current market conditions. The amount is determined on January 1 of each year.

The guaranteed portion of a VA loan is called an entitlement. The amount of entitlement relates to the amount VA will guarantee the lender against loss. Basically a veteran can borrow up to $417,000 with no downpayment. The actual money comes from the lender.

For loans over $417,000, the lender will most likely ask for a downpayment of around 25 percent of the remaining balance. For example:

Home: $450,000 (including all closing and other fees)

VA Home Loan: $417,000 including funding, closing, and other fees

Remainder: $33,000 that can either be paid using a downpayment provided by the veteran or the veteran must pay at least

25 percent of the difference to have the remainder added to their loan.

Confused? If you need help figuring out how much of an entitlement you are eligible for, or the limits on loans, work with the loan officer at the bank or ask a service officer of a Veterans Service Organization for a more detailed explanation.

There are advantages and disadvantages to a VA guaranteed loan. As with any financial decision, consider all your options before making a commitment.

The advantages of a VA loan:

- No downpayment
- Easier credit qualifying than conventional mortgage
- Lower closing costs
- No monthly mortgage insurance
- Loan is assumable

The disadvantages of a VA loan:

- VA loan includes funding fees (2 percent of the loan amount, slightly higher for reservists), although the fees may be rolled into the loan and are waived for vets with service-related disabilities. If you make a downpayment, the funding fee is reduced. Keep in mind that conventional mortgages also have closing costs.
- VA requires that the property meets certain minimum standards at appraisal. If the property doesn't meet those standards, and if the owner refuses to make required repairs, the buyer must either pay for the repairs himself, switch to conventional financing, or find another property.

What kinds of closing costs are permitted?

One advantage of a VA loan is the lower closing costs. While there can be no commission or brokerage fees charged for obtaining VA loans, here are the costs that are permissible: VA appraisal, credit report, survey, title search, recording fees, a 1 percent origination fee, and discount points. These can add up to a considerable out-of-pocket expense for the buyer because the closing costs and origination charge may not be included in the loan, except for VA refinancing loans. You will want to negotiate with your lender your interest rate, as well as the payment of discount points and other closing costs. For example, some mortgage brokers will waive the cost of a credit report. There are many VA-approved lenders—negotiate to get the best deal.

VA Loans: Not Just for Houses

You can use VA-guaranteed financing for a wide range of properties and for other purposes as well. They include

- Buying a single-family home or a townhouse or condominium unit in a VA-approved project.
- Building a home.
- Repairing, altering, or improving a home.
- Simultaneously purchasing *and* improving a home.
- Improving a home through installation of a solar heating and/or cooling system or other energy-efficient improvements.
- Refinancing an existing home loan.
- Refinancing an existing VA loan to reduce the interest rate and add energy-efficient improvements.
- Buying a manufactured (mobile) home and/or lot.
- Buying and improving a lot on which to place a manufactured home you already own and occupy.

- Refinancing a manufactured home loan in order to acquire a lot.

The property has to be in the United States, its territories, or possessions.

Can you use a VA loan to purchase a farm? No, but here's the exception. If you are buying a property that has a farmhouse on it and you plan to use that as your principal residence, then you can use a VA home loan. If you plan to farm the property, and that is to be your primary source of income, then you have to show that there is a reasonable chance of success. On the other hand, if you plan to use the residence and have another source of income, then choosing to farm the property becomes irrelevant. The Farmers Home Administration does offer financing and does give preference to veteran applicants.

Can you use a VA loan to buy or build a multi-family residence? Yes, up to four units if only one veteran is buying the property. If more than one vet is buying, then you are entitled to one additional family unit per vet buyer. Note: If you need the rental income to qualify for the loan, you are required to show that you have the background qualifications to be a successful landlord *and* that you have cash reserves to make the mortgage payments for six months without the rental income.

Generally, VA loans can't be used to purchase a cooperatively owned apartment because of the way those properties are financially structured and because it would require that all or almost all of the members of the cooperative were vets using their entitlements.

Who Qualifies for a VA Loan?

To determine if your service meets eligibility requirements, check the VA categories below. All classifications presume you have been discharged under other than dishonorable conditions (see chapter 2 for a full explanation of types of service discharges).

WARTIME SERVICE. Wartime eligibility includes service during:

World War II	9/16/1940 to 7/25/1947
Korea	6/27/1950 to 1/31/1955
Vietnam	8/5/1964 to 5/7/1975

For those who served in wartime, you must have at least 90 days on active duty and been discharged under other than dishonorable conditions. If you served less than 90 days, you may be eligible if you were discharged for a service-connected disability.

PEACETIME. Peacetime eligibility includes service during:

7/26/1947 to 6/26/1950
2/1/1955 to 8/4/1964
5/8/1975 to 9/7/1980 (enlisted)
5/8/1975 to 10/16/1981 (officer)

For those who served in these peacetime periods, you must have served at least 181 days of continuous active duty and been discharged under other than dishonorable conditions. If you served less than 181 days, you may still be eligible if you were discharged for a service-connected disability.

FOR ENLISTED SERVICE AFTER 9/7/1980; FOR OFFICER SERVICE AFTER 10/16/1981. If you began enlisted service after September 7, 1980, or officer service after October 16, 1981, you need to meet the following criteria in order to be eligible for a VA loan.

- You must have completed 24 months of continuous active duty or the full period (at least 181 days) for which you were ordered or called to active duty and been discharged under conditions other than dishonorable, OR
- You must have completed at least 181 days of active duty and been given a hardship discharge (10 USC 1173) or Early

Out (10 USC 1171), or have been determined to have a compensable service-connected disability
- ✦ You have been discharged with less than 181 days of service for a service-connected disability.

Some individuals may be eligible if they were released from active duty due to an involuntary reduction in force, certain medical conditions, or for the convenience of the government. Consult your local Veterans Affair officer to evaluate the specifics of your case.

GULF WAR—SERVICE DURING 8/2/1990 THROUGH THE PRESENT (end date to be determined). If you served on active duty during the period August 2, 1990, through the present, you must have

- ✦ Completed 24 months of continuous active duty or the full period (at least 90 days) for which you were called or ordered to active duty, and been discharged under conditions other than dishonorable, OR
- ✦ Completed at least 90 days of active duty and been given a hardship discharge (10 USC 1173) or an Early Out (10 USC 1173), or have been determined to have a compensable service-connected discharge, OR
- ✦ Been discharged with less than 90 days of service for a service-connected disability.

Some individuals may be eligible if they were released from active duty due to an involuntary reduction in force, certain medical conditions, or for the convenience of the government. Consult your local Veterans Affair officer to evaluate the specifics of your case.

IF YOU SERVED IN SELECTED RESERVES OR THE NATIONAL GUARD. You must have completed a total of six years in the Selected Reserves or National Guard (you must be a member of an active unit, attended required weekend drills and two-week active duty for training) AND

- Were discharged with an honorable discharge, OR
- Were placed on the retired list, OR
- Were transferred to the Standby Reserves or an element of the Ready Reserve other than the Selected Reserve after service characterized as honorable, OR
- Continue to serve in the Selected Reserves

You may still be eligible if you completed less than six years but were discharged for a service-connected disability.

Who Else Is Eligible for a VA Loan?

You may be able to establish eligibility if you are a United States citizen who served in the armed forces of a government allied with the United States in World War II. Also individuals with service as members in certain organizations such as Public Health Service officers, cadets at the United States Military, Air Force, or Coast Guard Academy, midshipmen at the United States Naval Academy, officers of National Oceanic and Atmospheric Administration, and merchant seamen with World War II service. Consult your local Veterans Affairs office.

The unmarried surviving spouse of a veteran who died on active duty or as the result of a service-connected disability is eligible for the home loan benefit. See chapter 12 for details.

Step-by-Step to a Home with a VA Loan

Smart homebuyers set up financing even before they go house hunting. This pre-planning allows you to move quickly once you find the right home for you. Of course, you can always find the property and then start the financing process in motion.

Remember: The VA loan can only be used for your principal place of residence.

What service doesn't meet eligibility requirements?

The following are not eligible for VA-guaranteed home loans: service in World War I, active duty for training in the Reserves, and active duty for training in the National Guard (unless "activated" under the authority of Title 10, U.S. Code, which is the United States Code for the Armed Forces, the governing military laws and powers).

However, those who have World War I and active duty for training status may qualify for HUD/FHA veterans' loans. This is a separate program and the VA's role is merely to determine the eligibility of the veterans and, if qualified, issue a Certificate of Veteran Status to be used to secure a HUD/FHA loan benefit for veterans.

Can I still qualify for a VA loan if I did not receive an honorable discharge?

Maybe. If you received a general discharge or a discharge under other than honorable conditions, eligibility for a VA loan is more difficult to attain. Consult your VA Regional Office.

1. *Obtain a Certificate of Eligibility.* If you think you are eligible for a VA-guaranteed home loan, your first step is to secure a certificate of eligibility. Submit an application (VA Form 26-1880) along with proof of your military service. Send to:

    VA Loan Eligibility Center
    P.O. Box 20729
    Winston-Salem, NC 27120
    1-888-244-6711
    nceligib@vba.va.gov

    Most lenders can furnish the forms and help you complete them. If the VA has sufficient data on you because you are already in the VA system (for example, you are receiving VA health care or educational benefits or vocational rehab), your lender may be able to obtain a certificate of eligibility for you via the Internet. The Automated Certificate of Eligibility (ACE) system can establish eligibility and issue an online Certificate of Eligibility. Ask your lender about this method of obtaining a certificate.

2. *Apply for the loan.* To get pre-approved for a VA loan, you will need to sign a release that permits the lender to obtain your credit report, as well as employment and bank verifications, and other information needed to complete the loan application.

   With this information, your lender can advise you about how much you should realistically plan on spending on a home. While VA loans offer good rates, no closing costs, and no mortgage insurance requirements, you will still have to be able to meet monthly house payments as well as your other obligations.

   Once you acquire pre-approval, you can begin the search for a house. Your VA loan can cover a variety of

What do I need to prove my military service?

If you were discharged after January 1, 1950, and before October 1, 1979, you'll need a photocopy of DD Form 214 (Certificate of Release or Discharge from Active Duty). If you were discharged after October 1, 1979, a photocopy of DD Form 214 copy 4 should be included.

What documentation do I need if I served in the Selected Reserves or National Guard? There is no single form used by the Reserves or National Guard that is similar to DD Form 214. You will have to provide documentation of at least six years of honorable service.

If you were discharged from the Selected Reserves or the National Guard, you will need to provide documentation of at least six years of honorable service. For service in the Army or Air Force National Guard, submit NGB Form 22, Report of Separation and Record of Service, or NGB Form 23, Retirement Points Accounting (or its equivalent). If you were discharged from the Selected Reserve, submit a copy of your latest annual points statement and evidence of honorable service.

Can I get a VA loan if I've had a bankruptcy?

It depends. Each case will be decided individually. You will not be eligible if you are in the midst of bankruptcy proceedings. Best case would be if you had gone through bankruptcy and it has been more than two years since the bankruptcy was discharged. Then, you have a good chance of the issue being disregarded. However, if the discharge has been within the last two years, you will have to provide evidence that you (and your spouse) have again established satisfactory credit *and* that the original bankruptcy was the result of circumstances beyond your control (for example, medical bills or unemployment). If the bankruptcy was discharged within the last year, it's unlikely that you can prove that you and your spouse are good credit risks; therefore, you will not be eligible for a VA loan.

properties, including single-family homes, condominiums, townhouses, even building a house.

3. *A VA Appraisal.* Once you've selected a home, bid on it, and both you and the seller have accepted the offer, you will need to call the VA and get a loan number and an appraiser.

   The VA appraiser will evaluate the home and compare it to other properties on the market. She will then determine the market value of the house and generate a report to the VA. After a review, the VA will issue a Certificate of Reasonable Value (CRV). The CRV establishes the maximum amount of the loan. Hopefully, you have selected a home within the price range already established before you began looking at properties.

   Remember: The VA appraisal does not take the place of a professional home inspection done by a certified home inspector. A VA appraisal is not a warranty that the home is problem-free. The VA requires the appraisal, but for your own protection, before you close escrow, consider a professional home inspection. The VA guarantees the loan, not the condition of the property.

4. *Sealing the deal.* Once you have the Certificate of Reasonable Value and your lender has the loan prepared, you will go to "closing," the final step in the sale/purchase of a home. The closing is usually held in a lawyer's office but in some locales, it may be held at the offices of the title company or escrow holder. At that time, the deed of title, financing papers, remaining funds due, and title insurance policies are exchanged.

   Remember: You cannot occupy the home until the loan closes.

What Kinds of Loans Are Available?

The VA will guarantee loans with a wide variety of repayment options. Talk to your lender about what works best for your financial circumstances. Here are some of the options.

- *Traditional Fixed Payment Mortgage.* You pay equal monthly payments for the life of the loan.

What happens to the loan if you die before it's paid off?

The VA guaranty does not pay off the balance of the loan if you should die before it's completely repaid. Your estate is then responsible for the loan, and your spouse or co-borrower must continue to make the payments until the loan is paid off or the property is sold and the loan is repaid at closing. You may want to consider mortgage life insurance, offered by private insurance companies, that pays off the remaining loan balance when the borrower dies.

- *Graduated Payment Mortgage.* You pay smaller monthly payments for the first few years, gradually increasing each year and then leveling off to larger than normal payments for the remainder of the loan term. The lower payments in the beginning of the loan term are the result of delaying a portion of the interest due on the loan each month and then adding that interest to the principal balance. This type of loan is helpful for the buyer who anticipates a significant increase in income in a few years (for example, a professional who is just beginning his career) or a buyer who anticipates reselling the property, at a profit, within a short time period. Caution: You will be required to provide a downpayment to secure the loan (unlike more traditional VA loans) because the maximum loan amount can't be more than the reasonable value of the property or the purchase price (whichever is less). Since the loan balance is increasing during the first years of the loan, you must give a downpayment in order to keep the loan balance from being larger than the reasonable value or purchase price.
- *Buy Downs.* At closing, the builder of a new home or the seller of an existing home "buys down" your mortgage payments by making a large lump sum payment upfront that is used to supplement your monthly payments for a certain short time period. This is used as an incentive for you to buy the property.
- *Growing Equity Mortgage (GEM).* You repay the mortgage in an accelerated fashion, thereby reducing the amount of interest you pay over the life of the loan. There is a gradual annual increase in the monthly payments *and* the increase is applied directly to the principal balance. You pay off the loan in 11 to 16 years instead of the traditional 30-year mortgage.

The Downlow on Downpayments

There was a time when conventional mortgages required a 20 percent downpayment to secure financing. Some sellers or housing communities still do. Although today there are conventional loans that have minimal (or no) downpayment requirements, a VA home loan has always had a no downpayment option.

There are some exceptions to this rule.

1. Some lenders may require a downpayment. Under those circumstances, if you don't have funds available or don't want to tie up your capital, consider applying to other VA-approved lenders.
2. If the purchase price of the property is greater than the reasonable value determined by the VA appraisal (see above), you will have to provide a downpayment so that the loan is for the amount approved by the VA. Caution: Think long and hard before buying a home at a price higher than the appraised value. Unless you have good reason to believe that the appraised value will eventually meet your purchase price, you may never recoup your investment.

Keep in mind that you may want to make a downpayment in order to lower your monthly mortgage payments and reduce the amount of interest you will pay over the life of the loan. On the other hand, if you are receiving high interest on your savings, you may prefer to keep the money in the bank to earn a greater return. Run the numbers (or ask your lender to help you) so that you know what you can afford and whether a downpayment, even if not required, makes sense.

How Vets and Non-Vets Can Buy Property Together

You may still be eligible for a VA home loan even if you purchase your principal residence with other buyers. Here are some other scenarios.

1. Buying property with other eligible veterans. Each vet will use up his entitlement based on his interest in the property. But the guaranty of the loan can't exceed either 40 percent of the loan amount or $36,000 (or $60,000 for certain loans over $144,000)—whichever is the lesser amount.
2. Buying property with your spouse who is also an eligible veteran. If both spouses are eligible vets, they may acquire a property together, but it doesn't increase the amount of the loan that can be guaranteed. The guaranty of the loan can't exceed either 40 percent of the loan amount or $36,000 (or $60,000 for certain loans over $144,000)—whichever is the lesser amount.
3. Buying property with a non-vet (not a spouse). If you purchase property with a non-vet (who is not your spouse) you can still be eligible for a VA loan. However, the loan guaranty can only be applied to veteran's part of the loan. You will need to work with your lender to determine if they are willing to accept this type of application. The VA would accept it, within the specified limits, but the lender may object.

VA Offers Refinancing Options

If you have a conventional mortgage, you may elect to refinance with a VA loan. The advantages of a VA loan have already been stated, and refinancing with this type of mortgage can be used for a multitude of purposes:

- To secure a lower interest rate
- To take out some of the equity you've built up in your home
- To pay off other debt obligations

VA Interest Rate Reduction Loan (IRRL)

If you currently hold a VA loan and want to refinance to get a lower interest rate, apply for a VA Interest Rate Reduction Loan (IRRL). This type of loan is fairly quick and easy. There are no out-of-pocket costs, no maximum loan amount, no monthly mortgage insurance, no appraisal required, and no income or credit check required. The following forms are needed to apply for an interest rate reduction loan:

VA Form 26-0285
VA Form 26-0286
VA Form 26-8320
VA Form 26-8998
VA Form 26-8923
VA Form 26-1820
VA Form 26-8937
HUD-1 Settlement Statement
VA Form 26-0503

There is a small funding fee, which can be rolled over into the loan itself.

VA Cash-Out or Debt Consolidation Refinance

If you want to take out some of the equity you've built up in your home, you can refinance your VA loan and cash out up to 90 percent of your home's value. You can use this money for home improvements, to pay off some debts, or other expenses.

Switching from Conventional to VA Loan

If you have a conventional mortgage on your home, you can decide to switch to a VA loan. Although there is a funding fee, you can roll over that charge into the cost of the loan. Again, the benefits of making the switch are

- No monthly mortgage insurance
- If you have poor credit, you may be able to get a better interest rate with a VA loan than with a conventional mortgage
- No out-of-pocket closing costs

Moving? Restore Your Entitlement for a New VA Loan

If you have used a VA loan to finance your residence, but now have decided to move, you may be able to restore your entitlement so that you can finance your new home with another VA loan. Restoration is not automatic. You must complete VA Form 26-1880 (available from any VA regional office or center). There are restrictions, but the advantages of a VA loan may be worth it. Here's how it works.

One time only, if you have repaid your VA loan *in full*, but have not disposed of the property, your entitlement may be restored to purchase a new home. Note the two important requirements: (1) you've repaid your loan in full *and* (2) you may only do this one time.

Otherwise, in order to restore your entitlement, you must have sold your home and repaid your VA loan in full. Unlike the one-time-only option above, you only get your entitlement restored if you meet both requirements: selling the property and repaying in full the loan.

Alternatively, if your buyer is a qualified veteran, he can agree to assume the outstanding balance on your loan and agree to substitute his entitlement for the same amount of entitlement as you originally used to get the loan. This property has to be the buyer's principal residence *and* the buyer still has to meet the income and credit requirements. To apply for substitution of entitlement, contact the VA office that guaranteed your loan.

If you cannot meet the requirements for restoring your entitlement, you may still be able to obtain another VA loan. That's because you may not have used up all of the entitlement with your original mortgage. For example, the current amount of entitlement available to each veteran is $36,000 (or $60,000 for certain loans over $144,000). But in previous years, the amount was significantly lower. So, for example, if you originally purchased a home when the entitlement was only $12,500, even if you have not paid off that loan, you still have $23,500 worth of entitlement remaining ($36,000 - $12,500 = $23,500).

Most lenders require that the guaranty is equal to 25 percent of the reasonable value or sales price of the property—whichever is less. If your remaining entitlement meets that, then probably no downpayment will be required. Otherwise, the lender will probably ask for a downpayment that in addition to the guaranty equals the 25 percent standard.

Time to Sell?

If you have decided to sell your home, you have two options. You can have the buyer secure a conventional mortgage and at closing, your VA loan will be paid off.

Or if your buyer is a qualified vet, he may assume your loan and

Retire your loan early

You have the option, at no penalty, of prepaying your VA loan. You can add a partial payment to any monthly installment, but it may not be less than one monthly installment or $100, whichever is less. Check with your lender.

take on the payments of that loan. However, for loans closed on or after March 1, 1988, the assumption has to be approved *in advance* by the lender or the VA. Usually this is a credit check of the buyer (to make sure that he has the financial ability to make the mortgage payments).

Which is better? Consider the advantages and disadvantages of each.

If your buyer secures a conventional mortgage:

- ✦ Your VA loan will be repaid in full at closing.
- ✦ You eliminate any worries about your purchaser defaulting on your original loan.
- ✦ Your entitlement may be restored.
- ✦ There is no prepayment penalty for paying off the loan before it is due.

On the other hand, the downside of your buyer using a conventional mortgage includes

- ✦ Your property has to be appraised (which might be a problem if the market has fallen).
- ✦ The closing costs tend to be higher.
- ✦ You may have to make repairs on your house in order for the buyer to secure a loan.

There are advantages to the scenario of your buyer assuming your VA loan.

- ✦ There is no appraisal required.
- ✦ There are low closing costs.
- ✦ There are no required repairs.
- ✦ There is fast and easy processing.

But should your buyer assume your VA loan, your entitlement can't be restored until the loan is paid off (unless the buyer is willing to substitute his available eligibility, which will restore yours). Otherwise, if he defaults on the loan, it's *your* entitlement that is affected.

In Conclusion

VA home loans have enabled many veterans to make the transition from renters to homeowners. Although VA loans provide veterans with the opportunity to buy, it's still important to do your homework to make sure the property is worth the investment and that you are financially able to make the loan repayments.

CHAPTER 11

Job Preference Eligibility and Entrepreneur Opportunities

The Federal and state Civil Service systems provide preferences to veterans. It's not a guarantee of employment, but may make the critical difference in landing a position. Veterans are also afforded some protection in the event of layoffs, for example, a reduction in force (RIF) in an agency. This chapter will provide a full review of what veterans need to know to take advantage of this benefit. Many companies in the private sector are also committed to employing veterans.

In this chapter you'll learn about the Department of Labor's *HireVetsFirst,* the government career website and job fairs for vets. You'll discover why vets, even those disabled during military service, are often in demand for private sector jobs. You'll also learn how to translate military skills to the private sector.

Finally, if you're interested in starting your own business, you'll find the help you need in the Small Business Administration's Veterans Business Outreach Program (VBOP). These are designed to provide entrepreneurial development services such as business training, counseling, and mentoring, and referrals for eligible veterans owning or considering, starting a small business.

Veterans Preference for Federal Civil Service Jobs

Ever since the Civil War, veterans have received some measure of preference for Federal government jobs. The justification is that veterans should not be penalized for the time they have spent in military service. Veterans also receive some preference for retention if there is a reduction in the workforce.

To secure a Civil Service job, you must conduct your own job search. Check listings for openings, and apply like any other individual searching for work. USAJOBS, www.usajobs.opm.gov, is the Federal government's official jobs site. It has the listings for openings in the Federal Civil Service, and you are able to search by job title, city, or state. America's Job Bank has been replaced by CareerOneStop, part of the Department of Labor, www.careeronestop.org. At this site, search Federal and state job banks, as well as private sector listings.

The veterans preference helps you in the hiring process and in the event there is a reducation in force. Once you are hired, your job performance determines any future promotions. Veterans preference does not affect performance reviews, reassignment, change to a lower grade, transfer or reinstatement, or raises.

To be eligible for veterans preference for Civil Service jobs:

- You must have an honorable or general discharge.
- Your military rank must be below major, lieutenant commander (or higher) unless you are disabled.
- Your military service must be more than Guard and Reserve active duty for training purposes.
- You must claim preference on your application or resume when applying for Federal jobs. If you are claiming a 10-point preference, you must complete SF-15, Application for 10-Point Veteran Preference.

Service Determines Types of Preference

Depending on your military service, you may receive an additional five or 10 points to your Civil Service examination score.

Application smarts

Your veterans preference eligibility is just one component of your job application. You may apply for a Federal Civil Service job with a resume, the Optional Application for Federal Employment (OF-612), or other written formats. Some jobs are filled online or the job announcement will give the specific format needed to apply. Read the instructions carefully.

Unless you use the OF-612 application, include the following information on your resume:

1. Job information including the announcement number, title, and grade.
2. Personal information—your full name, mailing address with zip code, day, evening, and cell phone numbers with area codes, Social Security number, country of citizenship, highest Federal grade held (if you've previously held a Federal Civil Service job). *In this section, be sure to list your veterans preference and reinstatement eligibility.*
3. Education—Name, city and state of high school and colleges/universities you attended, plus your major and type and year of degrees you received. If you didn't earn a degree, show the total number of credits you earned and indicate whether it was in semester or quarter hours.
4. Work experience—For each job you've held, create a listing that includes your title, duties, and accomplishments, employer's name and address, supervisor's name and phone number, starting and ending dates (month and year), hours per week, salary. In addition, indicate whether or not your current supervisor can be contacted.
5. Other qualifications you may have such as job-related training courses (title and year), job-related skills (for example, proficiency in software programs like Excel), job-related certificates and licenses, job-related honors and awards, and any special accomplishments.

Neatness counts. Avoid typos and misspellings. Proofread your resume at least twice.

Five-Point Preference

To receive an additional five-point preference, you must have served during one of these time periods:

- December 7, 1941, to July 1, 1955, OR
- For more than 180 consecutive days any part of which occurred after January 31, 1955, and before October 15, 1976, OR
- During the Gulf War from August 2, 1990, through January 2, 1992, OR
- In a campaign or expedition for which a campaign medal has been authorized, including El Salvador, Grenada, Haiti, Lebanon, Panama, Somalia, Southwest Asia, and Bosnia
- On active duty for a period of more than 180 consecutive days any part of which occurred during the period beginning September 11, 2001, and ending on the last date of Operation Iraqi Freedom (whenever that is declared either by Presidential Proclamation or by law)

Some additional requirements to qualify for a five-point preference:

- If you are a medal holder or Gulf War veteran who enlisted after September 7, 1980, or entered on active duty on or after October 14, 1982, you must have served continuously for 24 months or for the full period called or ordered to active duty. You do not have to have served in a combat zone in order to qualify for veterans preference if you were on active duty *during* the Gulf War.
- Service requirements do not apply to veterans with compensable service-connected disabilities OR to veterans separated for disability in the line of duty OR for hardship.

Ten-Point Preference

To receive an additional 10 points added to your examination score, you must meet these qualification requirements (and complete SF-15, Application for 10-Point Veteran Preference):

- You are a veteran (service at any time) who has a present service-connected disability OR is receiving compensation, disability retirement benefits OR pension from the military or the Department of Veterans Affairs
- You received the Purple Heart medal
- You are the unmarried spouse of certain deceased veterans who either served during a war or during the period of April 28, 1952, through July, 1, 1955, or in a campaign or expedition for which a campaign medal has been authorized; or died while on active duty that included service described as under conditions that would not have been the basis for other than an honorable or general discharge, OR the spouse of a veteran unable to work because of a service-connected disability
- You are the parent of a veteran who died in service OR who is permanently and totally disabled

How Does It Work?

There are three ways veterans can get jobs in the Civil Service: Competitive Appointment, Noncompetitive Appointment Under Special Authority, and Merit Promotion Selection under the Veterans Employment Opportunities Act (VEOA).

Veterans preference *does not* guarantee you a Federal job. Federal agencies can fill vacancies in ways other than from the list of eligibles. They can promote from within, transfer internally, reassign an existing employee, or reinstate a former employee. Veterans preference does provide a boost (either five or 10 points) to your Civil Service score. You must still:

- Meet the professional requirements of any job for which you apply
- Score at least 70 on the written examination *or* by an evaluation of your experience and education

If you are entitled to either a five- or 10-point preference, it will be added to your numerical rating at the time the score is first issued. The ratings system is used in different ways for different types of jobs.

For Scientific or Professional Jobs in Grade GS-9 or Higher

The names of everyone eligible are listed in order of their ratings, with the veterans preference augmentation already added. For example, if there were 10 applicants for a GS-9 scientific job, the ratings of all 10 applicants would be given to the supervisor. She would then choose among the top three–rated applicants. Unless your veterans preference score moved you into one of the top three positions, you would not be among the final three for consideration of the position.

For All Other Positions

Those veterans with 10-point preference who have compensable, service-connected disabilities of 10 percent or more, are *placed ahead* of the names of all other eligibles on a given job register. For those types of jobs, the names would be listed, by numerical rank, in this order: 10-point preference eligibles, 5-point preference eligibles, non-veterans.

Competitive Appointments

To land a job being filled by competitive appointment, the veteran must compete with all other applicants (veterans and nonveterans). This is the most common way of entering the Civil

Service. Generally you take a Civil Service exam and if you are an eligible veteran, you have an additional five or 10 points added to your score, depending on your status.

Here's the process for filling competitive appointments.

- The agency that wants to fill a job must report the vacancy to the Office of Personnel Management (OPM).
- A public announcement of the vacancy is posted and OPM also notifies state employment service offices.
- Applicants apply for the job and submit either a resume or application.
- OPM reviews the applicants' qualifications and ranks them according to job-related criteria.
- A list of eligible applicants is given to the selecting official of the agency with the vacancy who must then choose from among the top three high-scoring applicants. If you are a veteran, your score has already been increased by your eligibility preference. That may be enough to put you in the top three—but not necessarily.

Noncompetitive Appointment Under Special Authority

Agencies have the discretion, under the Veterans Recruitment Appointment (VRA), to skip the red tape and competitive examinations to appoint qualified disabled veterans to jobs. The veteran must be 30 percent or more disabled. This is a rarely utilized benefit, however.

The advantage of this appointment is that while it's made originally as an excepted position without the career rights given to employees who have been appointed under the competitive process, after two years of satisfactory service, the VRA-appointed employee is converted to a career-conditional appointment in the competitive Civil Service. Once an employee is designated career or career-conditional they acquire a competitive status automatically. This makes them eligible for other Civil Service positions.

The rule of three

"The rule of three" is shorthand for the selection process by which Federal and state agencies must hire new employees. Job applicants are ranked based on their Civil Service exam scores and experience. The three applicants with the highest scores are eligible for being hired based on the "rule of three." Officials of the Office of Personnel Management (or a designated agency) develop the applicant rankings, based on Civil Service exam results and experience evaluation. Veterans who are eligible for veterans preference have additional points added to their rank which *may* help to put them in the top three of qualified applicants. However, the additional points are simply added to their scores and do not insure a top three ranking.

An agency must choose from the top three candidates. The agency can't pass over a veteran who is preference eligible in favor of a lower ranking non-preference candidate. This means within the top three, if a veteran is in the top three, if his score is higher than an applicant who is not preference eligible, the agency must choose the veteran unless there are sound reasons that relate directly to the veteran's fitness. On the other hand, if there were not a veteran among the top three, the agency could choose any of those three applicants. It gets even more complicated because the agency does have the right to choose a lower-ranking preference eligible veteran over a compensably disabled veteran if both are among the rule of three.

Merit Promotion Selection Under the Veterans Employment Opportunities Act (VEOA)

For this type of job, the veteran competes with current Federal employees. The hiring agency can appoint an eligible veteran who has applied under an agency merit promotion announcement that is open to candidates outside the agency. This enables qualified veterans to compete for government positions that may have only been available to current Civil Service employees.

Additional Benefits for Job-Hunting Veterans

There are additional benefits available to veterans when searching for Civil Service jobs. While no benefit guarantees you a job, these may be helpful in the hunt for employment.

Applications After Exams Have Closed

You get additional time to file an application for vacant positions if you are a 10-point eligible veteran. That means that even if examinations have been closed for a job, you may still file an application for any vacant position if an appointment has been made from a competitive list of eligibles within the past three years. Contact the agency with the vacancy for further information. This doesn't guarantee you the job, but does insure that you will be considered for the position. In other words, even at the last minute, if a 10-point eligible files an application, he must be considered.

Veterans Preferred Jobs

Some Civil Service examinations are open only to those veterans who are preference eligible, as long as there are applicants available. These jobs are custodian, guard, elevator operator, and messenger. This special preference is only for the first job; that is, for veterans who are entering Civil Service for the first time.

How to Appeal an Agency Decision

You have the right to see why you were passed over for a job if you are a veteran who is (1) preference eligible and (2) among the top three candidates for a job. You also have the right to appeal if you believe that an agency has not given you the veterans preference you have earned. Before filing a complaint, however, discuss your concerns with your supervisor and/or the Federal agency personnel office that took the action. You may use a Veterans Service Organization to help you resolve your complaint.

If there is no resolution after discussing your complaint with the appropriate authority, here are the next steps to file a formal complaint.

If you believe that an agency has violated your rights under any statute or regulation relating to veterans preference, contact the Department of Labor's Veterans Employment and Training Service (VETS), www.dol.gov/elaws/vets/vetpref/complain.htm. Examples of these types of complaints include an agency that has not properly accorded them their veterans preference, an agency that failed to list jobs with state employment service offices as required by law, and an agency that failed to provide special placement consideration.

After the Department of Labor (DOL), Veterans Employment and Training Service (VETS) accepts your complaint, a VETS representative will work with the agency to resolve the complaint in a timely manner. If your case cannot be resolved within 60 days, on the 61st day you may close your case with VETS and appeal to the Merit System Protection Board (MSPB). However, if you and the VETS investigator agree, the case may remain open longer. When you are notified that VETS has closed your case, you have 15 days to foward an appeal to the MSPB. If the MSPB has not issued a decision within 120 days, you may seek judicial redress in the U.S. District Court.

Additionally, any veteran who feels they were not fairly considered for employment within the Civil Service may contact any Office of Personnel Management Service center for consideration of their complaint.

Veterans Preference During Reduction in Force

If there are layoffs (known as a reduction in force or RIF), veterans have preference for being retained over non-veterans. There are four criteria considered when ranking employees for retention: tenure (time in position), veterans preference, length of service, and performance.

When developing a reduction in force plan, the agency groups employees into three categories: Tenure Group I, Tenure Group II, and Tenure Group III. *Within each group, employees are then placed in a subgroup based on veterans status.*

- Subgroup AD—all preference eligibles who have a compensable service-connected disability of 30 percent or more
- Subgroup A—all other preference eligibles not in subgroup AD
- Subgroup B—all employees not eligible for veterans preference

Within each subgroup, the employees are ranked in descending order by the length of their Federal civilian and military service. Additional service is added based on the level of their performance ratings.

When there is a reduction in force, veterans are the last to be affected because they are listed ahead of non-veterans within each tenure group. However, it does not make them immune to being laid off. This benefit means only that they will be retained over employees without veterans preference—but that is clearly a valuable protection.

If you have any questions or problems with your veterans pref-

RIF and newly returned veterans

Immediately upon returning from active duty, if you have served for more than 180 days, you are protected from being laid off from a Federal Civil Service position for one year after your return. If you served for more than 30 days but less than 181 days, you are protected for six months.

erence in Civil Service jobs, contact a Veterans Service Organization and ask for help.

Private Sector Jobs for Veterans

Your military service has given you a set of skills that no amount of classroom experience can match. As Joseph J. Grano, Jr., Chairman of UBS Financial Services, Inc., testified before the House Committee on Veterans' Affairs: "While corporate battles are by no means the equivalent of real-life combat, they require many of the same skills to achieve success."

The website HireVetsFirst.com lists 10 reasons for employers to hire veterans:

1. *Accelerated learning curve.* Veterans have the proven ability to learn new skills and concepts. In addition, they can enter your workforce with identifiable and transferable skills, proven in real-world situations. This background can enhance your organization's productivity.
2. *Leadership.* The military trains people to lead by example as well as through direction, delegation, motivation, and inspiration. Veterans understand the practical ways to manage behaviors for results, even in the most trying circumstances. They also know the dynamics of leadership as part of both hierarchical and peer structures.
3. *Teamwork.* Veterans understand how genuine teamwork grows out of a responsibility to one's colleagues. Military duties involve a blend of individual and group productivity. Veterans also necessitate a perception of how groups of all sizes relate to each other and an overarching objective.
4. *Diversity and inclusion in action.* Veterans have learned to work side-by-side with individuals regardless of race, gender, geographic origin, ethnic background, religion, or economic status as well as mental, physical, or attitudinal

capabilities. They have the sensitivity to cooperate with many different types of individuals.

5. *Efficient performance under pressure.* Veterans understand the rigors of tight schedules and limited resources. They have developed the capacity to know how to accomplish priorities on time, in spite of tremendous stress. They know the critical importance of staying with a task until it is accomplished.
6. *Respect for procedures.* Veterans have gained a unique perspective on the value of accountability. They can grasp their place within an organizational framework, becoming responsible for subordinates' actions to higher supervisory levels. They know how policies and procedures enable an organization to exist.
7. *Technology and globalization.* Because of their experiences in the service, veterans are usually aware of international and technical trends pertinent to business and industry. They can bring the kind of global outlook and technological savvy that all enterprises of any size need to succeed.
8. *Integrity.* Veterans know what it means to do "an honest day's work." Prospective employers can take advantage of a track record of integrity, often including security clearances. This integrity translates into qualities of sincerity and trustworthiness.
9. *Conscious of health and safety standards.* Thanks to extensive training, veterans are aware of health and safety protocols both for themselves and the welfare of others. Individually, they represent a drug-free workforce that is cognizant of maintaining personal health and fitness. On a company level, their awareness and conscientiousness translate into protection of employees, property, and materials.
10. *Triumph over adversity.* In addition to dealing positively with the typical issues of personal maturity, veterans have frequently triumphed over great adversity. They likely

> have proven their mettle in mission-critical situations demanding endurance, stamina, and flexibility. They may have overcome personal disabilities through strength and determination.

In an interview describing the value civilian employers place on hiring military personnel, Navy Vice Adm. Patricia Tracey, former deputy assistant secretary of defense for military personnel policy, explained, "You can see particular head-to-head competition in the aviation career fields and high-tech career fields of all kinds. . . . For our mid-grade officer and enlisted leaders, though, there is high demand just for their leadership skills, almost no matter what their particular skill is."

Private Sector Programs for Veterans

Joseph J. Grano, Jr., pointed out: "I have no doubt in my mind that I owe a great deal of my career growth to many of the skills and leadership attributes that I acquired as a soldier for the United States of America. Indeed, discipline, the ability to quickly assess and react to your environment and efficient communication and interaction with your comrades are as important to success in the private sector as they are in the armed forces."

There has been a concerted effort in the private sector to hire veterans. Hire Vets First, www.hirevetsfirst.gov/, a website run under the aegis of the Department of Labor, promotes job fairs and opportunities for veterans. Here are some of the programs available to veterans.

Training Programs

The Department of Labor's Veterans Employment and Training Service (VETS), www.dol.gov/vets/welcome.html, provides grants to each state for employment and training services to eligible veterans primarily through Disabled Veterans' Outreach Program (DVOP) and Local Veterans' Employment Representative (LVER).

DVOP works directly with veterans with service-connected disabilitics to make them be competitive in the labor market.

LVERs are state employees located in the state employment service local offices. Their efforts are broad and include supervising the provision of services to vets including counseling, training, and identifying training and employment opportunities, as well as monitoring job listings from Federal contractors to see that eligible veterans get priority in referrals to these jobs.

Transition Assistance Program (TAP)

TAP workshops offer job-search assistance to veterans and their spouses. Since 1990 they have helped more than 1 million veterans and their spouses. Participants are taught how to compete effectively in the job market. The program includes how to write productive resumes and cover letters, interview techniques, and job-search tips. The employment needs of disabled veterans are also addressed.

Other Opportunities for Veterans

Many VSOs also have programs to help veterans in the transition from military service to the private sector. For example, the American Legion sponsors Transition Assistance Online (TAOnline), the largest single source of transition assistance information and tools for separating military, www.taonline.com/. This site assists transitioning military personnel, retirees, working spouses, and other job seekers from the military community to find jobs. The American Legion TAOnline Career Center offers thc opportunity for a job seeker to post his or her resume for free and apply to over 5,000 job ads from a wide variety of employers in locations around the world.

Corporate Gray Online is a military-specific employment website that links transitioning and former military members with employers nationwide, www.corporategray.com/. There is no fee to post your resume. Employers can post a job opening and use the Trial Resume Search at no charge.

Career One Stop, which replaces America's Job Bank, is sponsored by the Department of Labor and offers information on military transition, as well as more than 4,000 job listings, www.careeronestop.org/. Of special interest is the Military to Civilian Occupation Translator, www.acinet.org/acinet/moc/, an interactive site that helps veterans convert military skills to ones needed in the private sector.

Starting Your Own Business

Here's a very interesting statistic: the success rate of veteran-owned businesses is higher than for those owned by non-veterans. The skills, dedication, creativity, and perseverance learned in military service translate into making veterans successful entrepreneurs. "Veteran-owned businesses make significant contributions to the economy and because of the unique technical and leadership skills they acquire through military service, they [veterans] can become successful entrepreneurs," says Steven C., Preston, administrator for the Small Business Administration (SBA), a Federal agency.

Small businesses are the mainstay of the American economy.

- Nine out of 10 businesses are small firms.
- They produce approximately half of the U.S. gross national product.
- Over one-half of the nation's workforce is employed by small businesses.

Veteran-owned small businesses are a critical component of our economy. Some of these businesses are high-tech global corporations—and some are home-based sole proprietorships.

- Veterans own more than 14 percent of businesses in America.
- There are more than 4 million veterans who own small businesses.
- Service-connected disabled veterans own more than 235,000 of these small businesses.

The SBA guarantees more than $1 billion annually in loans for veteran-owned businesses. This is good for individual veterans who are looking for help to kick-start their businesses, but it's also good for our nation's economy. Small businesses are responsible for 60 to 80 percent of new jobs, helping to reduce unemployment.

The SBA Office of Veterans' Business Development is a key contact for veterans who need to learn the mechanics of starting, sustaining, and growing a small business. This agency provides distance-learning education in how to start—and expand—your own business, as well as training in finance, accounting, and contracting. There are Veterans Business Development Officers in the SBA District Offices in every state and territory throughout the nation (see Appendix J).

The Veterans Business Outreach Program (VBOP) can help you build a business from scratch. At Veterans Business Outreach Centers (VBOC) you can find workshops to help you plan and build a business. Some of the classes include

- *Pre-business plan workshops.* This class focuses on self-employment issues you need to address before you even begin developing a plan for your own business. Each client has the opportunity to work directly with a business counselor.
- *Concept assessments.* This class helps you assess the needs and requirements of an entrepreneur.
- *Business plan preparations.* A good business plan is the foundation of success. At VBOCs, you will find help devel-

oping a five-year business plan. It will include the legal form of the business, equipment requirements and cost, organizational structure, strategic plan, market analysis, and a detailed financial plan, including financial projections, budget projects, and funding requirements.

- *Comprehensive feasibility analysis.* VBOC counselors will analyze your business plan, identify the strengths and weaknesses, and help revise the strategic planning portions of your business plan.
- *Entrepreneurial training and counseling.* These programs are targeted to address the needs and concerns of service-disabled veterans who want to start their own businesses.
- *Mentorship.* VBOC counselors make *on-site* visits to veteran-owned businesses to ensure they are sticking to their business plan. VBOCs can also review monthly financial statements of veteran-owned businesses to see if the business plan needs to be revised or adjusted.

VBOCs can also provide help in training for international trade, franchising, Internet marketing, and accounting.

Loans for Veteran-Owned Small Businesses

Many small entrepreneurs apply for SBA loans to start their businesses. Veterans should consider applying for *Patriot Express Loans,* specially designated, streamlined financing with enhanced guaranty and interest rates for eligible veteran entrepreneurs. The advantage of these loans is that lenders may not charge more than 2.25 percent over prime for loans of less than seven years and 2.75 percent over prime for loans greater than seven years. Lenders may charge 1 percent more for loans of $50,000 or less and 2 percent more for loans of $25,000 or less. Contact your local SBA office for more details.

To be eligible for a Patriot Express Loan, you must meet SBA eligibility rules and the business must be 51 percent or more owned/controlled by:

- Veteran (s) (other than dishonorably discharged)
- Service-disabled veterans
- Active-duty military potential retiree within 24 months of separation and discharging active-duty member within 12 months of discharge (TAP eligible)
- Reservist and National Guard servicemember
- Current spouse of above or spouse of service member or veteran who died due to a service-connected disability

There are limitations on the types of businesses these loans can finance. Among those businesses *not* eligible for Patriot Express financing are agricultural and farm businesses; fishing and shore operations (including commercial fishing activities and the construction of new fishing vessels); medical facilities involving any type of extended care/assisted living situation; mines; applicants with operations, facilities, or offices located overseas (other than those strictly associated with the marketing and/or distribution of products exported from the United States); businesses engaged in teaching, instructing, counseling, or indoctrinating religion or religious beliefs; businesses that sell products, services, or presentation of any depiction or display of a prurient sexual nature or that presents any live performances of a prurient nature.

If You Already Own a Business

The SBA is a good resource to help you grow your business. There are programs to help you sell goods and services to the government, free or low-cost online training, business counseling, and specialized financing initiatives. You can get assistance in obtaining SBA financing for:

- Patriot Express Loans up to $500,000
- Major fixed-asset loans to purchase land and buildings
- Surety bond guarantees for construction contractors who are veterans
- Equity financing matching venture capitalists with veteran-owned small businesses
- Export assistance programs to help veteran-owned businesses become part of the global economy

In Conclusion

There are Federal and state laws that establish Civil Service job preference for veterans. In a tight job market, every bit of assistance can help, so take advantage of these opportunities. There are also companies in the private sector who will award preference to veterans. The Small Business Administration has loans and programs to help veterans who want to start their own businesses.

CHAPTER 12

Those Who Also Serve

Dependents of Veterans

Veterans benefits are not just for veterans. Your family can also benefit from your military service. This chapter will review the benefits available to dependents of eligible veterans. It includes a full discussion of CHAMPVA, the health care program *for the dependents* of certain eligible veterans.

The children and spouse of a veteran may also be eligible for Dependents' Educational Assistance (DEA). This chapter will review how they can receive the education and training they need to become independent and self-sufficient.

Also in this chapter, we will alert you to a hidden danger to your veterans disability payments should you divorce.

Finally, we will discuss life insurance options veterans have for the long-term protection of their loved ones.

VA Provides Health Care for Your Dependents

The spouse or children of certain veterans are eligible to participate in the Civilian Health and Medical Program of the Department of Veterans Affairs (CHAMPVA). This is a comprehensive health care program and the VA shares the cost of health care services and supplies with eligible beneficiaries. The CHAMPVA website is www.va.gov/hac.

It's important to distinguish CHAMPVA, a Veterans Affairs program, from TRICARE, which is a Department of Defense health care program (formerly known as CHAMPUS). TRICARE is a regionally managed health care program for active-duty and retired members of the uniformed services, their families, and survivors. While it may appear that some veterans are eligible for both TRICARE and CHAMPVA, keep in mind: if you are a military retiree or the spouse of a service member who was killed in action—you are to use TRICARE, that is your managed health care program.

Who Is Eligible for CHAMPVA?

You must be in one of the following four categories of individuals to be eligible for CHAMPVA:

1. The spouse or child of a *living* veteran who has been rated by a VA Regional Office to be permanently and totally disabled for a service-connected disability.
2. The surviving spouse or child of a veteran who died from a VA-rated service-connected disability.

Eligibility terms of CHAMPVA

- *Beneficiary:* A CHAMPVA-eligible spouse, widow (er), or child
- *Child:* Includes birth, adopted, stepchild; also helpless child as determined by a VA Regional Office
- *Helpless child:* A child who, before reaching the age of 18, becomes permanently incapable of self-support (A VA Regional Office makes this determination.)
- *Dependents:* A child, spouse, or widow(er) of a qualifying sponsor
- *Qualifying sponsor:* A veteran who is permanently or totally disabled from a service-connected condition, died as a result of a service-connected condition, was rated permanently and totally disabled from a service-connected condition at the time of death, or died on active duty and whose dependents are not otherwise eligible for TRICARE benefits

3. The surviving spouse or child of a veteran who was at the time of death rated permanently and totally disabled from a service-connected disability.
4. The surviving spouse or child of a military member who died in the line of duty, not due to misconduct—although in most of these cases, these family members are eligible for TRICARE, not CHAMPVA.

How About the Veteran?

A veteran, who is an eligible CHAMPVA-sponsor, is entitled to receive health care through the VA health care system. If a CHAMPVA sponsor is married to another eligible CHAMPVA sponsor, they are then both also eligible for CHAMPVA benefits. In those cases, each spouse may choose care from either the CHAMPVA system *or* the VA health care system. One reason a veteran might choose CHAMPVA for care rather than a VA medical facility would be because it's closer to home and more convenient. However, using a private medical provider would probably cost the veteran more money, simply because VA co-pays and fees are cheaper than what outside providers generally charge.

How to Use CHAMPVA

Each eligible family member will receive a CHAMPVA authorization card. You will present this card to your doctor (s) and at the pharmacy. Co-payment is based on a percentage of the CHAMPVA-allowable amount (rather than a fixed co-pay amount as is found in many private health care plans).

CHAMPVA covers most medically necessary health care including ambulance, ambulatory surgery, family planning, maternity, hospice, inpatient services, mental health services, outpatient services, pharmacy, skilled nursing care, and transplants. It does not cover long-term care like nursing homes.

Your Local VA Medical Center and CHAMPVA

Some local VA medical centers (VAMC) participate in the CHAMPVA Inhouse Treatment Initiative (CITI). This means that you may be able to get inpatient, outpatient, pharmacy, and mental health services at a nearby VA medical facility. (More than half of all VA medical facilities participate in CITI.) You can check the CHAMPVA website, www.va.gov/hac, to see if your local VA medical facility participates, or call, e-mail, or write for more information.

The advantage of using a participating VA medical center is that there is *no* co-pay and no deductible.

You must contact your local VA medical center and ask what services are available. The VAMC has the right to decide if they can accept you into their CITI program and if they can provide you with the care you need. The decision can change from time to time because of the VAMC workload. Generally if you are eligible for CHAMPVA and have Medicare or an HMO or PPO plan as your other health insurance, you can't participate in the CITI program, but it's up to the local VAMC to make that decision.

If You Can't Use the CITI Program

CHAMPVA does not have its own network of medical providers. If you must use a non-VA medical provider, you may have to do some research to find a doctor who will accept CHAMPVA. Most TRICARE providers will also accept CHAMPVA. Check the TRICARE website, www.tricare.osd.mil/standardprovider. You will find a list of providers in your area who accept TRICARE. Call and check to see if they also accept CHAMPVA.

Another resource? Most Medicare providers will accept CHAMPVA patients. Check www.medicare.gov for a list or simply ask the doctor's office when you call for an appointment. Moreover, any hospital that participates in Medicare, as well as any hospital-based health care professionals who are employed by or contracted by the hospital, must accept CHAMPVA.

Who Pays the Bill?

The amount you pay for your health care depends on where you seek care and whether the providers accept CHAMPVA. If you receive medical services from the VA under the CITI program, you will have no charge. Otherwise, you will be responsible for an annual deductible, as well as co-pay charges for medical and pharmaceutical services.

Unless you use CITI, for most outpatient care (doctor's appointments and pharmacy), you have an annual deductible of $50 per beneficiary or a maximum of $100 per family per year. The annual deductible must be paid before CHAMPVA will pay 75 percent of the allowable amount of subsequent bills.

Remember: CHAMPVA determines how much it considers an allowable amount for a medical service. That is not necessarily what the doctor charges. There is no co-payment charge for inpatient services, ambulatory surgery facility services, partial psychiatric day programs, hospice services, or services provided by VA medical facilities (CITI and Meds by Mail).

Catastrophic Cap Offers Protection

CHAMPVA has a $3,000 cap on out-of-pocket expenses on covered services and supplies in any calendar year. This is to limit your financial costs in the event of long-term illness or serious injury.

Here is the range of payment options for CHAMPVA participants.

NO CHARGE. There are no charges to you if you use CITI, that is you are enrolled in CHAMPVA and seek medical care at a Veterans Affairs medical center that is a participating CITI institution.

SOME CHARGE. If you use a non-VA medical provider who accepts "assignment" for CHAMPVA patients, the doctor has agreed to bill CHAMPVA directly for covered services, items, and supplies, and can only charge you up to the CHAMPVA deductible and the cost share amounts from you (generally 25 percent of the CHAMPVA allowable cost for the specific service).

FULL CHARGE. You have the option of going to a medical provider who does not accept CHAMPVA, but you will be responsible for the full bill. If you choose to use this medical provider, you must be ready to pay the full bill and will have to wait for a limited reimbursement from CHAMPVA.

Remember: The doctor's charges may be higher than what CHAMPVA allows for services. Furthermore, you will be reimbursed only CHAMPVA's share of the allowable amount and you will be responsible for your share of the allowable amount PLUS any charges over that allowable amount that the doctor has billed.

Where Does Medicare Fit In?

You can be enrolled in both Medicare Parts A and B, as well as CHAMPVA. You may not use, however, CHAMPVA's prescription plan by mail (Meds by Mail) if you are enrolled in Medicare Part D, which is a prescription drug plan.

Once you are enrolled in Medicare (it generally happens automatically 90 days prior to your 65th birthday), you will receive a Medicare card indicating both part A and part B coverage. To maintain your CHAMPVA eligibility, you must be enrolled in Medicare part B and must immediately send to CHAMPVA a copy of your Medicare card. Medicare then becomes your primary insurer and CHAMPVA becomes the secondary.

The requirement that you be enrolled in Medicare part B in order to maintain your CHAMPVA eligibility is conditional on when you became eligible for Medicare. It can be complicated. Here are the basic rules, but if you have questions, contact your regional VA office or a Veterans Service Organization for help.

You need Medicare Part B for CHAMPVA eligibility if you are in one of these groups:

- Under the age of 65, otherwise eligible for CHAMPVA, and entitled to Medicare Part A coverage
- Age 65 or older prior to June 5, 2001, became CHAMPVA eligible after June 5, 2001, and entitled to Medicare Part A coverage
- Age 65 or older prior to June 5, 2001, otherwise eligible for CHAMPVA, entitled to Medicare part A coverage, and enrolled in Medicare part B coverage as of June 5, 2001
- Age 65 on or after June 5, 2001, CHAMPVA eligible, and entitled to Medicare part A coverage

You do not need Medicare Part B to be eligible for CHAMPVA if you are age 65 or older prior to June 5, 2001, met all other eligibility requirements for CHAMPVA prior to June 5, 2001, and are entitled to Medicare Part A coverage.

Other Health Insurance (OHI) Impacts CHAMPVA

If you have other health insurance (other than Medicare, which is discussed above), such as a health maintenance organization (HMO) or preferred provider organization (PPO) coverage, you must submit a copy of the plan's co-payment information and schedule of benefits to CHAMPVA. Except for the types of coverage described below, CHAMPVA becomes a secondary provider behind your HMO or PPO.

If you qualify for one of these types of health insurance, your primary provider is CHAMPVA.

- Medicaid
- State Victims of Crime Compensation Program

- CHAMPVA supplemental health insurance (these are companies that offer supplemental policies to CHAMPVA, which makes the payment for the health service, and these plans cover the remaining out-of-pocket deductible and co-payments).

Here's a basic summary of how much you owe if you have OHI and CHAMPVA.

- If the medical service and supplies are covered by both your OHI and CHAMPVA: your OHI pays whatever its allowable amount is; CHAMPVA pays what you would have to pay up to the CHAMPVA allowable amount; and, most likely, you will have to pay nothing at all.
- If the medical services are covered by your OHI, but not by CHAMPVA: your OHI pays its allowable amount and CHAMPVA pays nothing; and you pay your OHI co-pay.
- If the medical services are not covered by your OHI, but are covered by CHAMPVA: your OHI pays nothing; CHAMPVA pays its allowable amount; and you pay your cost share for the type of services (usually 25 percent of the CHAMPVA allowable cost).

Dependents Gain Pharmacy Coverage

CHAMPVA operates Meds by Mail, which fills prescriptions by mail. It's an easy way to receive non-urgent, maintenance medications, as there are no co-payments, no deductible requirements, and no claims to file. Over-the-counter medications, except for insulin and insulin-related supplies, are not covered by CHAMPVA and not available from Meds by Mail.

To use Meds by Mail, complete the order form and profile form available at the website, www.va.gov/hac/forms/forms.asp or by calling 1-800-733-8387 to request the forms be mailed to you. Note: you should not use Meds by Mail for prescriptions that must be filled immediately.

If you are covered by Medicare Part D (Prescription Drug Coverage Plan), you cannot use Meds by Mail. If you are covered by Medicare parts A and B, but not Part D, you can use Meds by Mail. Similarly, if you choose to participate in any prescription benefit plan, you are no longer eligible for Meds by Mail.

CHAMPVA has a network of more than 45,000 pharmacies. An outpatient deductible is required, but once that is met, you will have to pay only your cost share of the prescription; there are no claims to file. You can find pharmacies in the CHAMPVA network at the website, www.va.gov/hac, click on For Beneficiaries, then click on the Pharmacies benefit under the CHAMPVA program. Or you can call 1-800-880-1377.

If you use a non-network retail pharmacy, your CHAMPVA authorization card is your proof of coverage. You will probably have to pay the full amount for the prescription. You can request reimbursement from CHAMPVA, but it's unlikely to be for the full amount you paid. CHAMPVA has a set price it pays for each medication, and it would only reimburse that amount less your co-pay.

Divorce, Property Division, and Veterans

The Uniformed Services Former Spouses' Protection Act permits state courts to divide military pensions based on state divorce law. It doesn't mandate that the pensions be divided, and it doesn't establish a uniform method of how to apply such a division. For example, some courts have awarded former spouses an amount based on the member's rank and pay at the time of the divorce. But other courts have based the amount on the member's rank and pay at the time of retirement, even if the divorce was finalized years earlier. There is no time limit for a former spouse to enter a claim for benefits, even if the divorce has been finalized. It's imperative that a division of military retirement benefits is clearly specified in a separation agreement.

Remember: The USFSPA provides that disability pay being received under Chapter 61 of USC 10 1201 et seq. is not to be included in the calculation of "disposable pay." (Military retirement pay has been defined as "disposable pay" for the purposes of the Uniformed Services Former Spouses' Protection Act.) Veterans receiving disability pay should be careful to check what is included in the calculation of disposable pay when arriving at a divorce settlement.

Dependents' Educational Assistance (DEA) Provides Learning Opportunities

Your children, and perhaps even your spouse, may be eligible for education and training opportunities because of your service to your country. The Dependents' Educational Assistance program offers up to 45 months of educational benefits, which may be used to earn a degree, finish a certificate program, complete an apprenticeship, or take on-the-job training. Spouses may also take correspondence courses, as well as the other approved courses and programs. If your dependents need to take a remedial or refresher course, they must seek approval of such classes, but they too may be covered.

There is a wide range of degree courses, training, and certificate programs that a student may pursue, but any program that a school or company offers for DEA students must be approved by the State Approving Agency (SAA) or the VA.

Who Is Eligible?

The son, daughter (including stepchildren and adopted children), or spouse of a veteran in one of these groups is eligible for Dependents' Educational Assistance.

- A veteran who died or is permanently and totally disabled as the result of a service-connected disability (The disability must arise out of active service in the armed forces.)

- A veteran who died from any cause while such service-connected disability was in existence
- A servicemember missing in action or captured in the line of duty by hostile forces
- A former prisoner of war, missing in action, or forcibly held by a foreign government or power
- A servicemember who is hospitalized or receiving outpatient treatment for a service-connected permanent and total disability and is likely to be discharged for that disability

Eligibility Requirements for Dependents

In order to qualify for DEA:

- You must be a son or daughter (includes adopted and stepchildren) between the ages of 18 and 26 and you may be married
- If you are a spouse, benefits end 10 years from the date the VA finds you eligible or from the date of the death of the veteran. If the servicemember died on active duty, the benefits of the surviving spouse end 20 years from the date of death. If your marriage to the veteran ends in divorce, your eligibility for DEA benefits stops on the date your divorce is finalized. But if you're in the middle of a semester (quarter), and the divorce occurs through no fault of yours, the VA will extend your eligibility to the end of the semester or quarter, or to the end of 12 weeks if the course isn't operated on a semester system.
- If you are a surviving spouse (the veteran has died) and you remarry, your DEA eligibility is affected. Check carefully the requirements because they depend on your age and date of remarriage.
    - If you remarry before the age of 57, your eligibility ends on the date of remarriage.

- If you remarried *after* November 30, 1999, and the marriage ends, your DEA eligibility may be reinstated.
- If you remarried after October 31, 1990, but before November 30, 1999, eligibility cannot be restored.
- If you are 57 or older and remarry on or after January 1, 2004, you are still eligible for DEA benefits.
- If you remarried after age 57 and before December 16, 2003, you must have applied *in writing* before December 16, 2004, in order to have your eligibility reinstated.

Also remember that children of a deceased veteran are entitled to receive death benefits until the age of 23 as long as they are in school. So, if you're eligible for DEA, you must decide which program to receive. If you elect DEA, the death benefits end when you start receiving DEA benefits. One solution: if your program is more than 45 months, defer the DEA benefits and continue to receive your death benefits while you are in school.

Contact a representative of the VA or a Veterans Service Organization to discuss the options and determine which works best for your circumstances.

If You Are in the Armed Forces

You may not use the DEA benefit while on active duty. You may use it for additional education or training after your discharge (which must not be under dishonorable conditions). The VA can extend your period of eligibility by the number of months and days equal to the time spent on active duty.

You may be eligible for DEA benefits and for your own veterans benefits under the Montgomery GI Bill—active-duty program. You cannot use more than one benefit at a time, but can use them consecutively. You are entitled to a maximum of 48 months of benefits. For example, under the Montgomery GI Bill program, you may be eligible for 30 months of benefits. You can then tap into 18 additional months using the DEA benefits program. Work with a representative of the VA or a Veterans Service Organization to maximize your benefits.

How Does DEA Affect the Veteran?

The spouse or surviving spouse may use DEA benefits without any negative impact on the benefits she receives as a dependent under the veteran's disability or death award.

However, if you are a son or daughter using DEA benefits, there is an impact on the veteran's income. Here's how. A veteran receives an additional dependent allowance for each child until the child reaches the age of 23, *as long as the child is in school.* However, if the child elects DEA, the additional allowance the veteran receives is stopped once the child begins receiving the DEA benefits.

To Apply for DEA

You can apply for DEA if you've selected a program you want to pursue or just to check your eligibility. Submit VA Form 22-5490, Application for Survivors' and Dependents' Educational Assistance. If you're eligible, you will receive a *Certificate of Eligibility* that tells

Special programs for disabled dependents

Physically or mentally disabled dependents, who are at least 14, are also eligible for DEA benefits for Special Restorative Training or Specialized Vocational Training. The disability must prevent the dependent from pursuing an educational program.

Special Restorative Training may include speech and voice correction, language retraining, lip reading, auditory training, Braille reading and writing, etc. Specialized Vocational Training focuses on specialized courses that lead to a vocation objective.

you how long you're eligible and how many months of benefits you can receive.

You can get a copy of the application online at www.gibill.va.gov. Click on Electronic Application. You can submit it electronically but must also print out a signature page and send it to the VA since an original signature is required to begin payments.

You can also receive a printed application form by downloading the entire application from the above website and completing it or by asking for an application form from the school or training facility you plan to attend.

If you know the program you want to pursue, you need to take a copy of the printed form to the certifying official for VA benefits at the school or training facility who will certify your enrollment.

Remember: To use your DEA benefits, make sure that the program you've chosen is approved for VA benefits. Check with the school's financial aid office, training facility employment office, or with the VA. Also be sure to have the school or training official certify your enrollment to the VA.

Earn While You Learn

If you are eligible for DEA, are a full-time or three-quarter-time student in a college degree program, or a vocational or professional program, you may also apply for a work-study allowance to earn extra money. The jobs are VA-related, such as processing VA paperwork at schools or in VA offices. The type of job you are offered is a combination of what is available and your interests.

There is competition for these jobs because there are other program participants who are also eligible for them (for example, Montgomery GI Bill Active Duty, Vocational Training and Rehabilitation for Veterans with Service-Connected Disabilities). Selection for these jobs is based on several factors, but the first priority is given to veterans with service-connected disabilities rated by the VA at 30 percent or more. Other factors include:

- Disability of the student
- Ability of the student to complete the work-study contract before the end of his eligibility to education benefits
- Job availability within normal commuting distance to the student

You will be paid an hourly wage equal to the Federal minimum wage or your state minimum wage, whichever is greater. If you get a VA work-study job at your college, your school may pay you the difference between the VA pay and the minimum wage that the school offers to its own work-study students. The total number of hours you may work can't be more than 25 times the number of weeks in your enrollment period. For example, if your term is 16 weeks long, you may work no more than 400 hours.

You can get an application for DEA Work-Study from any VA Regional Office, VA Vet Center, Veterans Service Organization, or Reserve Education and Incentives Officers, or download it at www.vba.va.gov/pubs/forms/22-8691.pdf.

Life Insurance to Protect Your Dependents

You may convert your Servicemembers' Group Life Insurance (SGLI) to a renewable, affordable term life insurance policy called Veterans' Group Life Insurance (VGLI). The policy is renewable every five years, regardless of health, and can be retained for life. A full description of the policy and benefits is available at www.insurance.va.gov.

If you want to obtain VGLI, *without proof of good health,* you must apply for VGLI within the first 120 days after separation from the service. Your SGLI coverage continues at no cost to you for 120 days and the VGLI takes effect on the 121st day. You have up to one year after the initial 120 days to apply for VGLI, but you will have to provide proof of good health in order to be eligible.

You should receive an application for VGLI within 60 days after separation, again within 120 days after separation when the SGLI free coverage period ends, and before the end of the 16-month application period. Applications are sent to the address listed on your DD Form 214 (or equivalent separation orders). Even if you don't receive an application, VGLI deadlines remain in force.

You cannot purchase more coverage than you had in SGLI at the time of separation, with a maximum of $400,000. You can convert VGLI to an individual permanent (whole life or endowment) policy using one of the 54 participating commercial insurance companies.

Life insurance for totally disabled veterans

If you are considered totally disabled at the time of separation, your coverage under SGLI continues without charge for two years after separation or until you are not considered totally disabled, whichever is the earlier date. This is called the SGLI Total Disability Extension.

At the end of the SGLI Total Disability Extension, you will be automatically billed for VGLI without proof of good health. You can still be granted coverage up to one year after SGLI coverage is terminated if you submit Form SGLV, evidence of insurability, and the initial premium. You can receive VGLI after having the SGLI Total Disability Extension without providing evidence of insurability. The new coverage will provide general insurance coverage.

ACCELERATED BENEFITS OPTION

Terminally ill patients can request up to 50 percent of their VGLI coverage in a lump sum. It will, of course, mean a reduced amount for the beneficiaries. An insured is considered to be terminally ill if he has a written medical prognosis of nine months or less to live. The insured must submit Form SGLV 8284, Servicemember/Veteran Accelerated Benefit Option Form.

Dependency and Indemnity Compensation (DIC) Offers More Assistance

Your family may be eligible for additional monthly compensation under the Dependency and Indemnity Compensation program. To qualify for DIC, you must be an eligible survivor of a veteran who died because of a service-related injury or illness.

If the death was not service related, the following conditions may still make you eligible.

- If at the time of death, the veteran was receiving VA disability compensation for a total disability for the last 10 years. This includes veterans who would have received VA compensation but didn't because they were receiving military retirement or disability pay
- If at the time of death, the veteran was receiving VA disability compensation for a total disability continuously since released from active service *for at least five years.*

Here are the requirements to be considered an eligible survivor.

Surviving spouse. You must have been married to the veteran for at least one year. If a child was born of the union, there is no time requirement as long as your marriage was valid and you lived with the veteran continuously until his death. If you separated, then the separation cannot have been your fault and you cannot have remarried. DIC compensation ends upon your remarriage. Entitlement to DIC may be restored if the remarriage is terminated by death or divorce.

Child. You must be the unmarried child of a deceased, DIC-eligible veteran who is under the age of 18 or between the ages of 18 and 23 and attending school.

Parents. DIC benefits are available to some parents of veterans with a service-connected disability or a veteran who died in service or as the result of a service-connected disability. Parents who are dependents may be entitled to receive a portion of the veterans compensation award or DIC if they are in financial need. Parents applying for this benefit need to submit a VA Form 21-535 to their VA Regional Office.

Helpless adult children. The children of veterans eligible for DIC may receive benefits if they were determined helpless or mentally disabled before the age of 18. Helpless adult children must submit VA Form 21-534 to apply for this benefit.

To receive DIC, you must complete VA Form 21-534, Application for Dependency and Indemnity Compensation, Death Pension, and Accrued Benefits by a Surviving Spouse or Child. Mail the form to the VA Regional Office serving your area.

In Conclusion

The families of veterans are also protected by VA. Medical and educational benefits are available to the spouse and children of eligible veterans. Life insurance, even for disabled veterans, is also available.

APPENDIX A

VA Forms

This is a complete listing of all VA forms.

NUMBER *(type)*	TITLE
SF26	Award/Contract
21-0512s-1	Section 306 Eligibility Verification Report (Surviving Spouse)
21-0519c-1	Improved Pension Eligibility Verification Report (Child or Children)
21-6898	Application for Amounts on Deposit for Deceased Veteran
10-0426a	Meds by Mail Patient Profile
10-0094f	Dental Education Affiliation Agreement
10-1170	Application for Furnishing Nursing Home Care to Beneficiaries of VA
10-1313-13	VHA Research and Development Letter of Intent Cover Page
21-0788	Information Regarding Apportionment of Beneficiary's Award
21-0760	VA Benefits in Brief
10-7959C	CHAMPVA—Other Health Insurance (OHI) Certificate
10-7959E	Claim for Miscellaneous Expenses
10-0094g	Associated Health Education Affiliation Agreement
28-8832	Application for Counseling
10-0094h	Education Affiliation Agreement—Non–VA Health Care Facility
10-7055	Application for Voluntary Service
SF-171	Application for Federal Employment
OF612	Optional Application for Federal Employment
10-0415	VA Geriatrics and Extended Care (GEC) Referral
29-541	Certificate Showing Residence and Heirs of Deceased Vet or Beneficiary
10-10EZ	Application for Health Benefits

NUMBER *(type)*	**TITLE**
21-8416b	Report of Medical, Legal and Other Expenses Incident to Recovery for Injury or Death
10-10M	Medical Certificate
10-0137	VA Advance Directive: Living Will and Durable Power of Attorney for Health Care
21-4706c	Court Appointed Fiduciary's Account
21-4718a	Certificate of Balance on Deposit and Authorization to Disclose Financial Record
10-1313-8	Investigator's Total VA and Non-VA Research/Development Support
26-6684	This form was discontinued 1/27/05
SF-424	Application for Federal Assistance
10-5345a-MHV	Individual's Request for Medical Record from MyHealtheVet
21a	Application for Accreditation as a Claims Agent
10-583	Claim for Payment of Cost of Unauthorized Medical Services
10-7078	Authorization and Invoice for Medical and Hospital Services
10-2511	Authority and Invoice for Travel by Ambulance or Other Hired Vehicle
21-22a	Appointment of Individual as Claimant's Representative
10-2065	Funeral Arrangements
21-0781a	Statement in Support of Claim for Service Connection for Post-Traumatic Stress Disorder (PTSD) Secondary to Personal Trauma
VAF-4597	Your Rights to Appeal our Decision
10-7959f-1	Foreign Medical Program (FMP) Registration Form
10-1245C	VA/Department of Defense Sharing Agreement
10-1313-5	R&D Program—Investigator's Biographical Sketch
10-1313A	Merit Review Board Summary Statement
10-8678	Application for Annual Clothing Allowance
26-8497a	Request for Verification of Deposit
10-0388-6	Certification of State Matching Funds to Qualify for Group 1 on Priority List
VA4107c	Your Rights to Appeal our Decision-Contested Claims
29-389	Notice of Lapse and Application for Reinstatement
5655blank	Financial Status Report (blank copy)
21-0789	Your Rights to Representation and a Hearing
OF8	Position Description

NUMBER *(type)*	TITLE
26-6705b	Credit Statement of Prospective Purchaser
10-0445	Occupational and Environmental Exposure History
21-526	Veteran's Application for Compensation and/or Pension
VA2793	Shop Data Sheet (Artificial Limbs)
22-8692a	Extended Student Work-Study Agreement
26-8629	Manufactured Home Loan Claim Under Loan Guaranty
FL 26-559	Statement of Holder or Servicer of Veteran's Loan
10-0094e	Medical Education Affiliation Agreement—VA Sponsor—Dentistry
21-534a	Application for Dependency and Indemnity Compensation by a Surviving Spouse or Child. In-Service Death Only
22-8864	Other On-the-Job Training and Apprenticeship Training Agreement and Standards
VA-2346	Request for Hearing Aid Batteries & Accessories
VAF-4078	Application for Promotion or Reassignment
VA4107VHA	Your Rights to Appeal Our Decision
22-8597	Fact Sheet on Approval of OJT Programs
VA2130	Inspection Sheet—Prosthetic Dealer
10-0137B	What You Should Know About Advance Directives
VAF-0220	Your Appellate Rights Relating to Our Denial of Your Motion for Reconsideration
VA9	Appeal to Board of Veterans' Appeals
10-0400	Request for VSO Access to CPRS (Computer Patient Record System)
10-0376a	Credentials Transfer Brief
26-8923	Interest Rate Reduction Refinancing Loan Worksheet
29-888	Insurance Deduction Authorization
10-1314	HSR&D Career Development Awardee Annual Progress Report
20-8206	VA Statement of Assurance of Complicance with Equal Opportunity Laws
10-0400a	CPRS Read-Only Rules for VSOs
21-4165	Pension Claim Questionnaire for Farm Income
28-0588	Vocational Rehab and Employment—Getting Ahead After You Get Out
26-4555c	Vets Supplemental Application for Assistance in Acquiring Specially Adapted Housing

NUMBER *(type)*	TITLE
28-1905	Authorization And Certification Of Entrance or Reentrance Into Rehabilitation and Certification of Status
VA0880b	Worksheet for Determining Percentages on Memorandum Service Level Expectations
10-1313-11	(RR&D) Scientific Merit Review Board Summary Statement
10-1313-4	R&D Program—Estimated Expenses of Program/Project
10-1313-6	R&D Program—Investigator's Biography
10-2478	Veterans Request for Refill of Medication
40-4970	Request for Disinterment
21-0512V-1	Section 306 Eligibility Verification Report (Veteran)
21-8941	REPS Annual Eligibility Report
29-0165	VA Matic Enrollment/ Change
28-1905m	Request for Supplies (Chapter 31—Vocational Rehabilitation)
10-1170	Application for Furnishing Nursing Home Care to Beneficiaries of VA
10-2570D	Dental Record Authorization and Invoice for Outpatient Service
10-2850B	Application for Residents
10-5588	State Home Report and Statement of Federal Aid Claimed
10-9009f	Depleted Uranium (DU) Program Checklist
10-0388-3	State Home Construction Grant Program Space Program Analysis—Nursing Home and Domiciliary
FL-10-426	Temporary Loan Follow-up Letter
21-4185	Report of Income from Property or Business
22-1999c	Certificate of Affirmation of Enrollment Agreement Correspondence Course
10-7959C	CHAMPVA—Other Health Insurance (OHI) Certificate
10-7959D	CHAMPVA Potential Liability Claim
21-0517-1	Improved Pension Eligibility Verification Report (Veteran with Children)
10-0094a	Medical Education Affiliation Agreement—School of Medicine
10-0094b	Medical Education Affiliation Agreement—Osteopathic Medicine
10-0094c	Medical Education Affiliation Agreement—Graduate Medical Education
10-0094d	Medical Education Affiliation Agreement—School of Dentistry
10-0143	Certification Regarding Drug-Free Workplace

NUMBER *(type)*	TITLE
10-0143a	Statement of Assurance of Compliance with Section 504 of the Rehabilitation Act
FL-10-90	Request to Firm to Submit Estimate of Cost of Purchase or Repair of Prosthetïc D
10-0144	Certification Regarding Lobbying
10-0144a	Statement of Assurance of Compliance with Equal Opportunity Laws
VA646	Statement of Accredited Representative in Appealed Case
FL-10-341a	Employment Reference for Title 38 Employee
21-0510	Eligibility Verification Report Instructions
08-6001a	Contract Progress Report
10-2406	Recommendation for Release of Patient in Home Other Than Patient's Own
10-0388-12	Certification Regarding Debarment, Suspension, Ineligibility, and Voluntary Exclusion—Lower Tier Covered Transactions
10-1313-5	Research and Development Program—Investigator's Biographic Sketch
10-1313-1	Merit Review Application
10-1313A	Merit Review Board Summary Sheet
10-2409	Patient Agreement with Hospital in Relation to Home Other Than Own
10-2410	Agreement to Provide Home Care to Patient
21-0519s-1	Improved Pension Eligibility Verification Report (Surviving Spouse with Children)
VAF-4597a	Your Rights to Appeal our Decision Concerning the Reasonableness of Your Fee Agreement
10-5345	Request for and Authorization to Release Medical Records
21-527	Income–Net Worth and Employment Statement Instructions
21-4171	Supporting Statement Regarding Marriage
10-6298	Architect—Engineer Fee Proposal
26-6393	Loan Analysis
24-0296	Direct Deposit Enrollment
10-3203	Consent for Use of Picture and/or Voice
20-572	Request for Change of Address/Cancellation of Direct Deposit
21-22	Appointment of Veterans Service Organization as Claimant's Representative

NUMBER *(type)*	TITLE
21-0506	Due Process Rights
21-0514-1	Parent's DIC Eligibility Verification Report
21-530	Application for Burial Benefits
21-534	DIC, Death Pension and Accrued Benefits by a Surviving Spouse or Child
21-535	Dependency and Indemnity Compensation by Parent (s)
21-601	Application for Accrued Amounts Due a Deceased Beneficiary
21-674	Request for Approval of School Attendance
4676a	Employee Supplemental Qualifications Statement
21-4138	Statement in Support of Claim
21-4142	Authorization and Consent to Release Information to the VA
21-4192	Request for Employment Info in Connection with Claim for Disability Benefits
21-4502	Application for Auto or Other Conveyance and Adaptive Equipment
21-4706b	Federal Fiduciary's Account
26-8149	Report of Automatic Manufactured Home and/or Lot Loan
21-8049	Request for Details of Expenses
26-6851	Notice of Intention to Foreclose
21-8764	Disability Compensation Award Attachment Important Information
21-8940	Veteran's Application for Increased Compensation Based on Unemployability
21-8951-2	Notice of Waiver of VA Comp or Pension to Receive Military Pay and Allowances
22-1995	Request for Change of Program or Place of Training
22-5490	Application for Survivors' and Dependents' Educational Assistance
22-5495	Change of Program or Place of Training Survivor's and Dependents' Educational Assistance
22-8691	Application for Work-Study Allowance
26-8736a	Non-Supervised Lender's Nomination and Recommendation of Credit Underwriter
VAF-0245	VA Records Center and Vault (RC&V) Reference Request
26-8791	VA Affirmative Marketing Certification
10-0137A	Your Rights Regarding Advance Directives
26-8812	VA Equal Opportunity Lender Certification

NUMBER *(type)*	TITLE
26-8844	Financial Counseling Statement
26-8903	Notice of Election to Convey and/or Invoice for Transfer of Property
26-8937	Verification of VA Benefits
28-1902	Counseling Record—Personal Information
28-8872a	Rehabilitation Plan—Continuation Sheet
28-8890	Important Information About Rehabilitation Benefits
29-336	Designation of Beneficiary—Government Life Insurance
29-1546	Application for Cash Surrender/Application for Policy Loan
29-4125	Claim for One Sum Payment (Government Life Insurance)
29-4364	Application for Service-Disabled Veterans Insurance
SGLV8283	Claim for Death Benefits (Servicemen and Veteran Group Life Insurance)
SGLV8285	Request for Insurance
SGLV8714	Application for Veterans' Group Life Insurance
21-0516-1	Improved Pension Eligibility Verification Report (Veteran with No Children)
26-8261a	Request for Certificate of Veteran Status
21-0307	Award Attachment for Certain Children with Disabilities Born of Vietnam Veterans
28-8872	Rehabilitation Plan
29-357	Claim for Disability Insurance Benefits
26-8106	Statement of Veteran Assuming Loan (Substitution of Entitlement)
21-2008	Application for United States Flag for Burial Purposes
21-4176	Report of Accidental Injury in Support of Claim for Compensation or Pension
21-0304	Application for Benefits for Certain Children with Disabilities Born of Vietnam and Korea Service Veterans
22-5281	Application for Refund of Educational Contributions
26-0286	VA Loan Summary Sheet
26-0592	Counseling Checklist for Military Homebuyers
26-1802a	HUD/VA Addendum to Uniform Residential Loan Application
26-1814	Batch Transmittal—Loan Code Sheet
26-6382	Statement of Purchaser or Owner Assuming Seller's Loan
26-6850a	Notice of Default and Intention to Foreclose

NUMBER *(type)*	TITLE
21-8416	Medical Expense Report
22-8873	Supplemental Information for Change of Program or Reenrollment after Unsatisfactory Attendance, Conduct or Progress
22-8889	Application for Educational Assistance Test Program Benefits
26-0285	VA Transmittal List
26-0503	Federal Collection Policy Notice
26-421	Equal Employment Opportunity Certification
26-1805	Request for Determination of Reasonable Value
26-1817	Request for Determination of Loan Guaranty Eligibility—Unremarried Surviving Spouses
26-1820	Report and Certification of Loan Disbursement
26-1839	Compliance Inspection Report
26-1843	Certificate of Reasonable Value
26-1844	Request for Acceptance of Changes in Approved Drawings and Specifications
26-1849	Escrow Agreement for Postponed Exterior Onsite Improvements
26-1852	Description of Materials
26-1859	Warranty of Completion of Construction
26-1880	Request for a Certificate of Eligibility
26-4555	Veterans Application in Acquiring Specially Adapted Housing or Special Home Adaptations Grant
26-6381	Application for Assumption Approval and/or Release from Personal Liability to the Government on a Home Loan
26-6681	Fee or Roster Designation—Application for Fee Personnel Designation
26-6705	Offer to Purchase and Contract of Sale
26-8497	Request for Verification of Employment
21-0781	Statement in Support of Claim for Service Connection for PTSD
VAF-0243	Diary Slip
26-6807	Financial Statement
26-6850	Notice of Default
26-6851	Notice of Intention to Foreclose
26-8599	Manufactured Home Warranty (Limited Warranty)
28-1905h	Trainee Request for Leave—Chapter 31, Title 38 U.S.C.
26-8630	Manufactured Home Loan Claim Under Loan Guaranty

NUMBER *(type)*	TITLE
26-8730	Used Manufactured Home Warranty (Limited Warranty)
26-8731a	Water-Plumbing Systems Inspection Report (Manufactured Home)
26-8731b	Electrical Systems Inspection Report (Manufactured Home)
26-8731c	Fuel and Heating Systems Inspection Report (Manufactured Home)
21-527	Income—Net Worth and Employment Statement
40-1330	Application for Standard Government Headstone or Marker
21-0513-1	Old Law and Section 306 Eligibility Verification Report
21-0518-1	Improved Pension Eligibility Verification Report—Surviving Spouse w/no Children
29-0563	Veterans Mortgage Life Insurance (VMLI)—Change of Address Statement
10-0388-1	Initial Application for State Home Construction and Acquisition
10-0388-2	Certification of Compliance w/the Provisions of Davis-Bacon Act (40 USC 276a to 276a-7)
10-0388-7	Certification Research Debarment, Suspension, Other . . . —Primary Covered Transactions
10-10d	Application for CHAMPVA Benefits
VAF-4597b	Your Rights to Appeal Decision on Your Motion for Review Clear and Unmistakable
10-3567	State Home Inspection
10-9009d	Depleted Uranium (DU) Questionnaire
10-6131	Daily Log—Formal Contract
VA0879	Speaker Request Form
3215	Application of Service Representative for Placement on Mailing List
29-0152	Application for Conversion—Government Life Insurance
10-0388-11	Memorandum of Agreement for a Grant to Construct or Acquire State Veterans Home
646	Statement of Accredited Representative in Appealed Case
20-8734	Equal Opportunity Compliance Review Report
40-0241	State Cemetery Data
10-10EC	Application for Extended Care Services
20-4274	Compliance Report of Proprietary Institutions
10-2407	Residential Care Home Program—Sponsor Application

NUMBER *(type)*	TITLE
21-4709	Certificate as to Assets
21-527	Income—Net Worth and Employment Statement Part A
VA0730e	Missing Child Care Subsidy Program Documents Form
10-0436	Application for an Off-Site Tissue Banking Waiver
21-0779	Request for Nursing Home Information in Connection with Claim for Aid and Attendance
21-8834	Application for Reimbursement of Headstone or Marker Expense
21-0784	Supplemental Income Questionnaire (for Philippine Claims Only)
28-1900	Disabled Veterans Application for Vocational Rehabilitation
VA0730f	Certification of Child Care Subsidy Payments
10-10SH	State Home Program Application for Veteran Care Medical Certificate
10-7959D	CHAMPVA Potential Liability Claim
21-4185	Report of Income from Property or Business
21-601	Application for Accrued Amounts Due a Deceased Beneficiary
10-7959A	CHAMPVA Claim Form
10-0361	Homeless Providers Grant and Per Diem Program
26-4555d	Veteran's Application for Assistance in Acquiring Special Housing Adaptations
26-6681	Fee or Roster Designation Application for Fee Personnel Designation
26-6807	Financial Statement
26-8084	Claim for Repurchase of Loan
5655	Financial Status Report
21-4176	General Instructions for Report of Accidental Injury in Support of Claim for Compensation or Pension Statement of Witness to Accident
21-530a	State Application for Interment Allowance Under 38 USC Chapter 23
21-530	Application for Burial Benefits
FL29-30a	Supplemental Disability Report
22-8889	Application for Educational Assistance Test Program Benefits
26-1839	Compliance Inspection Report
21-524	Statement of Person Claiming to Have Stood in Relation of Parent
26-6382	Statement of Purchaser or Owner Assuming Seller's Loan
26-6850	Notice of Default
20-8734a	Supplement to Equal Opportunity Compliance Review Report
21-0571	Application for Exclusion of Children's Income

NUMBER *(type)*	TITLE
21-6898	Application for Amounts on Deposit for Deceased Veteran
VA0880a	Memorandum of Service Level Expectations for Part-Time Physician on Adjustable Work
26-6850a	Notice of Default and Intention to Foreclose
26-8736	Application for Authority to Close Loans on Automatic Basis—Nonsupervise Lender
26-8844	Financial Counseling Statement
28-1902	Counseling Record—Personal Information
28-1905	Authorization and Certification of Entrance or Reentrance into Rehabilitation and Certification of Status
28-1905m	Request for Supplies (Chapter 31—Vocational Rehabilitation)
28-1905p	Annual Farm and Home Plan for Institutional On-Farm Course of Training
29-0188	Application for Supplemental Service Disabled Veterans (RH) Life Insurance
29-0532-1	VA Matic Authorization
29-0563	Veteran Mortgage Life Insurance—Change of Address Statement
29-4125a	Claim for Monthly Payment—National Service Life Insurance
29-4125k	Claim for Monthly Payment—United States Government Life Insurance (USGLI)
29-4499a	Notice—Payment Not Applied—Government Life Insurance
29-541	Certificate Showing Residence and Heirs of Deceased Veteran or Beneficiary
29-8146	Supplemental Physical Examination Report
VA4667b	Supervisory Appraisal of Employee for Promotion
26-8778	Present Status of Loan
26-6705d	Addendum to Offer to Purchase and Contract of Sale
22-8692	Student Work-Study Agreement (Student Services)
29-1549	Application for Change of Permanent Plan (Medical) (Change to a Policy with a Lower Reserve Value)
29-8158	Attending Physician's Statement
29-8160	Supplemental Physician Examination Report (Diabetes—Physician's Report)
29-8313-1	Disability Benefits Questionnaire

NUMBER *(type)*	TITLE
29-8485a	Application for Ordinary Life Insurance Replacement Insurance for Modified Life
FL29-459	Claim For Disability Insurance Benefits
FL29-551b	Reviewing Disability Insurance Benefits Claim
21-4140-1	Employment Questionnaire
21-0792	Fiduciary Statement in Support of Appointment
VA-3288	Request for and Consent to Release Information from Claimant's Records
SF15	Application for 10-Point Veteran Preference
10-0388-8	Certification Regarding Drug-Free Workplace Requirements for Grantees Other than Individuals
10-0388-10	Certification of Compliance with Federal Requirements—State Home Construction Grant
10-0388-13	Documents and Information Required for State Home Construction/ Acquisition—Post Grant Requirements
28-1905n	Farm Survey and Overall Farm and Home Plan Self-Proprietor/ Manager—Chapter 31
29-0543	Veteran Mortgage Life Insurance Inquiry
29-8485	Application for Ordinary Life Insurance Replacement Insurance for Modified Life
29-8636	Veterans Mortgage Life Insurance Statement
VA4107	Your Rights to Appeal Our Decision
10-1023	Information Regarding Possible Claim Against Third Party
10-0388	Documents and Information Required for State Home Construction and Acquisition Grant
21-4103	Information from Remarried Widow/er
29-888	Insurance Deduction Authorization (for deduction from benefit payments)
10-10EZR	Health Benefits Renewal Form
VAF-0120	VA Police Officer Pre-Employment Screening Checklist
21-8924	Application of Surviving Spouse or Child for REPS Benefits
10-2850C	Application for Associated Health Occupations
21-674b	School Attendance Report
10-2850A	Application for Nurses and Nurse Anesthetists

NUMBER *(type)*	TITLE
10-0379	Ecclesiastical Endorsing Organization Request to Designate Ecclesiastical Endorsing Official
20-8800	Request for VA Forms and Publications
VAF-40-1330	Application for Standard Government Headstone or Marker
22-1990	Application for VA Education Benefits
21-651	Election of Compensation in Lieu of Retired Pay or Waiver of Retired Pay to Secure Compensation from VA
21-527	Income-Net Worth Employment Statement Part B
21-526	Veteran's Application for Compensation and/or Pension
SF-50	Notification of Personnel Action
10-2850	Application for Physicians, Dentists, Podiatrists, Optometrists and Chiropractors
29-352	Application for Reinstatement
21-0501	Veterans Benefits Timetable
10-7055	Application for Voluntary Service
10-6056A	Lease
10-0408	VHA Fisher House Application
26-0551	Debt Questionnaire
21-686c	Declaration of Status of Dependents
28-1902w	Rehabilitation Needs Inventory (RNI)
VA0862	Claim for Credit of Annual Leave
21-4170	Statement of Marital Relationship
10-0388-14	Checklist of Major Requirements for State Home Construction/ Acquisition Grants
10-5345a	Individuals' Request for a Copy of Their Own Health Information
21-509	Statement of Dependency of Parent(s)
21-8834	Application for Reimbursement of Headstone or Marker Expense
26-1874	Claim Under Loan Guaranty
26-1874a	Claim Form Addendum—Adjustable Rate Mortgages
21-1775	Statement of Disappearance
21-509	Statement of Dependency of Parent(s)
FL26-567	Status of Loan Account—Foreclosure or Other Liquidation
26-0785	VA Lender Appraisal Processing Program (LAPP) Certification
10-0381	Civil Rights Discrimination Complaint

NUMBER *(type)*	TITLE
28-1905c	Monthly Record of Training and Wages
26-8084	Claim for Repurchase of Loan
10-0102	Career Development Application
10-0426	Meds by Mail Order Form CHAMPVA
10-0388-4	State Home Construction Grant Program-Adult Day Health Care
10-0388-5	Additional Documents and Information Required for State Home Construction and Acquisition Grants Application
10-0388-9	Certification Regarding Lobbying
10-7959f-2	Claim Cover Sheet—Foreign Medical Program (FMP)
29-380	Application for Protection Of Commercial Life Insurance Policy

APPENDIX B

Veterans Affairs Medical Centers

This is a complete listing of VA medical centers, by state. It includes contact information and the types of special programs at the facility.

Alabama

Birmingham VA Medical Center
700 S. 19th Street
Birmingham, AL 35233
205-933-8101 or 800-872-0328

Type of Facility

Tertiary care; 313 authorized beds

Special Programs

- Cardiac Catheterization
- Chemotherapy
- Geriatric Research, Education and Clinical Center (GRECC)
- Hemodialysis
- Home-Based Primary Care
- Mental Health Clinic
- Neurosurgery
- Nuclear Medicine
- Open Heart Surgery
- Palliative Care
- Research and Development
- Southeastern Blind Rehabilitation Center

Central Alabama Veterans Health Care System East Campus

2400 Hospital Road
Tuskegee, AL 36083-5001
334-727-0550 or 800-214-8387

Type of Facility

General medicine and surgery

Central Alabama Veterans Health Care System West Campus

215 Perry Hill Road
Montgomery, AL 36109-3798
334-272-4670 or 800-214-8387

Type of Facility

General medicine and surgery; 143 hospital beds, 160 nursing home care unit beds; 43 homeless domiciliary beds

Special Programs

Community Residential Care
Compensated Work Therapy (CWT)
Day Treatment
Health Care for Homeless Veterans (HCHV)
Home-Based Primary Care
Mental Health Intensive Case Management (MHICM)
Outpatient Substance Abuse Treatment (OSAT)
Preservation-Amputation Care and Treatment (PACT)
Psychosocial Residential Rehabilitation Treatment Program (PRRTP)
Respite Care
Visually Impaired Services Team (VIST)
Women Veterans Program

Tuscaloosa VA Medical Center

3701 Loop Road, East
Tuscaloosa, AL
205-554-2000 or 888-269-3045

Type of Facility

Long-term; mental health and outpatient primary care services

Special Programs

- Acute, Sustained Treatment and Rehab (STAR)
- Community Residential Care
- Compensated Work Therapy Transitional Residence (CWT-TR 12 beds)
- Dementia Program
- Dual Diagnosis
- Geriatric and Extended Care Services
- Health Care for Homeless Veterans
- Home and Community Programs
- Homeless Domiciliary (DRRTP—48 beds)
- Hoptel (on-station lodging program)
- Inpatient Mental Health Services
- Intermediate Medicine (inpatient) Services
- Mental Health Intensive Case Management
- Outpatient Mental Health Services
- Partial Hospitalization
- Post-Traumatic Stress Disorder Treatment Program
- Primary Care Services (Outpatient)
- Psycho-Geriatric Brief Stay Units
- Psycho-Geriatric Program
- PTSD (PRRP—15 beds)
- Residential Programs
- Skilled Nursing Home
- Substance Abuse (SARRTP—21 beds)
- Substance Use Disorders
- Women's Health and Mammography
- Vocational Rehabilitation

Alaska

Alaska VA Healthcare System and Regional Office

2925 DeBarr Road
Anchorage, AK 99508-2989
907-257-4700 or 888-353-7574

Type of Facility

Outpatient care; access to 20 MSU and 10 ICU beds through a VA/DoD Joint Venture with the 3rd Medical Group, Elmendorf Air

Force Base, Alaska; a VA-operated 50-bed domiciliary residential rehabilitation treatment program and 24-bed PRRTP

Special Programs

The following community-based outpatient clinics (CBOC) come under this facility:

Fairbanks, Alaska

Fairbanks VA Medical Clinic
Bassett Army Community Hospital
1060 Gaffney Road
Fort Wainwright, Alaska 99703
907-353-6370

Kenai, Alaska

Kenai VA Medical Clinic
11312 Kenai Spur Highway, Suite 39
Kenai, AK 99611
907-283-2231

Arizona

Carl T. Hayden VA Medical Center

650 E. Indian School Road
Phoenix, AZ 85012
602-277-5551 or 800-554-7174

Type of Facility

General medicine and surgery; 140 hospital (medical and surgical) beds, 104 nursing home beds, 48 mental health beds

Special Programs

Adult Day Health Care
Audiology and Speech Pathology
Cardiac Cath Lab
Community Residential Care

CT Scanner
Day Hospital
Day Treatment
Health Care for Homeless Veterans
Hemodialysis
Home-Based Primary Care
Mental Hygiene Clinic
MRI
Nuclear Medicine
PTSD
Pulmonary Function
Residential Care
Respiratory Care
SATU
Veterans Outreach Center
VIST

Northern Arizona VA Health Care System

500 N. Highway 89
Prescott, AZ 86313
928-445-4860 or 800-949-1005

Type of Facility

General medicine; 25 hospital beds, 85 ECRC beds; 120 domiciliary beds

Special Programs

American Indian Outreach
Dementia Special Care Unit
Domiciliary
Homeless Program
Hospice Unit

Southern Arizona VA Health Care System

3601 S. 6th Avenue
Tucson, AZ 85723
520-792-1450 or 800-470-8262

Type of Facility

General medicine and surgery; 155 hospital beds, 90 nursing home beds; 16 psychosocial residential rehabilitation treatment program (PRRTP) beds

Special Programs

Blind Rehabilitation Program
Cardiac Catheterization/Angioplasty
Cardiac Surgery
Evaluation and Brief Treatment PTSD Unit (EBTPU)
Geriatric Evaluation and Management Clinic
Geriatrics and Rehabilitation Center
Health Care for Homeless Veterans (HCHV)
Hematology/Oncology
Molecular Biology Department
Native American Outreach Program
Psychiatric Residential Rehabilitation Treatment Program (PRRTP) for Substance Abuse
Research Service
Spinal Cord Injury Clinic
Valley Fever Center for Excellence
VISN 18 Polytrauma Network Site

Arkansas

Central Arkansas Veterans Healthcare System Eugene J. Towbin Healthcare Center

2200 Fort Roots Drive
North Little Rock, AR 72114-1706
501-257-1000

Type of Facility

Primary care; extended care; rehabilitative care and mental health care; 395 beds

Special Programs

Adult Day Health Care
Ambulatory Surgery
Cardio/Thoracic
Comprehensive Homeless Center
Dental
Dermatology
Domiciliary
Drug and Alcohol
ENT
Gastroenterology
General Surgery
Geriatrics
GRECC
Hematology/Oncology
Home-Based Primary Care
Intermediate Medicine

Mental Health Services
Neurology
Neurosurgery
Nursing Home Care Unit
Open Heart Surgery
Ophthalmology
Orthopedics
Physical Medicine and Rehabilitation
Podiatry
Post-Traumatic Stress Disorder
Prosthetic & Sensory Aids Service
Pulmonary
Renal
Research
Respiratory Care
Respite Care
Short Stay Unit
Surgery
Urology
Vascular

Fayetteville VA Medical Center
1100 N. College Avenue
Fayetteville, AR 72703
479-443-4301 or 800-691-8387

Type of Facility

Primary and secondary care; 51 beds

Special Programs

Ambulatory Surgery Program
Cardiology and Surgical Clinics
Cardio-Pulmonary Function Lab
Dental Care
Diabetes
Echocardiography Services
Mental Hygiene
Optometry
Ultrasound
Urology
Women's Health

John L. McClellan Memorial Veterans Hospital
4300 W. 7th Street
Little Rock, AR 72205-5484
501-257-1000

Type of Facility

Tertiary care; 178 beds

Special Programs

Adult Day Health Care
Ambulatory Surgery
Cardio/Thoracic
Comprehensive Homeless Center
Dental
Dermatology
Domiciliary
Drug and Alcohol
ENT
Gastroenterology
General Surgery
Geriatrics
GRECC
Hematology/Oncology
Home-Based Primary Care
Intermediate Medicine
Mental Health Services
Neurology
Neurosurgery
Nursing Home Care Unit
Open Heart Surgery
Ophthalmology
Orthopedics
Podiatry
Physical Medicine and Rehabilitation
Post-Traumatic Stress Disorder
Prosthetic & Sensory Aids Service
Pulmonary
Renal
Research
Respiratory Care
Respite Care
Short Stay Unit
Surgery
Vascular
Urology

California

VA Central California Health Care System

2615 E. Clinton Avenue
Fresno, CA 93703
559-225-6100 or 888-826-2838

Type of Facility

General medicine and surgery; 114 authorized beds; 60 geriatric extended care unit beds

Special Programs

Abuse Treatment
Aids/HIV Services
Ambulatory Surgery
Amputation Care & Treatment (PACT)
Audiology

Comprehensive Cancer Care
Dementia Care
Diagnostic Radiology
Electroconvulsive Therapy
Electrophysiological Studies
Endocrinology
Gastroenterology
Geriatrics
Gulf War Syndrome Treatment Program
Homeless Veteran's Program
Home Based Primary Care (HBPC)
Interventional Radiology
Laparoscopic Surgery
Medical Research Projects
Mental Health Primary Care
Nuclear Medicine Prevention
PTSD Clinical Team (PCT) Unit
Pulmonary Function
Respite Care Sleep Lab
Smoking Cessation Substance
Speech Pathology
Visual Impairment (VIST)
Women's Wellness

VA Loma Linda Healthcare System

11201 Benton Street
Loma Linda, CA 92357
909-825-7084 or 800-741-8387

Type of Facility

General medicine, behavioral medicine, and NHCU; 248 beds

Special Programs

Alcohol and Drug Treatment
Cardiac Catheterization
Computerized Tomography
Dental
DOD/TRICARE/CHAMPVA
Hemodialysis
Magnetic Resonance Imaging
Mammography
Oncology
Post-Traumatic Stress Disorder Clinic
Sleep Disorder Clinic
Smoking Cessation Clinic
Visual Impairment Services Team
Vocational Rehabilitation
Women's Trauma Recovery Program
Women Veterans' Health Program

VA Long Beach Healthcare System

5901 E. 7th Street
Long Beach, CA 90822
562-826-8000 or 888-769-8387

Type of Facility

Tertiary care; 237 hospital beds; 90 spinal cord beds, 99 geriatric and nursing home beds

Special Programs

Cardiac Imaging Lab
Comprehensive Cancer Center
Preservation Amputation Care Treatment Program (PACT)
Radiation Therapy Program
Spinal Cord Injury Unit (SCI)
VA/CSULB Joint Studies Program
Women's Health Program

VA Greater Los Angeles Healthcare System (GLA)

11301 Wilshire Boulevard
Los Angeles, CA 90073
310-478-3711 or 800-952-4852

Type of Facility

General medicine and surgery; 953 authorized beds; 321 domiciliary beds, 226 NHCU beds

Special Programs

Automatic Implantable Cardioverter Defibrillator Center
Behavioral Improvement Program
Cardiac Catheterization
Comprehensive Women Veterans Health Center
Computer Tomography
Crisis Oriented Program Evaluation Service
Dialysis and Plasmapheresis Center
Dual Diagnosis Program for cocaine-abusing schizophrenics
Electrophysiology

Epilepsy Center
Gait Assessment and Falls Prevention Program
Geriatric Research Education and Clinical Center (GRECC)
Geropsychiatry
Gynecology Care, including Oncology and Pre-natal
Hospice Care
Immunodeficiency Clinical Care
Magnetic Resonance Imaging
Mental Illness Research Education and Clinical Center (MIRECC)
Neurosurgery
Nuclear Medicine Scanning and Imagery
Open Heart Surgery
Osteoporosis Center
Parkinson's Disease Research Education and Clinical Center (PDRECC)
Positron Emission Tomography
Post-Traumatic Stress Disorder Program
Prosthetics
Radiation Therapy
Spinal Cord Injury Program

Mather VAMC /VA Northern California Health Care System

10535 Hospital Way
Sacramento, CA 95655
916-366-5366 or 800-382-8387

Type of Facility

General medicine and surgery; 45 medical-surgical beds (Sacramento VAMC); 120 long-term care beds (Martinez VA Center for Rehabilitation & Extended Care)

Special Programs

Diagnostic Imaging (including CT Scan, PET Scan, MRI/MRA, Ultrasound)
General and Clinical Research Programs
General Clinical Research Center (GCRC)
Geriatrics Program
Home-Based Primary Care
Homeless Services
Long-Term Care (Extended Care, Neurocognitive Unit, Rehabilitation Program, Subacute Care, Transitional Care Unit, Respite and Palliative Care Programs)
Pain Clinic
PTSD Program
Substance Abuse/Methadone Program

Surgical and Major Surgical Subspecialties
Urgent Care
Women's Health Program

VA Palo Alto Health Care System

3801 Miranda Avenue
Palo Alto, CA 94304-1290
650-493-5000 or 800-455-0057

Type of Facility

A teaching hospital providing a full range of patient care

Special Programs

Allergy and Immunology
Andrology
Audiology
Blind Rehabilitation
Brain Injury Rehabilitation
Cardiology
Cardiothoracic
Coumadin
Dental
Dermatology
Diabetes
ENT
Endocrinology
Gastroenterology
General Internal Medicine
General Surgery
Geriatrics
Hand Surgery
Home-Based Primary Care
Immunology
Infectious Diseases
Nephrology
Neurology
Neurosurgery
Mental Health
Occupational Therapy
Oncology
Ophthalmology
Optometry
Orthopedics
Pathology and Lab Services
Pharmacy Services
Physical Therapy/PM&R
Plastic Surgery
Prosthetics/Orthotics
Pulmonary Medicine
Radiation Therapy
Radiology Services
Recreation Therapy
Rheumatology
Sleep Disorders
Smoking Cessation
Speech Pathology
Spinal Cord Injury
Substance Abuse
Urology
Vascular
Women's Health

VA San Diego Healthcare System

3350 La Jolla Village Drive
San Diego, CA 92161
858-552-8585 or 800-331-8387

Type of Facility

General medicine and surgery; 238 authorized rooms

Special Programs

- Alcohol/ Drug Research and Treatment Center
- Automated Prescription Filling System
- Barcode Medication Administration system (BCMA)
- Cardiac Catheterization & Electrophysiology Laboratory
- Cardiothoracic Surgery
- Clinical Diabetes Treatment & Research Program
- Computerized Medical Record (Computerized Patient Record System)
- Geropsychiatry
- Hepatitis C Program
- Hospital-Based Primary Care
- Magnetic Resonance Imaging (MRI)
- Mental Illness Rehabilitation, Education and Clinical Center
- Neurosurgery
- Nuclear Medicine
- Pain Management Program
- Positron Emission Tomography (PET) Scanner
- Post Development Clinic for Returning Combat Veterans
- Post-Traumatic Stress Disorder (PTSD) Program
- Research Center for AIDS & HIV Infection
- San Diego Center for Patient Safety
- Sleep Research
- Telemedicine
- Women Veterans Health Clinic

San Francisco VA Medical Center

4150 Clement Street
San Francisco, CA 94121-1598
415-221-4810 or 800-733-0502

Type of Facility

General medicine and surgery; 124 authorized beds and 120 NHCU beds; primary and specialty care is provided at the San Francisco facility, and primary and mental health care is provided at community-based outpatient clinics in Santa Rosa, Eureka, Ukiah, and in San Bruno; there is a specialized homeless veterans clinic at 401 3rd Street

Special Programs

Alcohol, Drug Abuse
Cardiac and Vascular Surgery
Clinical Cardiology
Dermatology
Endocrinology and Metabolism
Hematology/Oncology
Hepatology
Interventional Cardiology
Interventional Radiology
Mental Illness
Neurology and Neurosurgery
Ophthalmology
Oral Surgery
Orthopedics
Otolaryngology
Renal Dialysis
Urology

Colorado

VA Eastern Colorado Health Care System (ECHCS)

1055 Clermont Street
Denver, CO 80220
303-399-8020 or 888-336-8262

Type of Facility

General medicine and surgery; 128 hospital beds; 100 NHCU beds (Denver and Pueblo)

Special Programs

Audiology and Speech Pathology
Cardiology
Cardiothoracic
Dental
Dermatology
ENT
Gastroenterology
General

Geriatric Rehabilitation
Geriatrics
Gynecology
Hematology/Oncology
Homeless Program
Hospice
Imaging
Infectious Diseases
Medical
Mental Health
MHICM (MH Intensive Case Management)
MRI
Nephrology
Neurology
Neurosurgery
Nuclear Medicine
Orthopedics
Pathology and Laboratory Medicine
Physical Medicine and Rehabilitation
Podiatry
Prosthetic Treatment Center
PTSD Treatment
Pulmonary
Respite Care
Rheumatology
Substance Abuse
Surgical
Vascular

Grand Junction VA Medical Center
2121 North Avenue
Grand Junction, CO 81501
970-242-0731 or 866-206-6415

Type of Facility

General medicine and surgery; 23 acute medicine, surgery, and psychiatry beds; 30 transitional care unit beds

Special Programs

Ambulatory Surgery
Inpatient Psychiatry Care Unit
Intensive Care Unit
Mental Health Intensive Case Management
Transitional Care Unit

Connecticut

VA Connecticut Healthcare System Newington Campus

555 Willard Avenue
Newington, CT 06111
860-666-6951

Type of Facility

VA Connecticut comprises two campuses located in West Haven and Newington; 191 authorized beds

Special Programs

The Clinical Center for Excellence for Dialysis is the only veteran's dialysis center in Connecticut.

Single PhotoEmission Computerized Tomography SPECT, which provides state of the art imaging for medical care and research in biology, psychiatry, cardiology and oncology.

VA Connecticut is also designated a Clinical Program of Excellence for Seriously Mentally Ill veterans.

VA Connecticut Healthcare System West Haven Campus

950 Campbell Avenue
West Haven, CT 06516
203-932-5711

Delaware

Wilmington VA Medical Center

1601 Kirkwood Highway
Wilmington, DE 19805
302-994-2511 or 800-461-8262

Type of Facility

Primary and tertiary acute and extended care inpatient and outpatient, 60 hospital beds; 60 NHCU beds

Special Programs

Geriatric Evaluation & Management Program
Hemodialysis

District of Columbia

Washington DC VA Medical Center

50 Irving Street, NW
Washington, DC 20422
202-745-8000 or 888-553-0242

Type of Facility

Tertiary care; 158 acute care beds; 13 intermediate beds; 120 CNRC beds

Special Programs

Cardio-Thoracic Surgery
Eastern Pacemaker Surveillance Center
Geriatric Rehabilitation
Home Based Primary Care
Hospice and Palliative Care
Information Management Field Office
Institute for Clinical Research
National Media Development Center (CO)
Office of Special Projects (CO)
War Related Illness and Injury Study Center

Florida

Bay Pines VA Healthcare System

10000 Bay Pines Boulevard
Bay Pines, FL 33744
727-398-6661 or 888-820-0230

Type of Facility

General medicine; surgery; mental health; NHCU; and residential rehabilitation treatment program (domiciliary); 461 operating hospital beds; 142 operating NHCU beds; 104 operating domiciliary beds

Special Programs

Blind Rehabilitation Outpatient Service (BROS)
Day Treatment Program
Home-Based Primary Care
Hospice
Magnetic Resonance Imaging
Pulmonary Function Lab
Residential Rehabilitation Treatment Homeless Program
Respite Care
Sexual Trauma Recovery
Sleep Lab
Stress Treatment Program
Substance Abuse
VA Supportive Housing (VASH) Program
Veterans Outreach
Visual Impairment
Well Women's Program
Wound Care Program

James A. Haley Veterans' Hospital

13000 Bruce B. Downs Boulevard
Tampa, FL 33612
813-972-2000 or 888-716-7787

Type of Facility

Tertiary care; 327 authorized beds; 180 operating beds Tampa; 118 operating beds Orlando NHCU; 30 operating Orlando domiciliary beds

Special Programs

Cardiac Catheterization
Cardio-Pulmonary (Open Heart Surgery)
Coronary
Domiciliary (Orlando)
Electron Microscopy
Geriatric Psychiatry and Geriatric Medicine Hand/Orthopedic Surgery
Health Care for Homeless Veterans Program
Hemodialysis Center Self Dialysis
Home Dialysis Training
Hospital Based Primary Care

Intensive Care Units
Lithotripsy
Medical
Mental Health Clinic
Nuclear Medicine Service
Nursing Home Care Unit (Tampa and Orlando)
Outpatient Psychiatry
Partial Hospitalization—Acute Care
Partial Hospitalization—Extended Care
Plastic & Reconstructive Surgery
Post-Traumatic Stress Disorder (PTSD)
Radiation Therapy
Rehabilitation Medicine
Respiratory Therapy/Pulmonary Function Lab
Speech Pathology
Spinal Cord Injury Center
SCI Home Care
SCI Respiratory Dependency
Stereotactic Surgery
Surgical
Traumatic Brain Injury Center (TBIC)
Vietnam Veterans Outreach Centers (Tampa & Orlando)

Lake City VAMC, NF/SGVHS

619 S. Marion Avenue
Lake City, FL 32025-5808
386-755-3016 or 800-308-8387

Type of Facility

Secondary care facility; 38 operating hospital beds; 230 operating NHCU beds

Special Programs

Ambulatory Surgery
Amputee Clinic
Cardiac Telemetry
Cardiology
Dental
Echocardiology
EKG
Endoscopy
Eye Care Services (Optometry, Ophthalmology & Low Vision)
Hematology
Home-Based Primary Care
Homemaker/Home Health Aide
Internal Medicine
Medical Intensive Care Unit
Mental Health Clinic
Nursing Home Care Unit
Occupational Therapy
Oncology
Physical Therapy

Podiatry
Primary Care
Pulmonary Medicine
Radiology
Recreation Therapy
Respite Care
Speech Pathology
Surgery (General, Orthopedic, Urology)
Surgical Intensive Care Unit
Telemedicine/TeleHealth
Visual Impairment Center To Optimize Remaining Sight (VICTORS)
Visually Impaired Services Team (VIST)
Vocational Rehab
Women's Clinic

Malcom Randall VAMC, NF/SGVHS

1601 S. W. Archer Road
Gainesville, FL 32608-1197
352-376-1611 or 800-324-8387

Type of Facility

Tertiary care; general medicine, surgery and nursing home care, 251 operating hospital beds, 34 operating NHCU beds

Special Programs

Ambulatory Surgery
Amputee Clinic
Audiology
Blind Rehab
Cardiac Catheterization
Cardiac Telemetry
Cardiology
Cardiothoracic Intensive Care Unit
Dental
Dermatology
Dialysis
Echocardiology
EKG
Endocrinology and Metabolism
Endoscopy
Gastroenterology
Hematology
Home-Based Primary Care
Homemaker/Home Health Aide
Immunology
Infectious Diseases
Internal Medicine
Medical Intensive Care Unit
Mental Health Clinic
Nephrology
Neurology
Neurosurgery
Nursing Home Care Unit
Occupational Therapy
Oncology
Optometry

Otolaryngology (Ear, Nose, & Throat/ENT)
Physical Therapy
Podiatry
Primary Care
Prosthetics & Sensory Aids
Pulmonary Medicine
Radiology
Recreation Therapy
Respite Care
Rheumatology
Sleep Disorders
Speech Pathology
Surgery (Cardiac, General, Orthopedic, Plastic, Thoracic, Urology, Vascular)
Surgical Intensive Care Unit
Telemedicine/TeleHealth
VIST (Visually Impaired Services Team)
Vocational Rehabilitation
Women's Clinic

Miami VA Healthcare System

1201 N. W. 16th Street
Miami, FL 33125
305-575-7000 or 888-276-1785

Type of Facility

Tertiary care; 303 acute beds; 172 operating NHCU beds

Special Programs

Adult Day Health Care
AIDS Center
Ambulatory Surgical Center
Audiology and Speech Pathology
Cardiac Catheterization
Day Treatment Center
Electron Microscopy
GRECC
Hemodialysis Center
Hepatitis C Center of Excellence
Homeless Program
Hospital based Home Care
Maxillofacial Prosdontics
Neurosurgery
Nuclear Medicine
Open Heart Surgery
Oral Surgery and Implantology
Persian Gulf Family Support Program
Prosthetics Treatment Center
PTSD Program
Residential Care Program
Respiratory Care
SAMHSA (Substance Abuse Mental Health Services Administration)
Sleep Disorder Program
Spinal Cord Injury Center

Substance Abuse Center (Inpatient & Outpatient)
Supervoltage Therapy
UPBEAT (Unified Psychogeriatric Biopsychosocial Evaluation and Treatment)
Women's Health Center

West Palm Beach VAMC

7305 N. Military Trail
West Palm Beach, FL 33410-6400
561-422-8262 or 800-972-8262

Type of Facility

Primary and secondary health care; 270 medical center beds, 98 operating NHCU beds

Special Programs

Community Linkage Team
Dialysis Unit
ENT Clinic
Eye Clinic
ICU
Laboratory
Non-Invasive Cardiology
Non-Invasive Vascular
Outpatient

Georgia

Atlanta VA Medical Center

1670 Clairmont Road
Decatur, GA 30033
404-321-6111 or 800-944-9726

Type of Facility

Tertiary Care; 173 operational inpatient beds, 100 nursing home care beds

Special Programs

Alzheimer's Disease
Ambulatory Surgery
Angioplasty
Audiology Speech Pathology
Cardiac Catheterization and Open Heart Surgery
Comprehensive Cancer Center
Comprehensive Thallium Heart Imaging
Electroconvulsive Therapy
Electrophysiological Studies
Endocrinology
Geriatrics
Gulf War Syndrome Treatment Program
HIV/Aids
Homeless Veteran's Program
Home-Based Primary Care
Intensive Psychiatric Community Care Program
Interventional Radiology
Laparoscopic Surgery
Medical Research Projects
Mental Health Primary Care
Prevention, Amputation Care & Treatment (PACT)
PTSD Clinical Team (PCT) Unit
Pulmonary Function & Imaging
Rehabilitation Research and Development
Smoking Cessation
Substance Abuse Treatment
Visual Impairment
Women's Wellness

Augusta VA Medical Center

1 Freedom Way
Augusta, GA 30904-6285
706-733-0188 or 800-836-5561

Type of Facility

General medicine; surgery, and neuro-psychiatry; 470 authorized beds

Special Programs

Agent Orange
Ambulatory Surgery Center
Audiology
Blind Rehabilitation
Cardiac Catheterization Laboratory
Cardiopulmonary Rehabilitation
Domiciliary
Gulf War Registry
Homeless Chronically Mentally Ill
Hospice Unit
Intensive Psychiatric Community Care (IPCC)
Long-term Psychiatric Care

Magnetic Resonance Imaging (MRI)
Neurology
Open Heart Surgery
Post-Traumatic Stress Disorder
Pulmonary Function Laboratory
Respiratory Therapy
Respite Care
Restorative Nursing Home Care
SCI Hospital-based Home Care
Sleep Laboratory Program
Social Model for Alzheimer's Disease Care
Speech Pathology
Spinal Cord Injury Center (SCI)
Stroke Rehabilitation
Substance Abuse Treatment Program
Women's Health Clinic

Carl Vinson VA Medical Center

1826 Veterans Boulevard
Dublin, GA 31021
478-272-1210 or 800-595-5229

Type of Facility

General medicine and surgery; 34 medical and surgical beds; 161 nursing home care beds, 145 domiciliary care beds (including homeless veterans program)

Special Programs

Intensive Care Unit—7 beds
Mental Health Clinic
Outpatient Substance Abuse Treatment
Post-Traumatic Stress Disorder (PTSD)
Women's Health Clinic

Hawaii

VA Pacific Islands Health Care System

459 Patterson Road
Honolulu, HI 96819-1522
808-433-0600 or 800-214-1306

Type of Facility

Provides diagnostic, medical, mental health, and specialty care outpatient treatment

Special Programs

- Clinic Based Home Care
- Day Hospital
- Outpatient Clinic on Guam
- Pacific Center for PTSD
- Primary Care Clinics in Hawaiian Islands (Hawaii, Hilo/Kona, Kauai, Maui)
- Psychiatric Evaluation Team
- PTSD Clinical Team
- PTSD Research
- PTSD Residential Rehabilitation Program
- Rehabilitation Program
- Substance Abuse

Idaho

Boise VA Medical Center

500 W. Fort Street
Boise, ID 83702
208-422-1000

Type of Facility

Primary and secondary care; 46 hospital beds; 32 nursing home beds; 9 inpatient substance abuse beds

Special Programs

- Aging
- Cardiovascular Pharmacology
- Clinical Pharmacology
- Immuno-Pharmacology
- Infectious Diseases
- Neuro-Pharmacology
- Physician Diagnosis
- Pulmonary Physiology and Pharmacology

Illinois

Jesse Brown VA Medical Center

820 South Damen Avenue
Chicago, IL 60612
Phone: 312-569-6188
Fax: 312-569-6188

Type of Facility

Tertiary care; 205 authorized beds

VA Illiana Health Care System

1900 East Main Street
Danville, IL 61832-5198
Phone: 217-554-3000
Fax: 217-554 4552

Type of Facility

Primary, secondary, medical and surgical care, acute psychiatric care, extended long-term care and skilled nursing home care; 422 authorized beds, including 223 nursing home beds in the facility

Special Programs

Acupuncture
Alzheimer's Diagnostic Treatment Services
Compensated Work Therapy Program (CWT) for SMI Vets
CWT Transitional Residence (TR) House
Ex-POW Program
Grant & Per Diem Program
Healthcare for Homeless Veterans Program (HCVC)
Home Based Primary Care
Mental Health Clinic
Mental Health Intensive Case Management Program (MHICM)
Nursing Home Care Unit
OIF/OEF Outreach
Palliative Care
Post-Traumatic Stress Disorder Clinical team
Primary Care
Substance Abuse (Outpatient)
Visual Impairment Service Team

Edward Hines Jr. VA Hospital
5th Avenue and Roosevelt Road, P.O. Box 5000
Hines, IL 60141
Phone: 708-202-8387
Fax: 708-202-7998

Type of Facility

Tertiary care, 483 authorized beds

Special Programs

Blind Rehabilitation
Cardiovascular Surgery
Level 2 Poly-Trauma Center
Pathology
Radiology
Radiation Therapy
Residential Care
Spinal Cord Injury

Marion VA Medical Center
2401 West Main
Marion, IL 62959
Phone: 618-997-5311 or 866-289-3300

Type of Facility

General medical and surgery facility; 115 authorized beds

Special Programs

Dentistry
Geriatrics and Extended Care
Neurology
Oncology
Physical Medicine and Rehabilition
Primary Care
Psychiatry
Specialty Care and Long-Term Care in Medicine
Surgery

North Chicago VA Medical Center
3001 Green Bay Road
North Chicago, IL 60064
Phone: 847-0688-1900 or 800-393-0865
Fax: 224-610-3806

Type of Facility

Primary and secondary medical care, surgery and rehabilitation medicine; 159 operating hospital beds, 195 nursing home care beds, and 105 domiciliary beds that include homeless and alcohol/drug abuse programs

Indiana

VA Northern Indiana Health Care System–Fort Wayne Campus

2121 Lake Avenue
Fort Wayne, IN 46805
Phone: 260-426-5431 or 800-360-8387
Fax: 260-460-1336

Type of Facility

Primary and secondary medical and surgical care, chronic and acute psychitary care, nursing home care unit, extended care; 243 medical, surgical and mental health beds, 180 nursing home care unit beds

Special Programs

Adult Day Health Care
Combat Veterans Treatment
Dementia Unit
Home Based Primary Care
Mental Health Intensive Case Management
Post-Traumatic Stress Disorder Clinic Team
Substance Abuse Treatment Program

Richard L. Roudebush VA Medical Center (Indianapolis VA Medical Center)

1481 W. 10th Street
Indianapolis, IN 46202
Phone: 317-554-0000 or 888-878-6889

Type of Facility

Tertiary care; 170 authorized beds

Special Programs

- Alcohol and Drug Dependency Treatment (outpatient)
- Audiology and Speech Pathology
- Cardiac Catheterization
- Cardiac Surgery
- Champus/DOD Clinic
- Computerized Tomography/PET/MRI
- Electron Microscopy
- Home Based Primary Care
- Home Dialysis Program
- Homeless Program/HCMI Program
- Hoptel
- Inpatient Hemodialysis Center
- Laser Treatment/Therapy
- Mental Hygiene Clinic
- New Intensive Care Units
- Nuclear Medicine Services
- OEF/OIF
- Oral and Maxillofacial Surgery
- Orthopedic Services
- Persian Gulf Primary Care Clinic
- Polytrauma Center
- Prosthetics and Sensory Aids
- PT, OT, KT, and RT Services
- Pulmonary Function Laboratory
- Radiation/Oncology
- Women Veterans

VA Northern Indiana Health Care System—Marion Campus

1700 East 38th Street
Marion, IN 46953-4589
Phone: 765-674-3321 or 800-360-8387
Fax: 765-677-3124

Type of Facility

Primary and secondary medical and surgical care, chronic and acute psychiatry care, nursing home care unit, extended care; 243 medical, surgical and mental health beds, 180 nursing home care unit beds

Special Programs

- Adult Day Health Care
- Combat Veterans Treatment
- Dementia Unit
- Home Based Primary Care
- Mental Health Intensive Case Management Post Traumatic Stress Disorder Clinc Team
- Substance Abuse Treatment Program

Iowa

Des Moines Division—VA Central Iowa Health Care System

3600 30th Street
Des Moines, IA 50310-5774
515-699-5999 or 800-294-8387

Type of Facility

General medicine, surgical, neuropsychiatry and long-term care; 47 acute care beds, 38 domiciliary beds

Special Programs

- PTSD
- Alzheimer's Treatment
- Cardiac Catheterization
- Cardiac Rehabilitation
- Diagnostic Services
- Domiciliary
- Home-Based Primary Care
- Joint Replacement
- Laser Eye Surgery
- Mental Health Services
- Rehabilitation
- Substance Dependence Treatment
- VIST—Services for the visually impaired

Iowa City VA Medical Center

601 Highway 6 West
Iowa City, IA 52246-2208
319-338-0581 or 800-637-0128

Type of Facility

Tertiary care, medicine, neurology, surgery, and psychiatry; 93 authorized beds

Special Programs

- Burn Center
- Cardiac Bypass Surgery
- Cardiac Catheterization
- Complete Organ Transplantation
- Coronary and Peripheral Angioplasty

CT Scanning
Hemodialysis
Histocompatibility Typing
Hyperbaric Oxygen Chamber
Intensive Care Units
Interventional Radiology
Kidney and Gallstone Lithotripsy
Mohs' Surgery
MRI
Neurological Services
Nuclear Medicine Network
Oncology Services
Oral and Maxillofacial Surgery
Outpatient Substance Abuse Treatment Program
Palliative Care
PTSD Program
Radiation Therapy
Renal Transplantation
Respite Program
Services Offered Through Affiliate
Sleep Studies Laboratory
Visual Impairment Services Team
Women's Health Clinic

Knoxville Division—VA Central Iowa Health Care System

1515 W. Pleasant Street
Knoxville, IA 50138
641-842-3101 or 800-816-8878

Type of Facility

General medicine, surgical, neuropsychiatric, and long-term care; 226 nursing home care beds; 40 domiciliary beds; 34 psychiatric beds; 20 intermediate beds

Special Programs

Cardiac Catheterization
Cardiac Rehabilitation
Domiciliary
Home-Based Primary Care
Joint Replacement
Laser Eye Surgery
PTSD
Rehabilitation and Extended Care
Substance Dependence Treatment
VIST—Services for the visually impaired

Kansas

VA Eastern Kansas Health Care System—Dwight D. Eisenhower VA Medical Center
4101 S. 4th Street
Leavenworth, KS 66048-5055
913-682-2000 or 800-952-8387

Type of Facility

General medicine and surgery; 207 hospital beds; 38 nursing home beds, 178 domiciliary beds; 25 psychiatric residential rehabilitation treatment program beds

Special Programs

Cardiology
Dermatology
Gastroenterology
Geriatric Medicine
Infectious Disease
Internal Medicine
Pulmonology
Rheumatology

VA Eastern Kansas Health Care System—Colmery-O'Neil VA Medical Center
2200 S. W. Gage Boulevard
Topeka, KS 66622
785-350-3111 or 800-574-8387

Robert J. Dole Department of Veterans Affairs Medical and Regional Office Center
5500 E. Kellogg
Wichita, KS 67218
316-685-2221 or 888-878-6881

Type of Facility

General medicine and surgery; 81 authorized beds

Special Programs

- Ambulatory Day Surgery Program
- Mental Health Clinic
- Outpatient Post-Traumatic Stress Disorder
- Outpatient Substance Abuse Treatment
- Rehabilitative Medicine
- Visual Impairment Services
- Women's Clinic

Kentucky

Lexington VA Medical Center

1101 Veterans Drive
Lexington, KY 40502-2236
859-233-4511

Type of Facility

General medicine and surgery; 99 hospital beds, 61 NHCU beds

Special Programs

- Ambulatory Surgery
- Audiology/Speech Pathology
- Cardiac Cath Lab
- Cardiac Surgery
- Hemodialysis
- Home-Based Primary Care
- Inpatient and Outpatient Post-Traumatic Stress Disorder Programs
- Intensive Care
- Inpatient and Outpatient Substance Abuse Treatment Programs
- Low Vision and Visual Impairment Services
- Mental Health Clinic
- Polytrauma Unit
- Primary Care
- Women's Health

Louisville VA Medical Center

800 Zorn Avenue
Louisville, KY 40206
502-287-4000 or 800-376-8387

Type of Facility

Acute care; 114 beds

Special Programs

Ambulatory Surgery Unit
Audiology
Cardiac Rehabilitation
Geriatrics and Extended Care
Healthcare for the Homeless
Home-Based Primary Care
Hospice and Palliative Care
Mental Health Service Teams
Plastics
Primary Care
Prosthetic Treatment Center
Specialty Clinics
Spinal Cord Injury Clinic
Surgical Vascular Laboratory
Visual Impairment Service
Women's Healthcare

Louisiana

Alexandria VA Medical Center

2495 Shreveport Highway 71 North
Pineville, LA 71360
318-473-0010 or 800-375-8387

Type of Facility

Primary and secondary care

Special Programs

Adult Day Care Program
Alzheimer's Unit
Chemical Dependency Outpatient Program
Community Home Health
Community Nursing Home Care
Community Residential Care
Home-Based Primary Care
Homeless Program
Homemaker/Home Health Aide (H/HHA) Program
Nursing Home Care Unit
Social Detoxification Residential Treatment Program (SDRT)
Specialty Referral Facility-Psychiatry
Women Veterans Clinic

Overton Brooks VA Medical Center

510 E. Stoner Avenue
Shreveport, LA 71101-4295
318-221-8411 or 800-863-7441

Type of Facility

Tertiary care, medicine, surgery, neurology, and psychiatry; 112 beds

Southeast Louisiana Veterans Health Care System

1601 Perdido Street
New Orleans, LA 70112
800-935-8387; appts: 504-568-0811 x2929

Type of Facility

Acute care facility; 354 beds. An outpatient clinic offering primary care and mental health services is open at the New Orleans facility. The clinic is located on the ninth and tenth floors of the medical center's Lindy C. Boggs Transitional Care Unit at 1601 Perdido St., New Orleans, LA. Call 800-935-8387 for clinic appointments.

Maine

Togus VA Medical Center

1 VA Center
Augusta, ME 04330
207-623-8411 or 877-421-8263

Type of Facility

General medical, surgical, psychiatric, and geriatric-extended care services; 167 authorized/operating Beds, 67 medical/surgical/mental health beds, 100 nursing home beds

Special Programs

Day Hospital Post-Traumatic Stress Disorder Program
Day Treatment Program
Home-Based Primary Care
Home Health Services
Mental Health Intensive Case Management (MHICM)
Nursing Home Care Unit
Outpatient Chemical Dependence Recovery Program
Spinal Cord Injury Clinic
Visual Impairment Services

Maryland

Baltimore VAMC—VA Maryland Health Care System

10 North Greene Street
Baltimore, MD 21201
Phone: 410-605-7000 or 800-463-6295
Fax: 410-605-7901

Type of Facility

Tertiary care; 137 beds

Special Programs

Education and Clinical Center (GRECC)
Education and Clinical Center (MIRECC)
Geriatric Evaluation and Management Program
Geriatric Research
Home-Based Primary Care Program
Mental Illness Research
Multiple Sclerosis Center of Excellence
Outpatient Spinal Cord Injury Program
Refractory Congestive Heart Failure Program
Regional Neurosurgery Program
Women Veterans Evaluation and Treatment Program

Perry Point VA Medical Center

Perry Point, MD 21902
Phone: 410-642-2411 or 800-949-1003
Fax: 410-642-1161

Type of Facility

Mental health care; 470 beds

Special Programs

- Community-Based Health Care Program
- Domiciliary Care Program
- Geriatric Evaluation and Management Program
- Home-Based Primary Care Program
- Hospice Care Program
- Program (SARRTP)
- Substance Abuse Residential Rehabilitation Treatment
- Ventilator Care Program
- Women Veterans Evaluation and Treatment Program

Massachusetts

Edith Nourse Rogers Memorial Veterans Hospital

200 Springs Road
Bedford, MA 01730
781-687-2000 or 800-422-1617

Type of Facility

Geriatric care/psychiatry; 65 hospital beds; 345 nursing home beds, 40 domiciliary beds, 52 PRRTP beds

Special Programs

- Acute Inpatient Psychiatric Care
- Alzheimer's Inpatient and Outpatient Care
- The Geriatric Research Education Clinical Center (GRECC)
- The Mental Health Intensive Case Management Program (MHICM)
- Nursing Home Care
- Substance Abuse

Northampton VA Medical Center

421 N. Main Street
Leeds, MA 01053-9764
413-584-4040 or 800-893-1522

Type of Facility

Psychiatric, long-term care, and satellite outpatient clinics; 167 beds

Special Programs

Compensated Work Therapy/Transitional Living
Horticulture Therapy
Outpatient Substance Abuse Detox/Rehabilitation Programs
Palliative Care
Post-Traumatic Stress Disorder
Respite Care
Smoking Cessation
VA Outreach Center
Women Veterans Clinic

VA Boston Healthcare System, Brockton Campus
940 Belmont Street
Brockton, MA 02301
508-583-4500

Type of Facility

Tertiary care (West Roxbury Campus) and long-term care (Brockton Campus); 435 authorized hospital beds; 120 nursing home beds, 85 domiciliary beds

Special Programs

Geriatric Care (GRECC)
Homeless Veterans Treatment and Assistance
Persian Gulf Veterans Program
Post-Traumatic Stress Disorder (National Center for PTSD)
Preservation/Amputation Care and Treatment
Prosthetic and Sensory Aids Service
Readjustment Counseling Service
Seriously Mentally Ill Veterans
Spinal Cord Injury
Substance Abuse

VA Boston Healthcare System, Jamaica Plains Campus
150 S. Huntington Avenue
Jamaica Plains, MA 02130
617-232-9500

VA Boston Healthcare System, West Roxbury Campus
1400 VFW Parkway
West Roxbury, MA 02132
617-323-7700

Michigan

VA Ann Arbor Healthcare System
2215 Fuller Road
Ann Arbor, MI 48105
734-769-7100 or 800-361-8387

Type of Facility

General medicine, surgery, tertiary care referral center; 100 hospital beds; 38 nursing home beds

Special Programs

Alcohol/Substance Abuse
Cardiac Surgery and Catheterization
Cochlear Implantation
Computerized Axial Tomography
Hemodialysis
Intensive Psychiatric Community Care
Linear Accelerator
Magnetic Resonance Imaging
Neurosurgery
Nuclear Medicine Network
Nursing Home Care Unit
Outpatient Spinal Cord Injury
Positron Emission Tomography
Visual Impaired Services Team

Battle Creek VA Medical Center
5500 Armstrong Road
Battle Creek, MI 49015
269-966-5600 or 888-214-1247

Type of Facility

Mental health, primary care, physical medicine and rehabilitation, extended care, and long-term care; 243 hospital beds; 241 NHCU beds

Special Programs

- Contract Nursing Homes and Alcohol Halfway Houses
- Geriatric Evaluation Unit
- Mental Health Clinics
- Outpatient Alcohol/Drug Abuse Treatment Program
- Palliative Care Program
- Primary Care Clinic
- Residential Care Program
- Residential and Outpatient Post-Traumatic Stress Disorder Program
- Substance Abuse Residential Treatment Program
- Veterans Outreach Program

John D. Dingell VA Medical Center

4646 John R Street
Detroit, MI 48201
313-576-1000 or 800-511-8056

Type of Facility

General medicine and surgery; 108 authorized beds, 109 NHCU beds

Special Programs

- Acute/Medicine Surgery
- Cardiac Catheterization
- Comprehensive Cancer Center
- Comprehensive Psychiatry
- Healthcare for Homeless Veterans
- Hemodialysis
- HBPC
- Intensive Psychiatric Community Care
- NHCU
- Palliative/Respite Care
- PTSD Clinic
- Radiation Oncology
- Research/Education
- Sleep/Wake Center
- Women Veterans Center

Iron Mountain VA Medical Center

325 E. H Street
Iron Mountain, MI 49801
906-774-3300 or 800-215-8262

Type of Facility

General medicine and surgery; 17 acute care beds; 40 nursing home care beds

Special Programs

- Audiology and Speech Pathology
- Cardiology
- ENT
- General Surgery
- Geriatrics
- Intensive Coronary Care Unit (ICCU)
- Mental Health Service
- Nephrology
- Oncology
- Ophthalmology
- Optometry
- Orthopedics
- Podiatry
- Post-Traumatic Stress Disorder Clinical Team (PCT)
- Pulmonary Function Testing
- Substance Abuse Treatment Program (SATP)
- Urology

Aleda E. Lutz VA Medical Center

1500 Weiss Street
Saginaw, MI 48602
989-497-2500 or 800-406-5143

Type of Facility

General medicine and surgery; 33 hospital beds, 81 nursing home care beds

Special Programs

- Ambulatory Care
- Cardiology
- Computerized Axial Tomography Unit
- Diabetic Clinic
- Endocrinology
- GATE
- Homemaker/Home Health Services
- Hospice Care
- Infectious Diseases
- Medical Intensive Care
- Mental Health
- Nuclear Medicine Unit
- Oncology
- Optometry
- Outpatient Substance Abuse
- Physical Medicine & Rehabilitation
- Podiatry

Post-Traumatic Stress Treatment
Pulmonary Care
Speech/Language Pathology
Ultrasound
Urology

Minnesota

Minneapolis VA Medical Center

One Veterans Drive
Minneapolis, MN 55417
612-725-2000 or 866-414-5058

Type of Facility

Tertiary care; 237 authorized beds

Special Programs

Brain Sciences Center
Cardiac Surgery Program
Center for Chronic Disease Outcomes Research (CCDOR)
Chronic Hepatitis C Clinic
Domenici Research Center
Geriatric Research, and Education Clinical Center (GRECC)
Intensive Weight Management Program
Magnetoencephalography Instrument (MEG)
Orthopedics
Polytrauma Center
Spinal Cord Injury Center
Traumatic Brain Injury Center of Excellence
Women's Comprehensive Care Clinic

St. Cloud VA Medical Center

4801 Veterans Drive
St. Cloud, MN 56303
320-252-1670 or 800-247-1739

Type of Facility

Primary medical, mental health services and acute psychiatry; 225 operating beds; 15 psychiatry beds; 225 nursing home beds; 148 domiciliary & PRRTP beds

Special Programs

- Adult Day Health Care
- Dual Diagnosis
- Extended care
- Outpatient Programming for Seriously Mentally Ill
- Post-Traumatic Stress Disorder (PTSD)
- Psychiatric Residential Rehabilitative Treatment Program (PRRTP)
- Rehabilitation
- Residential Substance Abuse
- Ventilator Care
- Vocational Rehabilitation

Mississippi

VA Gulf Coast Veterans Health Care System

400 Veterans Avenue
Biloxi, MS 39531
228-523-5000 or 800-296-8872

Type of Facility

General medicine and surgery; 20 intermediate care beds; 20 mental health beds, 40 medical/surgical beds, 81 nursing home care unit beds, 81 domiciliary beds

Special Programs

- Day Treatment
- Graduate Training Program
- Home-Based Primary Care
- Homemaker/Home Health Aid (HHHA) Program
- Hospice
- Outpatient Substance Abuse Treatment
- Pain Management
- Post-Traumatic Stress Disorder Treatment (PTSD)
- Respite Care
- Spinal Cord Injury Program
- Telephone Advice Program (TAP)
- Veterans Industries Program
- Visual Impaired Services Team (VIST)
- Women Veterans Program

G.V. (Sonny) Montgomery VA Medical Center

1500 E. Woodrow Wilson Drive
Jackson, MS 39216
601-362-4471 or 800-949-1009

Type of Facility

Tertiary care; 163 hospital beds

Special Programs

Ambulatory Surgery
Infectious Diseases
Neurology
PTSD
Radiation Therapy
Readjustment Counseling
Substance Abuse

Missouri

Kansas City VA Medical Center

4801 Linwood Boulevard
Kansas City, MO 64128
816-861-4700 or 800-525-1483

Type of Facility

General medicine and surgery; 125 authorized beds

Special Programs

AIDS Program
Ambulatory Surgery
Compensated Work Therapy
Geriatric Evaluation and Management Program
Health Care for Homeless Veterans
Outpatient Services
Primary Care
PTSD Clinical Team
Regional Eye Center
Substance Abuse Treatment Unit
VICTORS
VIST

John J. Pershing VA Medical Center

1500 N. Westwood Boulevard
Poplar Bluff, MO 63901
573-686-4151

Type of Facility

Primary and secondary care; 18 internal medicine beds, 40 extended care unit beds

Special Programs

- Audiology
- Cardiology Clinic
- Dental
- Desert Storm Registry
- ENT Clinic
- Female Veteran Clinic
- General Surgery Clinic
- GI Clinic
- GU Clinic
- Mental Health Clinic
- Optometry Clinic
- Orthopedic Clinic
- PATCH (Patient Access to Community Health)
- Podiatry Clinic
- Substance Abuse Treatment Program
- Tele-Dermatology
- Tele-Diabetic
- Tele-Major Medical
- Tele-Nutrition
- Tele-Patient Education
- Tele-Pharmacy
- Tele-Psychiatry
- Tele-Psychology
- Veteran/Family PTSD Groups

St. Louis VA Medical Center—Jefferson Barracks Division

1 Jefferson Barracks Drive
Saint Louis, MO 63125-4101
314-652-4100 or 800-228-5459

Type of Facility

General medicine, surgery, and psychiatry; 355 authorized beds

Special Projects

Clinic of Jurisdiction for State of Missouri
Geriatric Research, Education and Clinical Center (GRECC)
Health Care for Homeless Veterans Program
Home-Based Primary Care
Inpatient and Outpatient Substance Abuse Treatment
Linear Accelerator
Magnetic Resonance Imaging
Major Psychiatric Disorders Program
Medical Research
Mental Hygiene Clinic
Neuropsychology
Nuclear Medicine Network
Nursing Home Care Unit
Positron Emission Tomography (PET)
Post-Traumatic Stress Disorder (PTSD)
Prosthetic Treatment Center
Senior Veterans (Geropsychiatry)
Spinal Cord Injury Program

St. Louis VA Medical Center—John Cochran Division
915 N. Grand Boulevard
Saint Louis, MO 63106
314-652-4100 or 800-228-5459

Harry S. Truman Memorial
800 Hospital Drive
Columbia, MO 65201-5297
573-814-6000 or 800-349-8262

Type of Facility

General medicine and surgery; 118 authorized beds

Special Programs

Cardiology (Diagnostic and Invasive)
Cardiovascular Surgery
Combined Medical/Surgical Intensive Care Unit
Geriatric Evaluation and Management
Hospice
Substance Abuse Treatment

Montana

VA Montana Health Care System

1892 Williams Street
Fort Harrison, MT 59636
406-442-6410

Type of Facility

General medicine and surgery; 50 general medicine, surgery, and psychiatry beds (Fort Harrison), 30 NHCU beds (Miles City)

Special Programs

- Cardiac Catheterization (Diagnostic & Interventional)
- Cardiology
- Cardiopulmonary Care (including sleep studies, EEG's)
- Chiropractic Care
- Community Based Clinics
- Consultant Services in Multiple Specialties
- Dental
- Dermatology
- ENT
- Gastroenterology
- Gynecology
- Lithotripsy
- Mental Health (including substance abuse treatment)
- Neurology
- Neurosurgery
- Nursing Home Care Unit
- Oncology (Medical)
- Ophthalmology
- Orthopedics
- Outpatient
- Pain Management—Interventional and Medical
- Palliative Care
- Podiatry
- Prosthetics and Sensory Aids
- Rehab Medicine
- Rehabilitative Care
- Respite Care
- Rheumatology
- Surgery-Outpatient Surgery
- Telemedicine (Psychiatry & Radiology, Palliative Care and Retinal Imaging)
- Urology
- Vascular
- VIST

Nebraska

Grand Island Division VA Nebraska Western Iowa Health Care System

2201 N. Broadwell Avenue
Grand Island, NE 68803-2196
308-382-3660 or 866-580-1810

Type of Facility

Ambulatory and extended care; 76 nursing home care beds; 18 residential substance abuse beds

Special Programs

Alzheimer's and Stroke Support Groups
Geriatrics Program
Interactive Television System
Post-Traumatic Stress Disorder (PTSD) outpatient program
Regional Audiology Center
Sleep Lab
Substance Abuse Treatment Program

Lincoln Division—VA Nebraska Western Iowa Health Care System

600 S. 70th Street
Lincoln, NE 68510
402-489-3802 or 866-851-6052

Type of Facility

Ambulatory care services

Special Programs

Alzheimer and Stroke Support Groups
Geriatrics Program
Interactive Television System
Post-Traumatic Stress Disorder (PTSD) Outpatient Program
Regional Audiology Center
Sleep Lab
Substance Abuse Treatment Program

Omaha Division—VA Nebraska Western Iowa Health Care System
4101 Woolworth Avenue
Omaha, NE 68105
402-346-8800 or 800-451-5796

Type of Facility

Tertiary care; 100 acute care beds, 8 residential substance abuse beds

Special Programs

- Alzheimer's and Stroke Support Groups
- Bariatric Surgery Program
- Interactive Videoconferencing System
- Post-Traumatic Stress Disorder (PTSD) Outpatient Program
- Regional Audiology Center
- Sleep Lab
- Substance Abuse Treatment Program

Nevada

VA Southern Nevada Healthcare System (VASNHS)
901 Rancho Lane
Las Vegas, NV 89106
702-636-3000 or 888-633-7554

Type of Facility

Primary Care

Special Programs

- Addictive Disorders Treatment Program
- Community-Based Outreach Center for Homeless Veterans
- Community Nursing Home and Skilled Home Care
- Diabetes Multidisciplinary Clinic
- Falls Program
- Gambling Addiction Treatment Program
- General Medical Assessment Team for Homeless/Transient Veterans
- Geriatric Neurology Clinic

Hearing Screening Program for NSC Veterans
Hepatitis C Clinic
HIV Primary Care
Home-Based Healthcare
Home Oxygen Therapy Program
Hospitalist Service
Mammography Unit
Mental Health Outreach to Henderson and Pahrump CBOC's
Movement Disorders Clinic
Outpatient Infusion Clinic
Pain Management Program
Post-Traumatic Stress Disorder (PTSD) Program
POW Clinic
Preoperative Medical Clearance Clinic
Pulmonary Oncology Clinic
Sleep Apnea Education Program
Spinal Cord Injury (SCI) Primary Care
Vascular and Orthopedic Surgery
Women's Clinic
Wound and Ostomy Care Program

VA Sierra Nevada Health Care System

1000 Locust Street
Reno, NV 89502
775-786-7200 or 888-838-6256

Type of Facility

Primary and secondary care; 62 hospital beds, 60 NHCU beds

Special Programs

Agent Orange
AIDS Clinic
Behavioral Medicine/Biofeedback
Day Treatment
Home-Based Primary Care
Ionizing Radiation
Persian Gulf
Respite Care
Sleep Apnea Clinic/Treatment
Telemedicine
Women's Health

New Hampshire

Manchester VA Medical Center
718 Smyth Road
Manchester, NH 03104
603-624-4366 or 800-892-8384

Type of Facility

Primary care

New Jersey

East Orange Campus of the VA New Jersey Health Care System
385 Tremont Avenue
East Orange, NJ 07018
973-676-1000

Type of Facility

General medicine, surgical, and psychiatry

Special Programs

Agent Orange
Allergy/Immunology Program
Audiology and Speech Pathology
Cancer Screening
Cardiac Catheterization Lab
CAT Scan
Comprehensive Integrated Inpatient Rehabilitation Program (CIIRP)
Day Treatment
Diabetes Education
Healthy Aging and Recovery Care Program (HARP)
Hemodialysis Program
Home-Based Primary Care
Homeless/Domiciliary Program
Infectious Diseases Unit
Linear Accelerator
Low Vision Center
Magnetic Resonance Imaging
Methadone Maintenance
Nuclear Medicine Unit3
Nursing Home Care
Pain Management Program
Persian Gulf Family Support Program
Post-Traumatic Stress Disorder (PTSD) Unit

Primary Care Program
Prosthetics Pulmonary Function Lab
Radiation Therapy
Rehabilitation Programs
Renal Program
Same Day Surgery
Sexual Dysfunction Unit
Sleep Studies Laboratory
Spinal Cord Injury Unit
Substance Abuse Treatment Unit (SATU)
Swallowing Program
War-Related Illnesses and Injuries Study Center
Women's Health Services

Lyons Campus of the VA New Jersey Health Care System

151 Knollcroft Road
Lyons, NJ 07939
908-647-0180

Type of Facility

General medicine, psychiatry, and long term care

New Mexico

New Mexico VA Health Care System

1501 San Pedro Drive, SE
Albuquerque, NM 87108-5153
505-265-1711 or 800-465-8262

Type of Facility

Primary, secondary, and tertiary health care

Special Programs

Cardiovascular Surgery
Endovascular Implants for Treatment of Abdominal Aortic Aneurysm
Home-Based Primary Care
Lithotriptor
Magnetic Resonance Imaging
Magnetoencephalography
Positron Emission Topography (PET) Imaging

- Psychosocial Residential Rehabilitation Treatment Program (PRRTP)
- Spinal Cord Injury Center
- Veterans Outreach Program

New York

Albany VA Medical Center: Samuel S. Stratton

113 Holland Avenue
Albany, NY 12208
518-626-5000

Type of Facility

Tertiary care; 156 authorized beds

Special Programs

- Adult Day Health Care
- Cardiac Catheterization
- Cardiac Rehabilitation
- Compensated Work Therapy
- Diagnostic Laboratory Medicine and Radiology
- Geriatric Assessment
- Hospice/Palliative Care
- Magnetic Resonance Imaging
- Memory Clinic
- Nuclear Medicine
- Nursing Home and Respite Care
- Post-Traumatic Stress Disorder
- Radiation Oncology
- Stereotactic Radiosurgery
- Tomography
- Women Veterans Health Program

Bath VA Medical Center

76 Veterans Avenue
Bath, NY 14810
607-664-4000 or 877-845-3247

Type of Facility

Secondary care; 440 authorized beds

Special Programs

Acute Medicine
Extended Care
Intermediate Medicine
Psychiatry

Brooklyn Campus of the VA NY Harbor Healthcare System

800 Poly Place
Brooklyn, NY 11209
718-836-6600

Type of Facility

Tertiary care medicine, surgery, psychiatry, residential substance abuse

Special Programs

Cardiac Surgery
Comprehensive Cancer Care Center
Dermatology
Dialysis Healthcare Center
HIV/AIDS
Laboratory Medicine and Radiology
Nephrology
Pathology
Psychiatry
Rehabilitation Medicine
Surgery

Canandaigua VA Medical Center

400 Fort Hill Avenue
Canandaigua, NY 14424
585-394-2000

Type of Facility

Secondary care; 276 authorized beds

Special Programs

Alcohol/Drug Rehabilitation
Domiciliary Program
Long-Term Care
Mental Health Intensive Case Management Program

Mental Health Care
Nursing Home Care
Post-Traumatic Stress Disorder Clinic
Respite Care

Castle Point Campus of the VA Hudson Valley Health Care System
Route 9D
Castle Point, NY 12511
845-831-2000 or 800-269-8749

Type of Facility

General medicine

Special Programs

Chemotherapy
Dental Clinic
Dermatology
Diabetes Education
Neurology
Oncology
Orthopedic Clinic
Physical Therapy
Primary Care
Rehabilitation Medicine
Rheumatology
Same Day Surgery
Social Work
Spinal Cord Injury

New York Campus of the VA NY Harbor Healthcare System
423 E. 23rd Street
New York, NY 10010
212-686-7500

Type of Facility

Tertiary care, medicine, surgery, and psychiatry

Special Programs

Cardiac Surgery
Cardiology
Dialysis Program
HIV/AIDS
Microvascular ENT Surgery
Mohs Surgery

Neurosurgery
Preservation and Amputation Care Team (PACT)
Prosthetic and Orthotic Lab
Prosthetic and Sensory Aids Service
Prosthetic Treatment Center
Rehabilitation Medicine
Urology Stone Center

Northport VA Medical Center

79 Middleville Road
Northport, NY 11768
631-261-4400 or 800-551-3996

Type of Facility

General medicine and surgery

Special Programs

Medical
Psychiatric
Rehabilitative
Skilled Nursing Care
Surgical

James J. Peters VA Medical Center (Bronx, NY)

130 West Kingsbridge Road
Bronx, NY 10468
718-584-9000 or 800-877-6976

Type of Facility

Tertiary care; 311 authorized beds, 120 nursing home care beds

Special Programs

AIDS
Alzheimer's Disease
Brain Bank
Geriatric Research Education Clinical Center (GRECC)
Mental Illness Research Education Clinical Center (MIRECC)
Metabolic Alterations in SCI Patients

Prosthetic Devices for Spinal Cord Injuries (SCI)
Psychiatry
Rehabilitation Research and Development Center
Renal Research
Spinal Cord Tissue Bank
Viral Oncogenesis

Franklin Delano Roosevelt Campus of the VA Hudson Valley Health Care System (Montrose)
2094 Albany Post Road, Route 9A,
Montrose, NY 10548
914-737-4400 ext. 2400 or 800-269-8749

Type of Facility

Geropsychiatric and substance abuse treatment

Special Programs

Agent Orange/Persian Gulf
Community Care
Dentistry
Diabetes Education
Domiciliary
Geriatric Assessment
Mental Health Clinic
Nutrition
Optometry
Podiatry
Positives Anonymous
Post-Traumatic Stress Disorder
Primary Care
Respite Care Program
Sexual Trauma Counseling
Social Work
Stress Management
Substance Abuse
Supportive Housing
Visually Impaired/Blind Rehabilitation
Vocational Testing and Career Counseling
Women's Health

Syracuse VA Medical Center
800 Irving Avenue
Syracuse, NY 13210
315-425-4400 or 800-792-4334

Type of Facility

Tertiary care; 164 authorized beds

Special Programs

Acute Medical
Neurological
Psychiatric Inpatient Care
Surgical

VA Western New York Healthcare System at Batavia

222 Richmond Avenue
Batavia, NY 14020
585-297-1000 or 888-798-2302

Type of Facility

Secondary care; 106 authorized beds

Special Programs

Geriatric and Rehabilitation Facility
Mental Health Services
Outpatient Services
Residential Care Post-Traumatic Stress Disorder Unit

VA Western New York Healthcare System at Buffalo

3495 Bailey Avenue
Buffalo, NY 14215
716-834-9200 or 800-532-8387

Type of Facility

Tertiary care; 167 authorized beds

Special Programs

Cancer Care
Cardiac Surgery
Cardiology
Long-Term Care Services
Medical
Mental Health
Surgical

North Carolina

Asheville VA Medical Center

1100 Tunnel Road
Asheville, NC 28805
828-298-7911 or 800-932-6408

Type of Facility

Tertiary care; 112 acute medical beds, 120 extended care beds

Special Programs

Home-Based Primary Care Program
Substance Abuse Residential Rehabilitation Treatment Program

Durham VA Medical Center

508 Fulton Street
Durham, NC 27705
919-286-0411 or 888-878-6890

Type of Facility

General medicine, surgery, and referral facility; 154 operating beds, 120 nursing home beds

Special Programs

Ambulatory Care
Audiology
Cardiac Catheterization
Cardiovascular Surgery
Coronary Care Unit
Electron Microscopy
Epidemiology Research and Information Center
Epilepsy Center
Geriatric Research, Education, and Clinical Center
GEROFIT Program
Health Services Research and Development
Hemodialysis
Home-Based Primary Care
Home Dialysis
Medical Intensive Care
Mental Health Clinic
Mental Illness Research, Education, and Clinical Center
MRI

National Center for Health Promotion and Disease Prevention
Neurodiagnostic Center
Neurosurgery
Pain Clinic
Post-Traumatic Stress Disorder
Psychiatric Emergency Services
Radiation Therapy
Research and Development Service
Respiratory Care
Respite Care
Speech Pathology
Surgical Intensive Care
Women's Comprehensive Health Care

Fayetteville VA Medical Center

2300 Ramsey Street
Fayetteville, NC 28301
910-488-2120 or 800-771-6106

Type of Facility

General medicine and surgery; 90 general medical, surgical and mental health beds, 69 long-term care beds

Special Programs

Acute Psychiatry
Amputee Clinic
Audiology and Speech Pathology
Chemical Addiction Rehabilitation Program
Combined 8-bed MICU, CCU, SICU
General Surgery
Geriatric Evaluation Management
Mental Hygiene
Nuclear Medicine
Nursing Home Care Unit
Physical Medicine and Rehabilitation
Primary Care
Prosthetics and Sensory Aids
Respite Care
Vet Center
Visually Impaired Service
Women's Health Care

Salisbury—W.G. (Bill) Hefner VA Medical Center

1601 Brenner Avenue
Salisbury, NC 28144
704-638-9000 or 800 469 8262

Type of Facility

General medicine and surgery; 159 hospital beds, 270 nursing home beds, 55 psychosocial, residential rehabilitation treatment program/substance abuse residential rehabilitation treatment program beds

Special Programs

Ambulatory Care
Care Coordination Home Telehealth
Geropsychiatric Unit
Homeless Veterans Treatment Program
Mental Health Clinic
MRI
Nuclear Medicine
Nursing Home Care Unit
Optometry/Low Vision Rehabilitation
Post-Traumatic Stress Disorder Program
Psychiatric Community Care Team
Psychiatric Emergency Services
Psychiatric Intensive Care Unit
Pulmonary Function Laboratory
Residential Substance Abuse Treatment Program
Sustained Treatment and Rehabilitation Unit
Women's Health Care

North Dakota

Fargo VA Medical Center

2101 Elm Street
Fargo, ND 58102
701-232-3241 or 800-410-9723

Type of Facility

General medicine and surgery; 59 authorized beds, 50 transitional care unit beds

Special Programs

Acute Psychiatry
Anatomic Pathology
Audiology
Blood Banking
Cardiology
Clinical Pharmacy

Gastroenterology
General Lab
ICU General (Medical and Surgical)
Infectious Diseases
Microbiology Lab
Nephrology
Neurology
Nuclear Medicine
Occupational Therapy
Oncology
Optometry
Outpatient Substance Abuse
Pharmacokinetics Lab
Physical Therapy
Prosthetics
Recreation Therapy
Rehabilitation Medicine
Respiratory Therapy
Speech Therapy
Voluntary Service

Ohio

Chillicothe VA Medical Center

17273 State Route 104
Chillicothe, OH 45601
740-773-1141 or 800-358-8262

Type of Facility

General Medicine, Neuro-Psychiatric and NHCU. 35 acute medical beds, 25 psychiatric beds, 25 psychosocial beds

Residential Rehabilitation Treatment Program (PRRTP) beds, 50 domiciliary beds, 162 NHCU beds

Special Programs

Acute Mental Health
Ambulatory Surgery Clinics
Audiology and Speech Pathology
Bone Density Studies
Care Coordination
Chronic Mental Health
Community-Based Outpatient Clinics
Community Nursing Home Care
Community Residential Care Program
Contract Adult Day Health Care
CT Scan
Diagnostic X-Ray
Domiciliary
Geriatric Evaluation and Management
Home-Based Primary Care
Home Health Aid

Hoptel
Hospice
Magnetic Resonance Imaging (MRI)
Medical Intensive Care Unit
Mental Health Clinics
Mental Health Intensive Case Management
Nuclear Medicine
Outpatient Medical Clinics
Outpatient Mental Health Clinics
Outpatient Physical Rehabilitation
PRRTP
PTSD Clinical Team
Respiratory Care
Respite Care
Sleep Studies
Substance Abuse Treatment Program
Telephome Care
Ultrasound
VA Nursing Home Care Unit
Women's Specialized Clinics

Cincinnati VA Medical Center
3200 Vine Street
Cincinnati, OH 45220
513-861-3100 or 888-267-7873

Type of Facility

Primary healthcare, specialized care, and mental health services

Dayton VA Medical Center
4100 W. 3rd Street
Dayton, OH 45428
937-268-6511 or 800-368-8262

Type of Facility

General medicine, surgery, mental health, and extended care; 120 medical, surgical, and mental health beds, 265 nursing home care beds, 115 domiciliary beds

Special Programs

- Adult Day Care
- Child Day Care On Site
- Community Nursing Home Care
- Domiciliary Homeless
- Geriatric Evaluation Management Unit
- Health Care for Homeless Veterans
- Hemodialysis
- Hospice Care
- Hospitality House On Site
- Hyperbaric Oxygen (Referral thru VA/DoD sharing)
- Medical and Surgical Sub-Specialties
- Mental Hygiene Clinic
- Nursing Home Care Unit
- Patient Health Education
- Polysubstance Abuse Treatment Program
- Post-Traumatic and Stress Disorder Unit
- Primary Care
- Radiation Therapy
- Referral Center for other VA Facilities
- Respite Care
- Same Day Surgery Unit
- Sleep Disorder Program
- Vietnam Veterans Outreach Center
- Women's Center for Health Promotion

Louis Stokes VA Medical Center

10701 E. Boulevard
Cleveland, OH 44106
216-791-3800

Type of Facility

Tertiary care; 285 hospital beds, 224 nursing home beds, 174 domiciliary beds

Special Programs

- Care of the Seriously Mentally Ill
- Center for Stress Recovery
- Functional Electrical Stimulation
- Geriatric Research Education and Care Center
- Hemodialysis
- HIV/AIDS Care
- Magnetic Resonance Imaging
- Nuclear Medicine
- Open Heart Surgery
- Pathology Reference Laboratory
- Radiation Therapy

Sleep Disorder Program
Spinal Cord Injury Care
Substance Abuse Care
Women's Health Programs

Oklahoma

Jack C. Montgomery VA Medical Center

1011 Honor Heights Drive
Muskogee, OK 74401
918-683-3261 or 888-397-8387

Type of Facility

General medicine and surgery; 187 authorized beds

Special Programs

Audiology
Behavioral Medicine, including Alcohol & Drug Treatment
Hospice
Nuclear Medicine
PTSD, and Homeless Veterans
Respite Care
SCI
SUD
VIST
Women Veterans Clinic

Oklahoma City VA Medical Center

921 N. E. 13th Street
Oklahoma City, OK 73104
405-270-0501 or 866-835-5273

Type of Facility

Tertiary care; 169 authorized beds

Special Programs

Abdominal Aortic Aneurysm (Endostent Repair)
Nuclear Medicine
Tri-Fab

Oregon

Portland VA Medical Center

3710 S. W. U.S. Veterans Hospital Road
Portland, OR 97239
503-220-8262 or 800-949-1004

Type of Facility

Primary care, acute med/surg, psychiatric, specialty medicine, nursing skilled care unit, and liver & renal transplant; 231 authorized beds

Special Programs

HCV Resource Center
Liver Transplant
MIRECC
MS Center for Excellence
National Center for Rehabilitative Auditory Research
PADRECC
Renal Transplant

VA Roseburg Healthcare System

913 N. W. Garden Valley Boulevard
Roseburg, OR 97470-6513
541-440-1000 or 800-549-8387

Type of Facility

Medical, surgical, and psychiatric; 143 authorized beds

Pennsylvania

Altoona—James E. Van Zandt VA Medical Center

2907 Pleasant Valley Boulevard
Altoona, PA 16602-4377
814-943-8164

Type of Facility

General medical with long-term care; 68 authorized beds

Special Programs

- 23-Hour Observation
- Ambulatory Surgery
- AmeriCorps Volunteer Program
- Behavioral Health Outpatient
- Dental
- Geriatrics
- Home Medical Equipment (HME)/Home Oxygen
- Home Telehealth
- Homeless Program
- Hoptel Services
- Hospice
- Inpatient Acute Care
- Intensive Care
- Nursing Home Care
- OIF/OEF Program/Case Manager
- Physical Medicine and Rehabilitation
- Primary Care
- Recreation
- Respite Care
- Senior Companion Program
- Specialty Care/Clinics
- Substance Abuse (Outpatient)
- Telemetry
- Transportation Program
- Veterans Outreach Program
- Visual Impairment Services Team (VIST)
- Volunteer Program
- Women's Health

Butler VA Medical Center

325 New Castle Road
Butler, PA 16001-2480
724-287-4781 or 800-362-8262

Type of Facility

Primary medical care; 172 authorized beds

Special Programs

- Adult Day Health Center
- Home Care—Primary Care
- Homeless Veterans Program
- Mental Health Outpatient Care
- Respite Care
- Substance Abuse Treatment (Residential and Outpatient)

Coatesville VA Medical Center
1400 Black Horse Hill Road
Coatesville, PA 19320-2096
610-384-7711

Type of Facility

Neuropsychiatric and extended/transitional care; 200 nursing home care unit beds, 80 domiciliary beds, 165 psychiatry beds, 106 intermediate medicine beds, 19 medical beds, 75 Substance Abuse Residential Rehabilitation Treatment Program (SAARTP) beds

Special Programs

Adult Day Health Care
Alzheimer's (Dementia Treatment)
Ambulatory Care
Cardiology (Consultation and Initial Treatment)
Community Nursing Home Program
Community Residential Care Program
Day Treatment
Dentistry (General)
Domiciliary Care
Geriatric Evaluation and Management
Homeless Chronically Mentally Ill
Infectious Diseases
Intensive Psychiatric Community Care (IPCC)
Intermediate Medicine
Internal Medicine
Medical Intensive Care Unit
Mental Health Clinic
Neurology
Nursing Home Care
On Grounds Community Residential Care
On Grounds Transitional Housing
Physical Therapy
Post-Traumatic Stress Disorder (PTSD)
Primary Care
Psychiatric Intensive Care
Psychiatry (General)
Pulmonary Medicine
Respite Care
Speech Pathology
Substance Abuse Treatment
Vocational Rehabilitation

Erie VA Medical Center

135 E. 38 Street
Erie, PA 16504
814-868-8661 or 800-274-8387

Type of Facility

General medicine and surgery; 78 authorized beds

Special Programs

- Audiology and Speech Pathology
- Cardiology
- CAT Scan
- Clinical Pharmacology
- Cooperative Health Education Program
- Day Treatment Program
- GEM Program
- General Surgery
- Hematology/Oncology
- Hospice Program
- Intensive Care
- Mental Hygiene Clinic
- Nursing Home Care
- Optometry
- Orthopedic
- Outpatient Substance Abuse Program
- Primary Medicine
- Psychiatry
- Pulmonary
- Rehabilitation Medicine
- Respite Care
- Ultrasound
- Urology
- Women Veterans Program
- Veterans Outreach Program

Lebanon VA Medical Center

1700 S. Lincoln Avenue
Lebanon, PA 17042
717-272-6621 or 800-409-8771

Type of Facility

General medicine and surgery; 49 hospital beds, 136 nursing home beds, 63 PRRTP beds

Special Programs

- Acute Psychiatry Inpatient including Detox
- Adult Day Health Care
- Ambulatory Surgery/Surgical Procedure Clinic
- Behavioral Health Outpatient
- Community Residential Care
- Dental
- Homeless Program
- Homemaker Home Health Care
- Home Medical Equipment (HME)/Home Oxygen
- Hoptel Services
- Hospice
- Hospital Based Primary Care
- Inpatient Acute Medicine and Surgical Care
- Intensive Care—Medical and Surgical
- Nursing Home Care
- OEF/OIF Outreach and Treatment Services
- Physical Medicine and Rehabilitation
- Primary Care
- Prison Outreach
- Recreation
- Respite Care
- Specialty Care/Clinics
- Speech Pathology
- Substance Abuse Treatment
- Telemetry
- Transportation Program
- VIST & Visual Impairment Services Outpatient Rehabilitation (VISOR)
- Vocational Rehabilitation
- Volunteer Program
- Women's Health

Philadelphia VA Medical Center

University and Woodland Avenues
Philadelphia, PA 19104
800-949-1001 or 215-823-5800

Type of Facility

Tertiary care and nursing home care unit; 135 hospital beds, 240 nursing home care unit beds

Special Programs

- Addiction Recovery Treatment Units
- Aortic Stent Surgery
- Brachytherapy
- Center of Excellence in Substance Abuse and Treatment

Center for Health Equity, Research and Promotion (CHERP)
Home-Based Primary Care
Mental Illness Research Education and Clinical Center (MIRECC)
Methadone Maintenance Program
Nursing Home Care Unit
Parkinson's Disease Research, Education and Clinical Center (PADRECC)
Radiation Therapy
Sleep Center
Women Veterans Program

VA Pittsburgh Healthcare System, H. John Heinz III Progressive Care Center
Delafield Road
Pittsburgh, PA 15260
866-482-7488 or 412-688-6000

Type of Facility

Progressive long-term care; 336 nursing home care unit beds

Special Programs

Dementia Unit
Fall Prevention
Geriatrics
Home-Based Primary Care
Hospice
Outpatient Primary and Specialty Care Clinics
Pain Management

VA Pittsburgh Healthcare System, Highland Drive Division
7180 Highland Drive
Pittsburgh, PA 15206
412-365-4900 or 1-866-4VAPITT or 866-482-7488

Type of Facility

Neuropsychiatric and homeless domiciliary; 180 authorized beds

Special Programs

Adult Day Health Care
Comprehensive Acute and Extended Psychiatric Care
Comprehensive Homeless Program
Comprehensive Substance Abuse
Post-Traumatic Stress Disorder (PTSD)
Regional Center for Treatment of Former Prisoners of War
Schizophrenia

VA Pittsburgh Healthcare System, University Drive Division
University Drive
Pittsburgh, PA 15240
866-482-7488

Type of Facility

General medicine and surgery; 146 general medicine and surgery beds

Special Programs

Audiology and Speech Pathology
Bariatric Surgery
Cardiac Catheterization/Angioplasty
Cardiac Surgery Referral Center
Computerized Axial Tomography (CAT Scan)
Dialysis
Electron Microscopy Hemodialysis Center including Home
Geriatric Care Referral Center
Intensive Care Units
Magnetic Resonance Imaging (MRI)
National Liver and Renal Transplant Center
Nuclear Medicine Pulmonary Function Lab
Oncology Referral Center
Open Heart Surgery
Pain Management
Positron Emission Tomography (PET Scan)
Radiation Therapy
Step-Down Unit
Telemetry Orthotic Lab
Visually Impaired Service Team
Women Veterans Care Program

Wilkes-Barre VA Medical Center
1111 East End Boulevard
Wilkes-Barre, PA 18711
570-824-3521 or 877-928-2621

Type of Facility

General medicine and surgery; 79 operating hospital beds, 165 nursing home care unit beds, and 10 substance abuse residential treatment program beds

Special Programs

23-Hour Observation Beds
American Diabetes Association National Standards for Diabetes Self-Management Education Program
Cardiopulmonary Rehabilitation Program
CARF Accredited Healthcare for Homeless Veterans Program
Contract Adult Day Health Care
Contract Home Health Care
Ex-POW
Hemodialysis Unit
HIV
Home-Based Primary Care
Home Hospice and Care Coordination
Homemaker/Home Health Aid
Hospice Unit
Mental Health Clinic
Outpatient Post-Traumatic Stress Disorder Program
Outpatient Respite
Persian Gulf
Polysomnography Laboratory
Same Day Surgery Program
Sexual Abuse and Behavior Management Modification
Short Procedure Unit
Substance Abuse Residential Rehabilitation Treatment Program (SARRTP)
VA Adult Day Health Care
Visual Impairment Services
Women's Health Program

Puerto Rico

VA Caribbean Healthcare System
10 Casia Street
San Juan, PR 00921-3201
787-641-7582 or 800-449-8729

Type of Facility

Tertiary care; 348 authorized beds

Special Programs

Alcohol and Drug Dependence Treatment
Cancer Center
Day Treatment Center
Hospital Based Care
Immunology Evaluation Clinic for HIV
Nursing Home
Open Heart Surgery
Post-Traumatic Stress Disorder Program
Pulmonary Function
Rehabilitation
Spinal Cord Injury

Rhode Island

Providence VA Medical Center

830 Chalkstone Avenue
Providence, RI 02908-4799
401-273-7100 or 866-590-2976

Type of Facility

General medicine and surgery; 143 authorized beds

Special Programs

ADA Recognized Diabetes Patient Self-Management Education Program
Dialysis
General Intensive Care Unit
Hospital-Based Home Care
Nuclear Imaging
Mental Health and Behavioral Sciences
Post-Traumatic Stress Disorder Clinical Team
Respiratory Diseases
Speech/Language Pathology
Substance Abuse Treatment Program (Outpatient)
Veterans Community Care Center
Visual Impairment Services

South Carolina

Wm. Jennings Bryan Dorn VA Medical Center

6439 Garners Ferry Road
Columbia, SC 29209-1639
803-776-4000

Type of Facility

General medicine and surgery; 122 general medicine, surgery and psychiatry beds, 94 nursing home care unit beds

Special Programs

Acute Psychiatry and Substance Abuse Treatment Program
General Medicine and Surgery
Health Care for Homeless Veterans Program
Home-Based Primary Care
Mental Health Intensive Case Management
Nursing Home Care and Intermediate Medicine
Tertiary Ophthalmological Care

Ralph H. Johnson VA Medical Center

109 Bee Street
Charleston, SC 29401-5799
843-577-5011 or 888-878-6884

Type of Facility

Primary, secondary, and tertiary care; 145 authorized beds

Special Programs

Adult Day Care
Audiology
Cardio-Thoracic Surgery
Community Contract Nursing Home
Community Residential Care
Compensated Work Therapy (CWT)
Dermatology
Electroconvulsive Therapy
Endocrinology
ENT

Gastroenterology
General Surgery
Geriatrics
Hematology/Oncology
Hemodialysis
Home-Based Primary Care (HBPC)
Homemaker Health Aide
Infectious Diseases
Inpatient Mental Health
Interventional Cardiology
Interventional Radiology
Mental Health Day Hospital
Mental Health Intensive Case Management (MHICM)
Nephrology
Neurology
Neurosurgery
Nursing Home Care Unit (NHCU)
Ophthalmology
Orthopedics
Physical Medicine and Rehabilitation
Podiatry
Primary Care
PTSD
Pulmonary Function Test
Pulmonary Services
Research Service
Sleep Studies
Smoking Cessation
Speech Pathology
Substance Abuse
Urology
Vascular Surgery
VIST Program
Women's Program

South Dakota

VA Black Hills Health Care System—Fort Meade Campus

113 Comanche Road
Fort Meade, SD 57741
605-347-2511 or 800-743-1070

Type of Facility

Primary, secondary, medical, surgical, tertiary, psychological, and long-term care; 54 hospital beds, 104 nursing home care unit beds, 160 domiciliary beds

Special Programs

Dialysis
Electroconvulsive Therapy (ECT)
Nursing Home Care Unit
Post-Traumatic Stress Disorder Residential Rehabilitation Program

Residential Rehabilitation Treatment Program (RRTP)
Substance Use and Post-Traumatic Stress (SUPT) Program
Veterans Industries Program at McLaughlin and Eagle Butte, South Dakota

VA Black Hills Health Care System—Hot Springs Campus

500 N. 5th Street
Hot Springs, SD 57747
605-745-2000 or 800-764-5370

Sioux Falls VA Medical Center

2501 W. 22nd Street
Sioux Falls, SD 57117-5046
605-336-3230 or 800-316-8387

Type of Facility

Tertiary care; 45 acute beds, 58 TCU beds

Special Programs

GEM Program
Hearing Aid Center
Home-Based Primary Care
Hospice Consultation Team
Mental Hygiene Clinic
Nuclear Medicine Unit
Optometry
Podiatry
PTSD Clinical Team
Sexual Assault Counseling
Spinal Cord Injury Team
Substance Abuse Treatment Program
Telemental Health
Transitional and Respite Care
Visual Impairment Treatment Team
Women's Health Clinic

Tennessee

Mountain Home VA Medical Center

Corner of Lamont and Sydney Streets
Mountain Home, TN 37684
423-926-1171 or 877-573-3529

Type of Facility

General medicine, surgery, and domiciliary; 111 hospital beds, 295 domiciliary beds, 120 nursing home care unit beds

Special Programs

Domiciliary Homeless Programs (In-patient and Outpatient)
Intensive Psychiatric Community Care
Post-Traumatic Stress Disorder Clinical Team
Primary Care
SICU/MICU/CCU Units
Substance Abuse
Vestibular and Balance Program
Veterans Outreach Center
Visual Impairment
Women's Health

Tennessee Valley Healthcare System—Alvin C. York (Murfreesboro) Campus

3400 Lebanon Pike
Murfreesboro, TN 37129
615-867-6000

Type of Facility

General medical and surgical, psychiatric, and long-term care; 347 authorized beds, 245 long-term care beds

Special Programs

Adult Day Health Care Program
Angiography Invasive Studies
Audiology/Speech Pathology
Community Residential Care Program
Dental

Extended Care Outreach program
Geriatric Research, Education and Clinical Center (GRECC)
Home Health Care Program
Hospice Program
Infectious Diseases
Mammography Services
Nursing Home Care Unit
Outpatient Substance Abuse Rehabilitation Program
Physical Medicine & Rehabilitation
Podiatry
Post-Traumatic Stress Disorder Program
Psychogeriatric Program
Psychological Testing
Sleep Lab Program
Spinal Cord Injury Support Clinic
Veterans Community Care Center
Visual Impairment Services Team
Women's Comprehensive Health Care Center

Tennessee Valley Healthcare System—Nashville Campus

1310 24th Avenue, South
Nashville, TN 37212-2637
615-327-4751 or 800-228-4973

Type of Facility

General medicine and surgery; 238 authorized beds

Special Programs

Angioplasty
Arthroscopic Surgery
Audiology/Speech Pathology
Brain Stem and Auditory Evoked Response Testing
Cardiac Catheterization
CT Scanning/MRI
Dental
Dermatology
Diabetic Education
Dialysis
Flow Cytometry
Geriatric Research, Education and Clinical Center (GRECC)
Head and Neck Surgery
Homeless Services and Outreach
Infectious Disease
Laser Surgery
Major Orthopedic Surgery
Neurology
Neuropsychiatric Testing
Open Heart Surgery
Ophthalmology
Organ Transplantation
Otolaryngology
Pain Clinic
Peripheral Vascular Surgery
Photopheresis
Post-Traumatic Stress
Retinal Screening

Veterans Affairs Medical Center, Memphis, Tennessee
1030 Jefferson Avenue
Memphis, TN 38104
901-523-8990 or 800-636-8262

Type of Facility

Tertiary referral center; 254 authorized beds, 19 SARRTP beds

Special Programs

Ambulatory Surgery
Audiology/Speech Pathology
Cardiology/Cardiac Cath
CT/MRI Scanning
Cytogenetic Referral Center
Day Treatment Center
Dermatology
Dialysis
Digital Angiography
Endoscopic Surgery
Extracorporeal Shock Wave Lithotripsy
Hemodialysis Center
Hospital Based Primary Care
Neurosurgery
Nuclear Medicine
Oncology/Hematology
Open Heart Surgery
Optometry Services
Oral Surgery and Implantology
Orthopedics
Pain Management
Prosthetic Treatment Center
Radiation Oncology
Research
Sleep Disorder Program
Spinal Cord Injury Center
Substance Abuse Treatment (Inpatient/Outpatient)
Veterans Outreach
Visual Impairment Support
Women's Center

Texas

Central Texas Veterans Health Care System—Olin E. Teague Veterans' Center
1901 Veterans Memorial Drive
Temple, TX 76504
254-778-4811 or 800-423-2111

Type of Facility

General medicine and surgery; 459 psychiatry beds, 408 domiciliary beds, 303 nursing home beds, 134 internal medicine beds, 44 surgery beds, 36 intermediate medicine beds, 20 PRRP beds, 15 blind rehabilitation beds

Special Programs

Audiology/Speech Pathology
Bar Code Medication Administration (BCMA)
Blind Rehabilitation
Computerized Patient Record System (CPRS)
Day Surgery
Dentistry
Domiciliary
Hospice
MRI/CAT Scan
Med/Surg ICU's
Nuclear Medicine
Oncology
PACT Clinic
Post-Traumatic Stress Disorder (PTSD)
Post-Traumatic Stress Disorder Residential Rehabilitation Program (PRRP)
Prosthetics/Orthotics Lab
Robotics Inpatient and Outpatient Pharmacy
Sleep Lab
Substance Abuse
Women Veterans' Clinic

Central Texas Veterans Health Care System—Waco VA Medical Center

4800 Memorial Drive
Waco, TX 76711
254-752-6581 or 800-423-2111

Michael E. DeBakey VA Medical Center

2002 Holcombe Boulevard
Houston, TX 77030-4298
713-791-1414 or 800-553-2278

Type of Facility

Primary health care; 343 hospital beds, 40 bed spinal cord injury Center beds, 120 transitional care unit for long-term care beds

Special Programs

Cardiovascular Surgery
Gastro-Intestinal Endoscopy
Nuclear Medicine
Ophthalmology
Radiation Therapy
Specialized Diagnostic Care
Surgery
Treatment of Spinal Cord Injury and Diseases

Kerrville VA Medical Center

3600 Memorial Boulevard
Kerrville, TX 78028
830-896-2020

Type of Facility

Medical, primary, and long-term care services; 226 authorized hospital beds, 154 nursing home care unit beds

Special Programs

Computerized Tomography Scanner
Extended Substance Abuse Treatment Program
Geriatric Evaluation and Management
Hospice Care

VA North Texas Health Care System: Dallas VA Medical Center

4500 S. Lancaster Road
Dallas, TX 75216
214-742-8387 or 800-849-3597

Type of Facility

General medicine and surgery; 300 plus–bed acute care medical center, 116 transitional care unit beds, 40 domiciliary care unit beds, 30 Spinal Cord Injury Center beds, 59 Psychiatric Residential Rehabilitation Treatment Program (PRRTP) beds

Special Programs

Adult Day Health Care
Agent Orange Evaluation
Cardiac Surgery
Geriatric Care
Hemodialysis
Magnetic Resonance Imaging
Persian Gulf Evaluation
Post-Traumatic Stress Disorder
Rehabilitation Medicine
Women Veteran Services

VA North Texas Health Care System: Sam Rayburn Memorial Veterans Center

1201 E. 9th Street
Bonham, TX 75418
903-583-2111 or 800-924-8387

Type of Facility

Primary health care, nursing home care, long-term rehabilitative care; 139 nursing home care unit beds, 224 domiciliary beds, 7 Psychiatric Residential Rehabilitation Therapy Program (PRRTP) beds

Special Programs

Audiology
Dental
Dermatology
ENT
Foot Care
GYN
Optometry
Podiatry
Spinal Cord Injury
Surgery
Telemedicine
Urology

Utah

VA Salt Lake City Health Care System

500 Foothill Drive
Salt Lake City, UT 84148
801-582-1565 or 800-613-4012

Type of Facility

Tertiary care; 121 authorized beds

Special Programs

- Geriatric Evaluation and Management Program
- Geriatric Research, Education, and Clinical Center (GRECC)
- Information Resources Management Field Office
- Organ Transplantation (Specializing in Heart Transplantation)
- Salt Lake Education Center

Vermont

White River Junction VA Medical Center

215 N. Main Street
White River Junction, VT 05009
802-295-9363 or 866-687-8387

Type of Facility

General medicine, surgery, psychiatric, and geriatric; 60 authorized beds

Special Programs

- Ambulatory Surgery Program
- CT Scan
- Dentistry
- Home-Based Primary Care
- Hospice
- Neurology
- Nuclear Medicine
- Oncology
- Optometry
- Orthopedics
- Podiatry
- PTSD Clinical Teams
- Respiratory Care
- Substance Abuse Treatment
- Veterans Integrated Community Care Program (VICC)

Virginia

Hampton VA Medical Center
100 Emancipation Drive
Hampton, VA 23667
757-722-9961

Type of Facility

General medicine and surgery; 175 medicine and surgery beds, 120 NHCU/ECRC beds, 200 domiciliary beds, 21 therapeutic residency beds

Special Programs

Compensated Work Therapy
Domiciliary Drug Abuse Program
Domiciliary Rehabilitative Residential Care
Extended Care Rehabilitation Center
Hemodialysis
Hospice
Mental Health Case Management
National Chaplain Center & National Chaplain Training Center
Oral Surgery
Outpatient Substance Abuse Treatment Program
Post-Traumatic Stress Disorder
ReHabitat—Domiciliary Homeless Program
Salvation Army—Transitional Residency Program
Sexual Trauma Program
Spinal Cord Injury and Disorders
Substance Abuse Vocational Employment Program
Transitional Residencies
Vocational Rehabilitation
Women's Health Program

Hunter Holmes McGuire VA Medical Center
1201 Broad Rock Boulevard
Richmond, VA 23249
804-675-5000 or 800-784-8381

Type of Facility

Tertiary care; 229 hospital beds, 98 nursing home beds, 100 spinal cord injury beds

Special Programs

- Cardiac Surgery
- Comprehensive Cancer Center
- Electrophysiology Lab
- Geriatric Evaluation Unit
- Heart/Lung Transplantation
- Hospice Unit
- Magnetic Resonance Imaging
- Medical/Surgical
- Primary Care
- Prosthetic Treatment Center
- Psychiatry
- Radiation Therapy
- Regional Audiology Center
- Spinal Cord Injury
- Traumatic Brain Injury

Salem VA Medical Center

1970 Roanoke Boulevard
Salem, VA 24153
540-982-2463 or 888-982-2463

Type of Facility

General medicine and surgery; 182 general medical, surgical, and psychiatry beds, 90 Extended Care Rehabilitation Center beds, 26 Substance Abuse Residential Rehabilitation Treatment Program (10 long-term substance abuse beds)

Special Programs

- 23 Hour Observation & Chest Pain Evaluation Unit
- AIDS/HIV Care
- Allergy Clinic
- Alzheimer's Clinic
- Anxiety Disorders Treatment Program
- Audiology and Speech Pathology
- Blind Rehab Clinic
- Cancer Program
- Cardiac Catheterization Lab
- Cardiac Rehabilitation
- Comprensated Work Therapy (CWT)
- Comprehensive Primary Care Services, including Mental Health
- Computerized Tomography Scanning (CT Scan)

Day Hospital
Day Treatment
Dementia Unit
Dermatology Clinic
Dialysis
Fee Basis Group Practice (Tazewell, Virginia; Danville, Virginia) (CBOCs)
Geriatric Evaluation Management Unit
Hemodialysis
Homeless Veterans Treatment and Assistance
Infectious Diseases
Intensive Care Unit
Interventional Radiology
Mental Health Clinic
Mental Health Intensive Case Management (MHICM)
MRI
Nephrology
Nuclear Medicine
OIF/OEF Team
Oncology
Ophthalmology
Outpatient Medical & Surgical Specialty Clinics
Post-Traumatic Stress Disorder Unit
Preservation Amputation Care & Treatment (PACT)
Preventive Care
Respite Care
Sleep Disorder Evaluation
Smoking Cessation Clinic
Spinal Cord Injury (SCI) (Outpatient Care)
Substance Abuse Residential Rehabilitation Treatment Program
Urology
Veterans Outreach Center
Women's Health Program

Washington

Portland VA Medical Center—Vancouver Campus

1601 East 4th Plain Boulevard
Vancouver, WA 98661
360-696-4061 or 800-949-1004

Spokane VA Medical Center

4815 N. Assembly Street
Spokane, WA 99205-6197
509-434-7000 or 800-325-7940

Type of Facility

Primary care, secondary care, and nursing home care; 46 hospital beds, 38 nursing home care beds

Special Programs

Health Care for Homeless Veterans
Hospice Care
Mental Health
Rural Mobile Clinic
Substance Abuse
Substance Abuse Residential Rehabilitation
Women Veterans Program
Vietnam Veterans Outreach Center

VA Puget Sound Health Care System
1660 S. Columbian Way
Seattle, WA 98108-1597
800-329-8387 or 206-762-1010

Type of Facility

Primary, tertiary (specialty) care, and nursing home; 230 acute care beds, 131 nursing home care unit beds, 60 domiciliary beds, 15 blind rehab beds, 30 residential rehab beds, 38 spinal cord beds

Special Programs

Alzheimer's Disease
Arthritis
Audiology and Speech Pathology
Blind Rehabilitation
Bone Marrow Transplantation
Cardiology
Comprehensive Cancer Care
Dementia Care
Dental Care
Deployment Health Clinic
Dermatology
Dialysis
Endocrinology
Ex-Prisoner of War Programs
Gastroenterology
General Internal Medicine
Geriatric Care
Hematology
Homeless Veteran Program
Infectious Diseases
Mental Health
Minority Veterans Outreach Programs
Multiple Sclerosis

Nephrology
Neurology
Nursing Home Care
Oncology
Ophthalmology & Optometry
Otolaryngology
Palliative Care
Parkinson's Disease
Physical & Occupational Therapy
Podiatry
Post Traumatic Stress Disorders
Primary Care
Prosthetics & Amputation Therapy Programs
Pulmonary Medicine
Radiation Oncology
Radiology
Readjustment Counseling
Recreation Therapy
Rehabilitation Medicine
Spinal Cord Injury Treatment
Substance Abuse Treatment
Surgery
Urology
Women's Health

VA Puget Sound HCS American Lake Division
9600 Veterans Drive
Tacoma, WA 98493
253-582-8440 or 800-329-8387

Jonathan M. Wainwright Memorial VA Medical Center
77 Wainwright Drive
Walla Walla, WA 99362
509-525-5200 or 888-687-8863

Type of Facility

Secondary care; 14 acute care beds, 30 nursing home care unit beds, 22 psychiatry and Substance Abuse Residential Rehabilitation Treatment Program beds

Special Programs

22-bed SARRTP/PRRTP

West Virginia

Beckley VA Medical Center
200 Veterans Avenue
Beckley, WV 25801
304-255-2121 or 877-902-5142

Type of Facility

General medicine and surgery; 26 medical beds, 2 surgical beds, 12 intermediate care rehabilitation beds, 50 extended care rehabilitation beds

Special Programs

Extended Care Rehabilitation Center
Homeless Veterans Outreach
ICU
Lithotripsy
Mental Health Clinic
Mobile MRI
Nuclear Medicine
Oncology Treatment Unit
Respiratory Care
Respite Care

Clarksburg—Louis A. Johnson VA Medical Center
One Medical Center Drive
Clarksburg, WV 26301
304-623-3461 or 800-733-0512

Type of Facility

General medicine, surgery, and psychiatry; 37 medicine beds, 7 surgery beds, 33 psychiatry beds, 27 nursing home beds

Special Programs

Acute Medicine
Acute Psychiatry
Ambulatory Surgery
Audiology
Behavioral Medicine (Including Substance Abuse, Telepsychiatry, PTSD, etc.)
Cardiology

Dental
Dermatology
Diabetes
ENT
Gastroenterology
General Internal Medicine
General Surgery
Gynecology
Hematology/Oncology
Infectious Diseases
Nephrology
Nursing Home Care
Nutrition
Occupational Therapy
Ophthalmology
Optometry
Pain
Physical Therapy
Podiatry
Primary Care
Prosthetics
PTSD Residential Rehabilitation Program (PRRP)
Pulmonology
Recreation Therapy
Rheumatology
Social Work
Speech Pathology
Substance Abuse Residential Rehabilitation Treatment Program (SARRTP)
Surgery
Urology
Vascular Surgery

Huntington VA Medical Center
1540 Spring Valley Drive
Huntington, WV 25704
304-429-6741 or 800-827-8244

Type of Facility

General medicine and surgery; 80 authorized beds

Special Programs

Acute Dialysis
Audiology & Speech Therapy
Cardiology, Cardiac Cath Lab and Electrophysiology
Clinical Pharmacy
Dental clinic and Oral/Maxillofacial surgery
Gastroenterology
Homeless Outreach
Infectious Diseases
Intermediate Medicine
Mental Health Clinic (Outpatient)
Neurology & EMG
Nuclear Medicine
Oncology/Hematology
Optometry

Outpatient Substance Abuse Treatment program
Pain Management
Podiatry
Primary Care
Prosthetics
PTSD Outpatient Clinic
Pulmonary
Rehabilitation Medicine, including Physical & Occupational Therapy
Research and Development
Spinal Cord Injury Primary Care and Support Team
Surgery, including ENT, Vascular, Thoracic, Urologic and Orthopedic
Telemedicine and Telemental Health
Visually Impaired Support Team (VIST)
Women's Health

Martinsburg VA Medical Center

510 Butler Avenue
Martinsburg, WV 25405
304-263-0811 or 800-817-3807

Type of Facility

General medical, surgical, long-term care, rehab and domiciliary; 69 hospital beds, 178 nursing home care unit beds, 312 domiciliary beds

Special Programs

Alcohol-Drug Rehabilitation Unit
Audiology and Speech Pathology
Homeless Domiciliary Program
Inpatient Hospice (Palliative Care)
Intensive Care Unit
Medical Center and Domiciliary-Based Substance Abuse Programs
Mental Hygiene Clinic
Nuclear Medicine
Post-Traumatic Stress Disorder-Residential Rehab (PTSD-PRRP) Program
Primary Care
Pulmonary Function Lab
Same-Day Surgery
Traumatic Brain Injury-Community Re-Entry

Wisconsin

William S. Middleton Memorial Veterans Hospital

2500 Overlook Terrace
Madison, WI 53705-2286
608-256-1901

Type of Facility

General medicine and surgery; 87 authorized beds

Special Programs

Addictive Disorders Community Housing Support Program
Addictive Disorders Treatment Program
Cardiac Catheterization Lab
Compensated Work Therapy/Vocational Rehabilitation
CT Scan
Digital Subtraction Angiography
Evoked Potential Lab
Epilepsy Center
GEU (Outpatient)
GRECC
Heart/Lung Organ Transplantation
Mental Health Intensive Case Management
MRI
Open Heart Surgery
Sleep/Wake Lab
Substance Abuse Residential Rehabilitation Treatment Program
Women's Stress Disorder Treatment Program

Tomah VA Medical Center

500 E. Veterans Street
Tomah, WI 54660
608-372-3971 or 800-872-8662

Type of Facility

Acute care, mental health, long-term care and rehabilitation; 271 authorized beds

Special Programs

Compensated Work Therapy/ Transitional Residency (CWT/TR)
PTSD—Residential Program (PRRTP)
Substance Abuse—Residential Program (PRRTP)

Clement J. Zablocki Veterans Affairs Medical Center
5000 W. National Avenue
Milwaukee, WI 53295-1000
414-384-2000 or 888-469-6614

Type of Facility

Primary, secondary, and tertiary care; 168 authorized beds, 113 geriatric beds, 356 domiciliary beds

Special Programs

Cardiac Surgery
Comprehensive Cancer Care
Geriatric Evaluation and Management Program
Interventional Radiology
Palliative Care Program
Pathology/Laboratory Medicine
Post-Traumatic Stress Disorder
Psychiatric Rehabilitation
Radiation Therapy
Spinal Cord Injury Unit
Substance Abuse Rehabilitation
Telemedicine Program

Wyoming

Cheyenne VA Medical Center
2360 E. Pershing Boulevard
Cheyenne, WY 82001
307-778-7550 or 888-483-9127

Type of Facility

General medicine and surgery; 21 hospital beds

Special Programs

- Audiology
- ENT
- Gastroenterology
- General Surgery
- Geriatrics
- Health Care for Homeless Veterans
- Home-Based Primary Care
- Hospice Care
- Infectious Diseases
- Intensive Care
- Intermediate Medicine
- Internal Medicine
- Long-Term Care
- Magnetic Resonance Imaging (MRI)
- MHICM
- Nuclear Medicine
- Ophthalmology
- Optometry
- Orthopedics
- Podiatry
- Post-Combat Trauma Program
- Psychiatry
- Respite Care
- Rheumatology
- Substance Abuse Treatment
- Transitional Care
- Urology

Sheridan VA Medical Center

1898 Fort Road
Sheridan, WY 82801
307-672-3473 or 866-822-6714

Type of Facility

Psychiatry, general medicine, and long-term care; 199 authorized beds

Special Programs

- Domiciliary Residential Rehabilitation Treatment Program for Homeless Veterans
- Inpatient and Outpatient Primary Care Services
- Inpatient, Outpatient, and Residential Mental Health Services
- Mental Health Intensive Case Management Program (MHICM)
- Post-Traumatic Stress Disorder
- Seriously Mentally Ill
- Sleep Laboratory
- Substance Abuse

APPENDIX C

Veteran Centers by State

This is a listing, by state, of all Vet Centers. See Chapter 5 for a description of the services provided by Vet Centers.

Alabama

Birmingham Vet Center
1500 5th Avenue South
Birmingham, AL 35233
205 731 0550

Mobile Vet Center
2577 Government Boulevard
Mobile, AL 36606
251-478-5906

Alaska

Anchorage Vet Center
4201 Tudor Centre Drive, Suite 115
Anchorage, AK 99508
907-563-6966

Kenai Vet Center Satellite
Building F, Suite 4, Red Diamond Center
43335 Kalifornsky Beach Road
Soldotna, AK 99669
907-260-7640

Fairbanks Vet Center
540 4th Avenue, Suite 100
Fairbanks, AK 99701
907-456-4238

Wasilla Vet Center
851 E. West Point Drive, Suite 111
Wasilla, AK 99654
907-376-4318

Arizona

Chinle Vet Center Outstation
P.O. Box 1934
Chinle, AZ 86503
928-674-3682

Hopi Vet Center Outstation 2
1 Main Street, Room 123
Keams Canyon, AZ 86034
928-738-5166

Phoenix Vet Center
77 E. Weldon, Suite 100
Phoenix, AZ 85012
602-640-2981

Prescott Vet Center
161 South Granite Street, Suite B
Prescott, AZ 86303
928-778-3469

Tuscon Vet Center
3055 N. First Avenue
Tucson, AZ 85719
520-882-0333

Arkansas

Little Rock Vet Center
201 W. Broadway Street, Suite A
North Little Rock, AR 72114
501-324-6395

California

Anaheim Vet Center
859 S. Harbor Boulevard
Anaheim, CA 92805
714-776-0161

Chico Vet Center
280 Cohasset
Chico, CA 95928
530-899-8549

Concord Vet Center
1899 Clayton Road, Suite 140
Concord, CA 94520
925-680-4526

Corona Vet Center
800 Magnolia Avenue, Suite 110
Corona, CA 92879-3123
951-734-0525

East Los Angeles Vet Center
5400 E. Olympic Boulevard, Suite 140
Commerce, CA 90022
323-728-9966

Fresno Vet Center
3636 North 1st Street, Suite 112
Fresno, CA 93726
559-487-5660

Los Angeles Veterans Resources Center
1045 W. Redondo Beach Boulevard, Suite 150
Gardena, CA 90247
310-767-1221

Northbay Vet Center
6225 State Farm Drive, Suite 101
Rohnert Park, CA 94928
707-586-3295

Oakland Vet Center
1504 Franklin Street, Suite 200
Oakland, CA 94612
510-763-3904

Pacific Western Vet Center Regional Office
420 Executive Court North, Suite G
Fairfield, CA 94534
707-646-2988

Peninsula Vet Center
2946 Broadway Street
Redwood City, CA 94062
650-299-0672

Redwoods Vet Center
2830 G Street, Suite A
Eureka, CA 95501
707-444-8271

Sacramento Vet Center
1111 Howe Avenue, Suite 390
Sacramento, CA 95825
916-566-7430

San Bernardino Vet Center
155 West Hospitality Lane, Suite 140
San Bernardino, CA 92408
909-890-0797

San Diego Vet Center
2900 Sixth Avenue
San Diego, CA 92103
619-294-2040

San Francisco Vet Center
505 Polk Street
San Francisco, CA 94102
415-441-5051

San Jose Vet Center
278 N. 2nd Street
San Jose, CA 95112
408-993-0729

Sepulveda Vet Center
9737 Haskell Avenue
Sepulveda, CA 91343
818-892-9227

San Marcos Vet Center
One Civic Center Drive, Suite 140
San Marcos, CA 92069
760-744-6914

Ventura Vet Center
790 E. Santa Clara Street, Suite 100
Ventura, CA 93001
805-585-1860

Santa Cruz County Vet Center
1350 41st Avenue, Suite 102
Capitola, CA 95010
831-464-4575

West Los Angeles Vet Center
5730 Uplander Way, Suite 100
Culver City, CA 90230
310-641-0326

Colorado

Boulder Vet Center
2336 Canyon Boulevard, Suite 103
Boulder, CO 80302
303-440-7306

Ft. Collins Vet Center Outstation
1100 Poudre River Drive (Lower Level)
Ft. Collins, CO 80524
970-221-5176

Colorado Springs Vet Center
416 E. Colorado Avenue
Colorado Springs, CO 80903
719-471-9992

Western Mountain Regional Office
789 Sherman Street, Suite 570
Denver, CO 80203
303-393-2897

Denver Vet Center
7465 E. First Avenue, Suite B
Denver, CO 80230
303-326-0645

Connecticut

Hartford Vet Center
30 Jordan Lane
Wethersfield, CT 06109
860-563-2320

New Haven Vet Center
141 Captain Thomas Boulevard
West Haven, CT 06516
203-932-9899

Norwich Vet Center
2 Cliff Street
Norwich, CT 06360
860-887-1755

Delaware

Wilmington Vet Center
VAMC, Building 3
1601 Kirkwood Highway
Wilmington, DE 19805
302-994-1660

Florida

Ft. Lauderdale Vet Center
713 N.E. 3rd Avenue
Ft. Lauderdale, FL 33304
954-356-7926

Jacksonville Vet Center
300 E. State Street
Jacksonville, FL 32202
904-232-3621

Ft. Myers Vet Center Outstation
Lee County Veterans Service Office
2072 Victoria Avenue
Ft. Myers, FL 33901
239-938-1100

Key Largo Vet Center Outstation
105662 Overseas Highway
Key Largo, FL 33037
305-451-0164

Miami Vet Center
8280 NW 27th Street, Suite 511
Miami, FL 33122
305-718-3712

Orlando Vet Center
5575 S. Semoran Boulevard, Suite 36
Orlando, FL 32822
407-857-2800

Palm Beach Vet Center
Spectrum Center
2311 10th Avenue, N., Suite 13
Lake Worth, FL 33461
561-585-0441

Pensacola Vet Center
4501 Twin Oaks Drive, Suite 104
Pensacola, FL 32506
850-456-5886

Sarasota Vet Center
4801 Swift Road, Suite A
Sarasota, FL 34231
941-927-8285

Southeast Vet Center
RCS, 10B/RC3A VA Medical Center, Building T203
Bay Pines, FL 33744
727-398-9343

St. Petersburg Vet Center
2880 1st Avenue North
St. Petersburg, FL 33713
727-893-3791

Tallahassee Vet Center
548 Bradford Road
Tallahassee, FL 32303
850-942-8810

Tampa Vet Center
8900 N. Armenia Avenue, Suite 312
Tampa, FL 33604
813-228-2621

Georgia

Atlanta Vet Center
1440 Dutch Valley Place, Suite 1100
Box 55
Atlanta, GA 30324
404-347-7264

Savannah Vet Center
308 A Commercial Drive
Savannah, GA 31406
912-652-4097

Guam

Guam Vet Center
222 Chalan Santo Papa Reflection Center, Suite 201
Hagatna, GU 96910
671-472-7160

Hawaii

Hilo Vet Center
120 Keawe Street, Suite 201
Hilo, HI 96720
808-969-3833

Honolulu Vet Center
1680 Kapiolani Boulevard, Suite F-3
Honolulu, HI 96814
808-973-8387

Kailua-Kona Vet Center
73-4976 Kamanu Street, Suite 207
Kailua-Kona, HI 96740
808-329-0574

Kauai Vet Center
3-3367 Kuhio Highway, Suite 101
Lihue, HI 96766
808-246-1163

Maui Vet Center
35 Lunalilo Street, Suite 101
Wailuku, HI 96793
808-242-8557

Idaho

Boise Vet Center
5440 Franklin Road, Suite 100
Boise, ID 83705
208-342-3612

Pocatello Vet Center
1800 Garrett Way
Pocatello, ID 83201
208-232-0316

Illinois

Chicago Heights Vet Center
1600 Halsted Street
Chicago Heights, IL 60411
708-754-0340

Chicago Veterans Resource Center
2038 W. 95th Street, Suite 200
Chicago, IL 60643-1116
773-881-9900

East St. Louis Vet Center
1265 N. 89th Street, Suite 5
East St. Louis, IL 62203
618-397-6602

Evanston Vet Center
565 Howard Street
Evanston, IL 60202
847-332-1019

Oak Park Vet Center
155 S. Oak Park Avenue
Oak Park, IL 60302
708-383-3225

Peoria Vet Center
3310 N. Prospect Road
Peoria, IL 61603
309-688-2170

Quad Cities Vet Center
1529 46th Avenue, Suite 6
Moline, IL 61265
309-762-6954

Rockford Vet Center Outstation
4960 E. State Street, Suite 3
Rockford, IL 61108
815-395-1276

Springfield Vet Center
1227 S. Ninth Street
Springfield, IL 62703
217-492-4955

Indiana

Evansville Vet Center
311 N. Weinbach Avenue
Evansville, IN 47711
812-473-5993

Ft. Wayne Vet Center
528 W. Berry Street
Fort Wayne, IN 46802
260-460-1456

Gary Area Vet Center
6505 Broadway Avenue
Merrillville, IN 46410
219-736-5633

Indianapolis Vet Center
3833 N. Meridian Street, Suite 120
Indianapolis, IN 46208
317-927-6440

Iowa

Cedar Rapids Vet Center Satellite
1642 42nd Street NE
Cedar Rapids, IA 52402
319-378-0016

Sioux City Vet Center
1551 Indian Hills Drive, Suite 204
Sioux City, IA 51104
712-255-3808

Des Moines Vet Center
2600 Martin Luther King Parkway
Des Moines, IA 50310
515-284-4929

Kansas

Wichita Vet Center
413 S. Pattie
Wichita, KS 67211
316-265-3260

Kentucky

Lexington Vet Center
301 E. Vine Street, Suite C
Lexington, KY 40507
859-253-0717

Louisville Vet Center
1347 S. Third Street
Louisville, KY 40208
502-634-1916

Louisiana

New Orleans Veterans Resource Center
2200 Veterans Boulevard, Suite 114
Kenner, LA 70062
504-464-4743

Shreveport Vet Center
2800 Youree Drive, Building 1, Suite 105
Shreveport, LA 71104
318-861-1776

Maine

Bangor Vet Center
352 Harlow Street, In-Town Plaza
Bangor, ME 04401
207-947-3391

Portland Vet Center
475 Stevens Avenue
Portland, ME 04103
207-780-3584

Caribou Vet Center
456 York Street, York Street Complex
Caribou, ME 04736
207-496-3900

Sanford Vet Center
628 Main Street
Springvale, ME 04083
207-490-1513

Lewiston Vet Center
29 Westminster Street, Parkway Complex
Lewiston, ME 04240
207-783-0068

Maryland

Aberdeen Vet Center Outstation 2
223 W. Bel Air Avenue
Aberdeen, MD 21001
410-272-6771

Baltimore Vet Center
1777 Reisterstown Road, Suite 199
Baltimore, MD 21208
410-764-9400

Cambridge Vet Center Outstation 1
830 Chesapeake Drive
Cambridge, MD 21613
410-228-6305

Mid Atlantic Vet Center
305 W. Chesapeake Avenue, Suite 510
Towson, MD 21204
410-828-6619

Elkton Vet Center
103 Chesapeake Boulevard, Suite A
Elkton, MD 21921
410-392-4485

Silver Spring Vet Center
1015 Spring Street, Suite 101
Silver Spring, MD 20910
301-589-1073

Massachusetts

Boston Vet Center
665 Beacon Street, Suite 100
Boston, MA 02215
617-424-0665

New Bedford Vet Center
468 North Street
New Bedford, MA 02740
508-999-6920

Brockton Vet Center
1041 Pearl Street, Suite L
Brockton, MA 02301
508-580-2730

Springfield Vet Center
1985 Main Street, Northgate Plaza
Springfield, MA 01103
413-737-5167

Lowell Vet Center
73 E. Merrimack Street
Lowell, MA 01852-1206
978-453-1151

Worcester Vet Center
691 Grafton Street
Worcester, MA 01604
508-753-7902

Michigan

Dearborn Vet Center
2881 Monroe Street, Suite 100
Dearborn, MI 48124-3475
313-277-1428

Detroit Vet Center
4161 Cass Avenue
Detroit, MI 48201
313-831-6509

Grand Rapids Vet Center
1940 Eastern Avenue, S.E.
Grand Rapids, MI 49507
616-243-0385

Michigan Upper Peninsula
2831 N. Lincoln Road
Escanaba, MI 49829
906-789-9732

Minnesota

Duluth Vet Center
405 E. Superior Street
Duluth, MN 55802
218-722-8654

St. Paul Veterans Resource Center
2480 University Avenue
St. Paul, MN 55114
651-644-4022

Mississippi

Biloxi Vet Center
288 Veterans Avenue
Biloxi, MS 39531
228-388-9938

Jackson Vet Center
1755 Lelia Drive, Suite 104
Jackson, MS 39216
601-965-5727

Missouri

Central Vet Center
1 Jefferson Barracks Drive
Building 50, Room 2N52
St. Louis, MO 63125
314-894-5717

St. Louis Vet Center
2901 Olive
St. Louis, MO 63103
314-531-5355

Kansas City Vet Center
301 E. Armour Boulevard, Suite 305
Kansas City, MO 64111
816-753-1866

Montana

Billings Vet Center
1234 Avenue C
Billings, MT 59102
406-657-6071

Missoula Vet Center
500 N. Higgins Avenue
Missoula, MT 59802
406-721-4918

Nebraska

Lincoln Vet Center
920 L Street
Lincoln, NE 68508-2228
402-476-9736

Omaha Vet Center
2428 Cuming Street
Omaha, NE 68131-1600
402-346-6735

Nevada

Las Vegas Vet Center
1919 S. Jones Boulevard, Suite A
Las Vegas, NV 89146
702-251-7873

Reno Vet Center
1155 W. 4th Street, Suite 101
Reno, NV 89503
775-323-1294

New Hampshire

Manchester Vet Center
103 Liberty Street
Manchester, NH 03104
603-668-7060

Northeast Vet Center
15 Dartmouth Drive, Suite 204
Auburn, NH 03032
603-623-4204

New Jersey

Jersey City Vet Center
115 Christopher Columbus Drive,
Suite 200
Jersey City, NJ 07302
201-748-4467

Newark Vet Center
2 Broad Street, Suite 703
Bloomfield, NJ 07003
973-748-0980

Trenton Vet Center
934 Parkway Avenue, 2nd Floor
Ewing, NJ 08618
609-882-5744

Ventnor Vet Center
6601 Ventnor Avenue, Suite 105
Ventnor, NJ 08406
609-487-8387

New Mexico

Albuquerque Vet Center
1600 Mountain Road NW
Albuquerque, NM 87104
505-346-6562

Santa Fe Vet Center
2209 Brothers Road, Suite 110
Santa Fe, NM 87505
505-988-6562

Farmington Vet Center Satellite
4251 E. Main, Suite B
Farmington, NM 87402
505-327-9684

New York

Albany Vet Center
17 Computer Drive West
Albany, NY 12205
518-626-5130

Brooklyn Veterans Resource Center
25 Chapel Street, Suite 604
Brooklyn, NY 11201
718-624-2765

Babylon Vet Center
116 West Main Street
Babylon, NY 11702
631-661-3930

Buffalo Vet Center
564 Franklin Street, 2nd Floor
Buffalo, NY 14202
716-882-0505

Bronx Vet Center
130 W. Kingsbridge Road, Suite 7A-13
Bronx, NY 10468
718-367-3500

Harlem Vet Center
55 W. 125th Street, 11th Floor
New York, NY 10027
212-426-2200

Manhattan Vet Center
32 Broadway, Suite 200
New York, NY 10004
212-742-9591

Queens Vet Center
75-10B 91 Avenue
Woodhaven, NY 11421
718-296-2871

Rochester Vet Center
1867 Mount Hope Avenue
Rochester, NY 14620
585-232-5040

Staten Island Vet Center
150 Richmond Terrace
Staten Island, NY 10301
718-816-4499

Syracuse Vet Center
716 E. Washington Street, Suite 101
Syracuse, NY 13210
315-478-7127

White Plains Vet Center
300 Hamilton Avenue, 1st floor
White Plains, NY 10601
914-682-6250

North Carolina

Charlotte Vet Center
223 S. Brevard Street, Suite 103
Charlotte, NC 28202
704-333-6107

Fayetteville Vet Center
4140 Ramsey Street, Suite 110
Fayetteville, NC 28311
910-488-6252

Greensboro Vet Center
2009 S. Elm-Eugene Street
Greensboro, NC 27406
336-333-5366

Greenville Vet Center
150 Arlington Boulevard, Suite B
Greenville, NC 27858
252-355-7920

Raleigh Vet Center
1649 Old Louisburg Road
Raleigh, NC 27604
919-856-4616

North Dakota

Bismarck Vet Center Outstation
1684 Capital Way
Bismarck, ND 58501
701-224-9751

Minot Vet Center
1400 20th Avenue SW
Minot, ND 58701
701-852-0177

Fargo Vet Center
3310 Fiechtner Drive, Suite 100
Fargo, ND 58103-8730
701-237-0942

Ohio

Cincinnati Vet Center
801B W. 8th Street, Suite 126
Cincinnati, OH 45203
513-763-3500

Dayton Vet Center
6th Floor, East Medical Plaza
627 Edwin C. Moses Boulevard
Dayton, OH 45408
937-461-9150

Cleveland Heights Vet Center, 205
2022 Lee Road
Cleveland, OH 44118
216-932-8471

McCafferty Vet Center Outstation
4242 Lorain Avenue, Suite 201
Cleveland, OH 44113
216-939-0784

Columbus Vet Center
30 Spruce Street
Columbus, OH 43215
614-257-5550

Parma Vet Center
5700 Pearl Road, Suite 102
Parma, OH 44129
440-845-5023

Oklahoma

Oklahoma City Vet Center
1024 NW 47th Street, Suite B
Oklahoma City, OK 73118
405-270-5184

Tulsa Vet Center
1408 S. Harvard Avenue
Tulsa, OK 74112
918-748-5105

Oregon

Eugene Vet Center
1255 Pearl Street, Suite 200
Eugene, OR 97402
541-465-6918

Portland Vet Center
8383 N.E. Sandy Boulevard, Suite 110
Portland, OR 97220
503-273-5370

Grants Pass Vet Center
211 S. E. 10th Street
Grants Pass, OR 97526
541-479-6912

Salem Vet Center
617 Chemeketa Street, NE, Suite 100
Salem, OR 97301
503-362-9911

Pennsylvania

Erie Vet Center
Renaissance Centre
1001 State Street, Suite 102
Erie, PA 16501
814-453-7955

McKeesport Veterans Resource Center
2001 Lincoln Way
McKeesport, PA 15131
412-678-7704

Harrisburg Vet Center
1500 N. Second Street, Suite 2
Harrisburg, PA 17102
717-782-3954

Philadelphia Vet Center
801 Arch Street, Suite 102
Philadelphia, PA
215-627-0238

Pittsburgh Vet Center
2500 Baldwick Road
Pittsburgh, PA 15205
412-920-1765

Scranton Vet Center
1002 Pittston Avenue
Scranton, PA 18505
570-344-2676

Williamsport Vet Center
805 Penn Street
Williamsport, PA 17701
570-327-5281

Puerto Rico

Arecibo Vet Center
50 Gonzalo Marin Street
Arecibo, PR 00612-4702
787-879-4510

Ponce Vet Center
35 Mayor Street, Suite 1
Ponce, PR 00730-3726
787-841-3260

San Juan Vet Center
Cond. Medical Center Plaza
Suite LC 8, 9 & 11, Urb. La Riviera
Rio Piedras, PR 00921
787-749-4409

Rhode Island

Providence Vet Center
2038 Warwick Avenue
Warwick, RI 02889
401-739-0167

South Carolina

Charleston Vet Center
5603-A Rivers Avenue
N. Charleston, SC 29406
843-747-8387

Columbia Vet Center
1513 Pickens Street
Columbia, SC 29201
803-765-9944

Greenville Vet Center
14 Lavinia Avenue
Greenville, SC 29601
864-271-2711

South Dakota

Pine Ridge Vet Center Outstation
P.O. Box 910
105 E. Highway 18
Martin, SD 57747
605-685-1300

Rapid City Vet Center
621 6th Street, Suite 101
Rapid City, SD 57701
605-348-0077

Sioux Falls Vet Center
601 S. Cliff Avenue, Suite C
Sioux Falls, SD 57104
605-330-4552

Tennessee

Chattanooga Vet Center
951 Eastgate Loop Road, Building 5700, Suite 300
Chattanooga, TN 37411
423-855-6570

Johnson City Vet Center
1615A Market Street
Johnson City, TN 37604
423-928-8387

Knoxville Vet Center
2817 E. Magnolia Avenue
Knoxville, TN 37914
865-545-4680

Memphis Vet Center
1835 Union, Suite 100
Memphis, TN 38104
901-544-0173

Nashville Vet Center
1420 Donelson Pike, Suite A-5
Nashville, TN 37217
615-366-1220

Texas

Amarillo Vet Center
3414 Olsen Boulevard, Suite E
Amarillo, TX 79109
806-354-9779

Austin Vet Center
1110 West William Cannon Drive, Suite 301
Austin, TX 78745
512-416-1314

Corpus Christi Vet Center
4646 Corona, Suite 250
Corpus Christi, TX 78411
361-854-9961

Dallas Vet Center
10501 N. Central, Suite 213
Dallas, TX 75231
214-361-5896

E1 Paso Vet Center
1155 Westmoreland, Suite 121
E1 Paso, TX 79925
915-772-0013

Ft. Worth Vet Center
1305 W. Magnolia Street, Suite B
Ft. Worth, TX 76104
817-921-9095

Houston Vet Center
701 N. Post Oak Road, Suite 102
Houston, TX 77024
713-682-2288

Houston Vet Center
503 Westheimer
Houston, TX 77006
713-523-0884

Laredo Vet Center
6020 McPherson Road, Suite 1A
Laredo, TX 78041
956-723-4680

Lubbock Vet Center
3208 34th Street
Lubbock, TX 79410
806-792-9782

McAllen Vet Center
801 Nolana Loop, Suite 140
McAllen, TX 78504
956-631-2147

Midland Vet Center
3404 W. Illinois, Suite 1
Midland, TX 79703
432-697-8222

San Antonio Vet Center
231 W. Cypress Street, Suite 100
San Antonio, TX 78212
210-472-4025

South Central Vet Center
4500 S. Lancaster Road, Building 69
Dallas, TX 75216
214-857-1254

Utah

Provo Vet Center Satellite
1807 N. 1120 West
Provo, UT 84604
801-377-1117

Salt Lake Vet Center
1354 E. 3300 South
Salt Lake, UT 84106
801-584-1294

Vermont

South Burlington Vet Center
359 Dorset Street
South Burlington, VT 05403
802-862-1806

White River Junction Vet Center
Gilman Office, Building 2
222 Holiday Inn Drive
White River Junction, VT 05001
802-295-2908

Virgin Islands

St. Croix Vet Center Satellite
The Village Mall, RR 2 Box
10553 Kingshill
St. Croix, VI 00850
340-778-5553

St. Thomas Vet Center Satellite
Buccaneer Mall, Suite 8
St. Thomas, VI 00802
340-774-6674

Virginia

Alexandria Vet Center
8796 Sacramento Drive, Suites D & E
Alexandria, VA 22309
703-360-8633

Norfolk Vet Center
2200 Colonial Avenue, Suite 3
Norfolk, VA 23517
757-623-7584

Richmond Vet Center
4902 Fitzhugh Avenue
Richmond, VA 23230
804-353-8958

Roanoke Vet Center
350 Albemarle Avenue, SW
Roanoke, VA 24016
540-342-9726

Washington

Bellingham Vet Center
3800 Bryon Avenue, Suite 124
Bellingham, WA 98229
360-733-9226

Tacoma Vet Center
4916 Center Street, Suite E
Tacoma, WA 98409
253-565-7038

Seattle Vet Center
2030 9th Avenue, Suite 210
Seattle, WA 98121
206-553-2706

Yakima Valley Vet Center
1111 N. 1st Street, Suite 1
Yakima, WA 98901
509-457-2736

Spokane Vet Center
100 N. Mullan Road, Suite 102
Spokane, WA 99206-6848
509-444-8387

Washington, DC

Washington Vet Center
1250 Taylor Street, NW
Washington, DC 20011
202-726-5212

West Virginia

Beckley Vet Center
101 Ellison Avenue
Beckley, WV 25801
304-252-8220

Charleston Vet Center
521 Central Avenue
Charleston, WV 25302
304-343-3825

Huntington Vet Center
3135 16th Street Road, Suite 11
Huntington, WV 25701
304-523-8387

Morgantown Vet Center
1083 Greenbag Road
Morgantown, WV 26508
304-291-4303

Logan Vet Center Outstation
21 Veterans Avenue
Henlawson, WV 25624
304-752-4453

Princeton Vet Center
905 Mercer Street
Princeton, WV 24740
304-425-5653

Martinsburg Vet Center
900 Winchester Avenue
Martinsburg, WV 25401
304-263-6776

Wheeling Vet Center
1206 Chapline Street
Wheeling, WV 26003
304-232-0587

Wisconsin

Madison Vet Center
147 S. Butler Street
Madison, WI 53703
608-264-5342

Milwaukee Vet Center
5401 N. 76th Street
Milwaukee, WI 53218
414-536-1301

Wyoming

Casper Vet Center
1030 N. Poplar, Suite B
Casper, WY 82601
307-261-5355

Cheyenne Vet Center
3219 E. Pershing Boulevard
Cheyenne, WY 82001
307-778-7370

APPENDIX D

Women's Veterans Organizations and Services

Below are services and benefits, on the Federal and state level, created for women veterans. Those are in addition to the services and benefits available to all veterans. There is a special department within the VA for women's issues, as well as eight Women Veterans Comprehensive Health Centers.

Veterans Affairs

Women's Veterans Health Strategic Healthcare Group (13E)
810 Vermont Avenue, N. W.
Washington, DC 20420

VHA Office of Women Veterans Health: 202-273-8577
Dept. of Veterans Affairs Office of the Center for Women Veterans: 202-273-6193

Veterans can apply for VA health care enrollment by completing VA Form 10-10EZ, which may be obtained by contacting any VA health care facility or by calling toll free at 877-222-8387. You may access the form on the internet at www.va.gov and click on online applications.

Services available for women veterans include counseling for sexual trauma, Pap smears, mammography and general reproductive health care (including birth control and treatment of menopause), maternity and infertility benefits, evaluation and treatment for osteoporosis, substance abuse treatment, evaluation and treatment for Post-Traumatic Stress Disorder (PTSD). Also available are programs for homeless women veterans, victims of domestic violence, and vocational rehabilitation. Every VA medical center has a women veterans program manager who is available to assist women veterans. Women veterans interested in receiving care at the VA are encouraged to contact the nearest VA medical center and ask for the Women Veterans program manager.

Comprehensive Health Centers

There are eight Women Veterans Comprehensive Health Centers in the VA system. These centers develop new and enhanced programs focusing on the unique health care needs of women veterans.

VA Medical Center
Boston, MA
617-232-9500, Ext. 4276

VA Medical Center
Tampa, FL
813-972-2000, Ext. 3678

VA Medical Center
Philadelphia, PA
215-823-4496

VA Medical Center
Durham, NC
919-286-0411, Ext. 5073

Va Medical Center
Chicago, IL
312-569-6168

VA Medical Center
San Francisco, CA
415-221-4810, Ext. 2174

VA Medical Center
Minneapolis, MN
612-725-2030

VA Medical Center
West Los Angeles, CA
310-478-3711

Additional Benefits and Services for Women Veterans

As a veteran, you may be entitled to one or more of the following benefits. Contact your local VA regional office, medical center, or vet center for more information.

- Disability compensation for service-related disabilities
- Disability pension for non-service-related disabilities
- Education assistance programs

- Work-study allowance
- Vocational rehabilitation and counseling
- Insurance
- Home loan benefits
- Medical inpatient and outpatient care
- Substance abuse treatment and counseling
- Sexual trauma and assault counseling
- Nursing home care

National Cemetery Administration

Women veterans discharged from the U.S. Armed Forces under conditions other than dishonorable are eligible for burial in a VA national cemetery. Call 1-800-827-1000 to speak with a Veterans Benefits counselor.

Help for Homeless Veterans

The Department of Veterans Affairs has awarded grants to eight community-based homeless veteran service providers to support programs designed specifically for women veterans, including those with dependent children. The grants are funded under the VA Homeless Providers Grant and Per Diem Program. The programs funded under this "special needs" GPD program are:

California: Long Beach, United Veterans Initiative, 562-388-7810; Los Angeles, Salvation Army, 310-478-3711; San Diego, Vietnam Veterans of San Diego, 619-497-6123; Santa Rosa, Vietnam Veterans of California, 707-578-8387.

Florida: Tampa, Agency for Community Treatment Services, 813-246-4899

Massachusetts: Leeds, United Veterans of America, 413-584-4040

Ohio: Cleveland, West Side Catholic Center, 216-636-4741

Pennsylvania: Philadelphia Veterans Multi-Service and Education Center, 215-923-2600

Women's Army Corps Veterans Association

The association focuses on VA hospital volunteer work and community service in the local and national community. Volunteers serve in 50 VA hospitals and nursing homes where veterans are patients. website:www.armywomen.org

ELIGIBILITY: Current, former or retired women members of the Army who have served honorably on active duty in the Army of the United States (AUS), Regular Army (RA), Army National Guard (ANG) and the United States Army Reserve (USAR) the Army Nurse Corps (ANC), the Women's Army Auxiliary Corps (WAAC), or the Women's Army Corps (WAC) in commissioned, warrant, non-commissioned, or enlisted status for 90 days or more, after May, 14 1942.

VERIFICATION OF ELIGIBILITY.

Honorable Discharge/Certificate of Service
DD Form 214 (Report of Separation)
Official Retirement Order

- Active Duty—provide a statement from custodian of personnel records, that service is being performed under honorable conditions (facsimile of army identification card)
- United States Army Reserve and United States National Guard—provide a statement from custodian of personnel records, that service is being performed under honorable conditions (facsimile of army identification card).

Women in Military Service for America Memorial Foundation

Department 560
Washington, DC 20042-0560
703-533-1155
hq@womensmemorial.org
www.womensmemorial.org

The Women's Memorial at Arlington National Cemetery is a unique, living memorial honoring all military women—past, present, and future—and is the only major national memorial honoring women who have served in our nation's defense during all eras and in all services.

Eligibility as a "Member" includes living or deceased women veterans; Active Duty, Reserve, Guard, and US Public Health Service uniformed women; and women in the Coast Guard Auxiliary and the Civil Air Patrol.

Eligibility as a "We Also Served Member" member includes women who served overseas during conflicts, in direct support of the armed forces, in organizations such as the Red Cross, USO, and Special Services. Those in the US Public Health Service Cadet Nurse Corps are included in a special Honor Roll of Cadet Nurses.

Idaho

Office of Veterans Advocacy

805 W. Franklin Street, Room 201
Boise, ID 83702
208-334-1245
info@veterans.idaho.gov
www.veterans.idaho.gov

Professional benefits counseling and advocacy is offered through a network of state veteran service officers. These officers can advise and assist you in applying for a variety of Department of Veterans Affairs (VA) benefits and services.

Massachusetts

Women Veterans' Network

Department of Veterans' Services
600 Washington Street, Suite 1100
Boston, MA 02111
617-210-5781
dvswomen@vet.state.ma.us
www.mass.gov/veterans

Women's Veterans' Homelessness Program

VA Boston Healthcare System
Women's Health Sciences Division (116B-3)
150 S. Huntington Avenue
Boston, MA 02130
857-364-4027 (Lauren Dever, LICSW)
or 857-364-4940 (Meredith Powers-Lupa, LICSW)

This program provides case management and health services to homeless women and their children in Boston and the surrounding areas. It also offers services for those at-risk for homelessness.

TRUST House
857-364-4149 (Tracy Sweeney, LICSW)

TRUST (Transitional Residence Utilizing Support and Treatment) House is a therapeutic residential program that offers secure and aforable housing along with a communal atmosphere in a treatment-focused setting in Jamaica Plain. The treatment program involves individual and group therapy, case management, paid work experiences through Veterans Industries Vocational Program, house meetings, and recreational community outings. The TRUST House specializes in the treatment of women with PTSD as well as depression, substance abuse, anxiety, dissociation, and homelessness.

Women's Integrated Treatment and Recovery Program
VA Boston Healthcare System
Brockton Campus
940 Belmont Street
Brockton, MA 02301
774-826-1833

This treatment program is designed to help women veterans who have both Post-Traumatic Strees Disorder (PTSD) and a Substance Use Disorder (SUD). Designed to fill the gap between short-term inpatient and long-term outpatient and residential programs, the program offers approximately eight weeks of specialized, intensive treatment based on individual needs and strengths.

United Veterans of America, Inc.
Northampton VA Medical Center
421 North Main Street
Leeds, MA 01053-9764
413-584-4040, Ext. 2288

UVA has a house on the Northampton VA campus that is especially for women veterans. The UVA program provides resident veterans with treatment and recovery from drug and alcohol addictions along with medical services. Contact UVA for information on admission criteria and the application process.

Massachuestts Veterans, Inc.
Cambridge/Canterbury Street
Worcester, MA 01603
508-791-5348, Ext. 124

MVI has a women's housing program that offers an alcohol and drug-free environment coupled with case management services.

Women's Dorms at Chelsea Soldiers' Home
91 Crest Avenue
Chelsea, MA 02150
817-884-5660

The Chelsea Soldiers' Home has a private and secure dormitory wing specifically for female veterans who can live in an independent setting and who require minimal assistance with the activities of daily living.

Homeless Women Veterans' Outreach and Case Management Program
VA Boston Healthcare System
150 S. Huntington Avenue (116B-3)
Boston, MA 02130
857-364-4027

Wisconsin Women Veterans

Wisconsin Department of Veterans Affairs
301 W. Mifflin Street
Madison, WI 53703
800-947-8387
http://dva.state.wi.us/womenvets.asp

To address the needs of women veterans in Wisconsin, the Wisconsin Department of Veterans Affairs (WDVA) remains committed to providing advocacy for women veterans; encouraging and supporting recognition of women veterans' contributions to Wisconsin and the nation; providing outreach for women veterans' programs and issues, and uniting Wisconsin women veterans so their voices may be heard.

Women Veterans' Clinics

The following VA medical centers serving Wisconsin veterans have women veterans' clinics. Ask for the Women's Health Clinic when you call.

- Madison (Middleton VA Hospital) 608-256-1901
- Milwaukee (Zablocki VA Medical Center) 414-384-2000
- Tomah (Great Lakes Health Care System) 608-372-3971
- Minneapolis, MN (Minneapolis VA Medical Center) 612-725-2000
- Iron Mt. MI (Iron Mountain VA Medical Center) 906-774-3300

APPENDIX E

Nursing Homes for Veterans

This is a complete list, by state, of nursing homes for veterans.

Alabama

Bill Nichols State Veterans Home
1784 Elkahatchee Road
Alexander City, AL 35010
256-329-0868

William F. Green State Veterans Home
P.O. Box 1461
300 Faulkner Drive
Bay Minette, AL 36507

Floyd E "Tut" Fann State Veterans Home
2701 Meridian Street
Huntsville, AL 35811
256-851-2807

Alaska

Alaska State Veterans and Pioneers Home
250 E. Fireweed
Palmer, AK 99645-6699
907-745-4241

Anchorage Pioneer Home
923 W. 11th Avenue
Anchorage, AK 99501
907-276-3414

Arizona

Arizona State Veterans Home
4141 N. Third Street
Phoenix, AZ 85012
602-248-71550

Arkansas

Arkansas Veterans Home
4701 West 20th Street
Little Rock, AR 72204
501-296-1885

California

Veterans Home of California—Barstow
100 E. Veterans Parkway
Barstow, CA 92311-7003
760-252-6200

Veterans Home of California—Chula Vista
700 E. Naples Court
Chula Vista, CA 91911
619-482-6010

Veterans Home of California—Yountville
100 California Drive
Yountville, CA 94599
707-944-4500

Colorado

Colorado State Veterans Center
P.O. Box 97
Homelake, CO 81135
719-852-5118

Colorado State Veterans Center
P.O. Box 1420
Rifle, CO 81650
970-625-0842

Colorado State Veterans Nursing Home
903 Moore Drive
Florence, CO 81226
719-784-6331

Colorado State Veterans Nursing Home—Fitzsimmons
1919 Quentin Street
Aurora, CO 80010

Colorado State Veterans Nursing Home
23500 U.S. Highway 160
Walsenburg, CO 81089
719-738-5133

Connecticut

Connecticut Department of Veterans Affairs
287 West Street
Rocky Hill, CT 06067
860-721-5818

Delaware

Delaware Veterans Home
100 Delaware Veterans Boulevard
Milford, DE 19963
302-424-6000

Florida

Alexander "Sandy" Nininger State Veterans' Nursing Home
8401 W. Cypress Drive
Pembroke Pines, FL 33025
954-985-4824

Baldomero Lopez Veterans Nursing Home
6919 Parkway Boulevard
Land-o-Lakes, FL 34639
813-558-5000

Clifford Chester Sims State Veterans' Nursing Home
4419 Tram Road
Springfield, FL 32404
850-747-5401

Emory Bennett Memorial Veterans' Home
1920 Mason Avenue
Daytona Beach, FL 32117
386-274-3460

Douglas Jacobson State Veterans' Nursing Home
21281 Grayton Terrace
Port Charlotte, FL 33954
941-613-0919

Robert H. Jenkins, Jr. Veterans' Domiciliary Home of Florida
751 S.E. Sycamore Terrace
Lake City, FL 32025
386-758-0600

Georgia

Georgia War Veterans Home
2249 Vinson Highway
Milledgeville, GA 31061
478-445-4516

Hawaii

Yu Kio Okutsu Veterans Home
1180 Waianuenue Avenue
Hilo, HI 96720
808-961-1500

Idaho

Idaho State Veterans Home—Boise
320 Collins Road
Boise, ID 83702
208-334-5000

Idaho State Veterans Home—Lewiston
821-21st Avenue
Lewiston, ID 83501
208-799-3422

Idaho State Veterans Home—Pocatello
1957 Alvin Ricken Drive
Pocatello, ID 83201
208-236-6340

Illinois

Illinois Veterans' Home
1015 O'Conor Avenue
LaSalle, IL 61301
815-223-0303

Illinois Veterans' Home
792 N. Main
Anna, IL 62906-1627
618-833-6302

Illinois Veterans Home
One Veterans Drive
Manteno, IL 60950
815-468-6581

Illinois Veterans Home at Quincy
1707 North 12th Street
Quincy, IL 62301
217-222-8641

Iowa

Iowa Veterans Home
1301 Summit Street
Marshalltown, IA 50158-5485
641-752-1501

Kansas

Kansas Soldiers' Home
714 Sheridan
Unit 128
Fort Dodge, KS 67843
620-227-2121

Kansas Veterans' Home
1220 World War II Memorial Drive
Winfield, KS 67156
620-221-9479

Kentucky

Eastern Kentucky Veterans Center
200 Veterans Drive
Hazard, KY 41701
606-435-6196

Western Kentucky Veterans Center
926 Veterans Drive
Hanson, KY 42413
270-322-9087

Thomson Hood Veterans Center
100 Veterans Drive
Wilmore, KY 40390
859-858-2814

Louisiana

Louisiana War Veterans' Home
4739 Highway 10
Jackson, LA 70748
225-634-5265

S. E. Louisiana War Veterans' Home
P.O. Box 511
Reserve, LA 70084
985-651-2762

N.E. Louisiana War Veterans' Home
6700 Highway 165 North
Monroe, LA 71203
318-362-4206

South West Louisiana War Veterans' Home
P.O. Box 80
Jennings, LA 70546
337-824-2829

N. W. Louisiana War Veterans' Home
Box 8570
Bossier City, LA 71113
318-741-2763

Maine

Maine Veterans Home
310 Cony Road
Augusta, ME 04330
207-622-2454

Maine Veterans Home
290 U.S. Route 1
Scarborough, ME 04074
207-883-7184

Maine Veterans' Home—Bangor
44 Hogan Road
Bangor, ME 04401
207-942-2333

Maine Veterans' Home
477 High Street
South Paris, ME 04281
207-743-6300

Maine Veterans Home
163 Van Buren Road, Suite 2
Caribou, ME 04736
207-498-6074

Maine Veterans' Home
1 Veterans Way
RR 1, Box 11
Machias, ME 04654
207-255-0162

Maryland

Maryland Veterans Home
29449 Charlotte Hall Road
Charlotte Hall, MD 20622
301-884-8171

Massachusetts

Soldiers' Home in Holyoke
110 Cherry Street
Holyoke, MA 01040
413-532-9475

Soldiers' Home in Massachusetts
91 Crest Avenue
Chelsea, MA 02150
617-884-5660

Michigan

D.J. Jacobetti Home For Veterans
425 Fisher Street
Marquette, MI 49855
906-226-3576

Grand Rapids Home for Veterans
3000 Monroe, N.W.
Grand Rapids, MI 49505
616-364-5400

Minnesota

Minnesota Veterans Home
1821 North Park Street
Fergus Falls, MN 56537
218-736-0400

Minnesota Veterans Home
5101 Minnehaha Avenue South
Minneapolis, MN 55417-1699
612-721-0600

Minnesota Veterans Home
1200 East 18th Street
Hastings, MN 55033-3680
651-438-8504

Minnesota Veterans Home
45 Banks Boulevard
Silver Bay, MN 55614
218-226-6300

Minnesota Veterans Home
1300 N. Kniss
P.O. Box 539
Luverne, MN 56156
507-283-1100

Mississippi

Mississippi Veterans Home
3466 Highway 80 East
P.O. Box 5949
Pearl, MS 39288-5949
601-576-4850

Mississippi Veterans Home
3261 Highway 49
Collins, MS 39428
601-765-0403

Mississippi Veterans Home
120 Veterans Boulevard
Oxford, MS 38655
662-236-7641

Missouri

Missouri Veterans Home
2400 Veterans Memorial Drive
Cape Girardeau, MO 63701
573-290-5870

Missouri Veterans Home
I Veterans Drive
Mexico, MO 65265-1890
573-581-1088

Missouri Veterans Home
1600 S. Hickory Street
Mt. Vernon, MO 65712
417-466-7103

Missouri Veterans Home
620 N. Jefferson
St. James, MO 65559
573-265-3271

Missouri Veterans Home
10600 Lewis 7 Clark Boulevard
St. Louis, MO 63136
314-340-6389

Missouri Veterans Home
1300 Veterans Road
Warrensburg, MO 64093
660-543-5064

Missouri Veterans Home
1111 Euclid
Cameron, MO 64429
816-632-6010

Montana

Eastern Montana Veterans Home
2000 Montana Avenue
Glendive, MT 59330
406-377-8855

Montana Veterans Home
P.O. Box 250
Columbia Falls, MT 59912
406-892-3256

Nebraska

Grand Island Veterans Home
2300 W. Capital Avenue
Grand Island, NE 68803-2097
308-385-6252

Thomas Fitzgerald Veterans Home
15345 W. Maple Road
Omaha, NE 68116-5175
402-595-2180

Norfolk Veterans Home
600 E. Benjamin Avenue
Norfolk, NE 68701-0836
402-370-3177

Western Nebraska Veterans Home
1102 W. 42nd Street
Scottsbluff, NE 69361
308-632-0300

Nevada

Nevada State Veterans Home
100 Veterans Memorial Drive
Boulder City, NV 89005
702-332-6864

New Hampshire

New Hampshire Veterans Home
139 Winter Street
Tilton, NH 03276
603-527-4400

New Jersey

New Jersey Memorial Home
524 N. W. Boulevard
Vineland, NJ 08360
856-405-4200

New Jersey Veterans Memorial Home
P.O. Box 3013
Edison, NJ 08818-3013
732-452-4102

New Jersey Veterans Memorial Home
Box 608
One Veterans Drive
Paramus, NJ 07653-0608
201-967-7676

New Mexico

Fort Bayard Medical Center
P.O. Box 36219
Fort Bayard, NM 88036
505-537-3302

New Mexico Veterans' Home
P.O. Box 927
Truth or Consequences, NM 87901
505-894-4200

New York

Long Island State Veterans Home
100 Patriots Road
Stony Brook, NY 11790-3300
637-444-VETS

New York State Veterans Home—Oxford
4211 State Highway 220
Oxford, NY 13830-4305
607-843-3100

New York State Veterans Home—Batavia
220 Richmond Avenue
Batavia, NY 14020
716-345-2000

New York State Veterans Home—St. Albans
178-50 Linden Blvd.
Jamaica, NY 11434-1467
718-481-6268

New York State Veterans Home—Montrose
198 Albany Post Road
Montrose, NY 10548
914-788-6000

North Carolina

State Veterans Nursing Home
214 Cochran Avenue
Fayetteville, NC 28301
910-630-4257

North Dakota

North Dakota Veterans Home
1400 Rose Street
Lisbon, ND 58054
701-683-6501

Ohio

Ohio Veterans Home
3416 Columbus Avenue
Sandusky, OH 44870-5598
419-625-2454

Ohio Veterans Home—Georgetown
2003 Veterans Boulevard
Georgetown, OH 45121
937-378-2900

Oklahoma

Lawton / Ft. Sill Veterans Center
501 S.E. Flowermound Road
Lawton, OK 73501
580-351-6511

Oklahoma Veterans Center
P.O. Box 489
Ardmore, OK 73402
580-223-2266

Oklahoma Veterans Center
P.O. Box 1668
Norman, OK 73070
405-360-5600

Oklahoma Veterans Center
P.O. Box 988
Claremore, OK 74018
918-342-5432

Oklahoma Veterans Center
P.O. Box 1688
Talihina, OK 74571
918-567-2251

Oklahoma Veteran Center
200 E. Fairlane
Sulphur, OK 73086
580-622-2144

Oklahoma Veteran Center
P.O. Box 1209
Clinton, OK 73601
580-331-2200

Oregon

Oregon State Veterans Home
700 Veterans Drive
Dalles, Or 97058
541-296-7152

Pennsylvania

Delaware Valley Veterans' Home
2701 Southampton Road
Philadelphia, PA 19154-1205
215-965-5900

Pennsylvania Soldiers' & Sailors' Home
560 East Third Street
P.O. Box 6239
Erie, PA 16512-6239
814-871-4531

Gino J. Merli Veterans' Center
401 Penn Avenue
Scranton, PA 18503
570-961-4300

Southeastern Pennsylvania Veterans' Center
1 Veterans Drive
Spring City, PA 19475-1230
610-948-2400

Hollidaysburg Veterans Home
P.O. Box 319
Hollidaysburg, PA 16648
814-699-5201

Southwestern Veterans' Center
7060 Highland Drive
Pittsburgh, PA 15206-1297
412-665-6706

Puerto Rico

Casa Del Veterano
115 Bo. Amuelas
Carr 592, Km. 5. 6
Juana Diaz, PR 00795
787-837-6574

Rhode Island

Rhode Island Veterans Home
480 Metacom Avenue
Bristol, RI 02809-0689
401-253-8000

South Carolina

Richard M. Campbell Veterans Nursing Home
4605 Belton Highway
Anderson, SC 29621-7755
803-261-6734

Veterans' Victory House Nursing Home
2461 Sidneys Road
Walterboro, SC 29488
843-538-3000

South Dakota

Michael J. Fitzmaurice South Dakota Veterans Home
2500 Minnekahta Avenue
Hot Springs, SD 57747-1199
605-745-5127

Tennessee

Tennessee Veterans Home
P.O. Box 10299
Murfreesboro, TN 37129
615-895-8850

Tennessee State Veterans Home
2865 S. Main Street
Humboldt, TN 38343
901-784-8405

Texas

Texas State Veterans Home
1300 Seven Oaks Road
Bonham, TX 75418
903-640-8387

Texas State Veterans Home
1424 MLK Jr. Lane
Temple, TX 76504
254-791-8280

Utah

Utah State Veterans Nursing Home
700 Foothill Boulevard
Salt Lake City, UT 84113
801-584-1900

Vermont

Vermont Veterans Home
325 N. Street
Bennington, VT 05201
802-442-6353

Virginia

Virginia Veterans Care Center
4550 Shenandoah Avenue
Roanoke, VA 24017
540-982-2860

Washington

Washington Soldiers' Home
P.O. Box 199
Orting, WA 98360
360-893-4500

Washington Veterans Center
P.O. Box 698
Retsil, WA 98378
360-895-4700

Spokane Veterans Home
222 East 5th Avenue
Spokane, WA 99202
509-344-5770

West Virginia

The West Virginia Veterans Home
512 Water Street
Barboursville, WV 25504
304-736-1027

Wisconsin

Wisconsin Veterans Home
N2665 County Road QQ
King, WI 54946-0600
715-258-5586

Wisconsin Veterans Home
21425 C Spring Street
Union Grove, WI 53182
262-878-5668

Wyoming

Veterans Home of Wyoming
700 Veterans' Lane
Buffalo, WY 82834
307-684-5511

APPENDIX F

Cemeteries for Veterans (National and State)

This is a complete listing of cemeteries for veterans. See Chapter 8 for a full discussion of VA burial benefits.

National Cemeteries

ALABAMA

Fort Mitchell National Cemetery
553 Highway 165
Fort Mitchell, AL 36856

Mobile National Cemetery
1202 Virginia Street
Mobile, AL 36604

ALASKA

Fort Richardson National Cemetery
Building 997, Davis Highway
P.O. Box 5-498
Fort Richardson, AK 99505

Sitka National Cemetery
803 Sawmill Creek Road
Sitka, AK 99835

ARIZONA

National Memorial Cemetery of Arizona
23029 North Cave Creek Road
Phoenix, AZ 85024

Prescott National Cemetery
VAMC, 500 Highway 89 North
Prescott, AZ 86313

ARKANSAS

Fayetteville National Cemetery
700 Government Avenue
Fayetteville, AR 72701

Little Rock National Cemetery
2523 Confederate Blvd
Little Rock, AR 72206

Fort Smith National Cemetery
522 Garland Avenue and South 6th Street
Fort Smith, AR 72901

CALIFORNIA

Fort Rosecrans National Cemetery
P.O. Box 6237
San Diego, CA 92166

Sacramento Valley VA National Cemetery
5810 Midway Road
Dixon, CA 95620

Golden Gate National Cemetery
1300 Sneath Lane
San Bruno, CA 94066

San Francisco National Cemetery
1 Lincoln Boulevard, Presidio of San Francisco
San Francisco, CA 94129

Los Angeles National Cemetery
950 S. Sepulveda Boulevard
Los Angeles, CA 90049

San Joaquin Valley
National Cemetery
32053 W. McCabe Road
Santa Nella, CA 95322

Riverside National Cemetery
22495 Van Buren Boulevard
Riverside, CA 92518

COLORADO

Fort Logan National Cemetery
4400 W. Kenyon Avenue
Denver, CO 80236

Fort Lyon National Cemetery
15700 County Road HH
Las Animas, CO 81054

CONNECTICUT

There are no national cemeteries in Connecticut.

DELAWARE

There are no national cemeteries in Delaware.

FLORIDA

Barrancas National Cemetery
Naval Air Station, 80 Hovey Road
Pensacola, FL 32508-1054

South Florida VA National Cemetery
6501 S. State Road 7
Lake Worth, FL 33467

Bay Pines National Cemetery
10,000 Bay Pines Boulevard, North
Bay Pines, FL 33504-0477

Saint Augustine National Cemetery
104 Marine Street
St. Augustine, FL 32084

Florida National Cemetery
6502 SW 102nd Avenue
Bushnell, FL 33513

GEORGIA

Georgia National Cemetery
2025 Mount Carmel Church Lane
Canton, GA 30114

Marietta National Cemetery
500 Washington Avenue
Marietta, GA 30060

HAWAII

National Memorial Cemetery of the Pacific
2177 Puowaina Drive
Honolulu, HI 96813-1729

IDAHO

There are no national cemeteries in Idaho.

ILLINOIS

Abraham Lincoln National Cemetery
27034 S. Diagonal Road
Elwood, IL 60421

Mound City National Cemetery
Highway Junction 37 and 51
Mound City, IL 62963

Alton National Cemetery
600 Pearl Street
Alton, IL 62003

Quincy National Cemetery
36th and Maine Street
Quincy, IL 62301

Camp Butler National Cemetery
5063 Camp Butler Road
Springfield, IL 62707

Rock Island National Cemetery
Building 118, Rock Island Arsenal
Rock Island, IL 61299

Danville National Cemetery
1900 E. Main Street
Danville, IL 61832

INDIANA

Crown Hill National Cemetery
700 W. 38th Street
Indianapolis, IN 46208

New Albany National Cemetery
1943 Ekin Avenue
New Albany, IN 47150

Marion National Cemetery
VAMC, 1700 E. 38th Street
Marion, IN 46952

IOWA

Keokuk National Cemetery
1701 J Street
Keokuk, IA 52632

KANSAS

Fort Leavenworth National Cemetery
395 Biddle Boulevard
Fort Leavenworth, KS 66027

Leavenworth National Cemetery
P.O. Box 1694
Leavenworth, KS 66048

Fort Scott National Cemetery
900 E. National Avenue
Fort Scott, KS 66701

KENTUCKY

Camp Nelson National Cemetery
6980 Danville Road
Nicholasville, KY 40356

Lexington National Cemetery
833 West Main Street
Lexington, KY 40508

Cave Hill National Cemetery
701 Baxter Avenue
Louisville, KY 40204

Mill Springs National Cemetery
Nancy, KY 42544

Danville National Cemetery
277 N. First Street
Danville, KY 40442

Zachary Taylor National Cemetery
4701 Brownboro Road
Louisville, KY 40207

Lebanon National Cemetery
20 Highway 208
Lebanon, KY 40033

LOUISIANA

Alexandria National Cemetery
209 East Shamrock Street
Pineville, LA 71360

Baton Rouge National Cemetery
220 North 19th Street
Baton Rouge, LA 70806

Port Hudson National Cemetery
20978 Port Hickey Road
Zachary, LA 70791

MAINE

Togus National Cemetery
VA Medical and Regional Office Center
Togus, ME 04330

MARYLAND

Annapolis National Cemetery
800 West Street
Annapolis, MD 21401

Baltimore National Cemetery
5501 Frederick Avenue
Baltimore, MD 21228

Loudon Park National Cemetery
3445 Frederick Avenue
Baltimore, MD 21228

MASSACHUSETTS

Massachusetts National Cemetery
Off Connery Avenue
Bourne, MA 02532

MICHIGAN

Fort Custer National Cemetery
15501 Dickman Road
Augusta, MI 49012

Great Lakes National Cemetery
4200 Belford Road
Holly, MI 48442

MINNESOTA

Fort Snelling National Cemetery
7601 34th Avenue, South
Minneapolis, MN 55450-1199

MISSISSIPPI

Biloxi National Cemetery
P.O. Box 4968
Biloxi, MS 39535-4968

Corinth National Cemetery
1551 Horton Street
Corinth, MS 38834

Natchez National Cemetery
41 Cemetery Road
Natchez, MS 39120

MISSOURI

Jefferson Barracks National Cemetery
2900 Sheridan Road
St. Louis, MO 63125

Jefferson City National Cemetery
1024 East McCarty Street
Jefferson City, MO 65101

Springfield National Cemetery
1702 East Seminole Street
Springfield, MO 65804

NEW HAMPSHIRE

There are no national cemeteries in New Hampshire.

NEW JERSEY

Beverly National Cemetery
916 Bridgeboro Road
Beverly, NJ 08010

Finns Point National Cemetery
Ft. Mott Road
Salem, NJ 08079

NEW MEXICO

Fort Bayard National Cemetery
P.O. Box 189
Fort Bayard, NM 88036

Santa Fe National Cemetery
501 North Guadalupe Street
Santa Fe, NM 87501

NEW YORK

Bath National Cemetery
VA Medical Center
San Juan Avenue
Bath, NY 14810

Gerald B.H. Solomon Saratoga National Cemetery
200 Duell Road
Schuylerville, NY 12871-1721

Calverton National Cemetery
210 Princeton Boulevard
Calverton, NY 11933-1031

Long Island National Cemetery
2040 Wellwood Avenue
Farmingdale, NY 11735-1211

Cypress Hills National Cemetery
625 Jamaica Avenue
Brooklyn, NY 11208

Woodlawn National Cemetery
1825 Davis Street
Elmira, NY 14901

NEVADA

There are no national cemeteries in Nevada.

NORTH CAROLINA

New Bern National Cemetery
1711 National Avenue
New Bern, NC 28560

Salisbury National Cemetery
501 Statesville Boulevard
Salisbury, NC 28144

Raleigh National Cemetery
501 Rock Quarry Road
Raleigh, NC 27610

Wilmington National Cemetery
2011 Market Street
Wilmington, NC 28403

NORTH DAKOTA

There are no national cemeteries in North Dakota.

OHIO

Dayton National Cemetery
VAMC, 4100 W. Third Street
Dayton, OH 45428-1088

Ohio Western Reserve National Cemetery
P.O. Box 8
10175 Rawiga Road
Rittman, OH 44270

OKLAHOMA

Fort Gibson National Cemetery
1423 Cemetery Road
Fort Gibson, OK 74434

Fort Sill National Cemetery
2648 NE Jake Dunn Road
Elgin, OK 73538

OREGON

Eagle Point National Cemetery
2763 Riley Road
Eagle Point, OR 97524

Willamette National Cemetery
11800 SE Mt. Scott Boulevard
Portland, OR 97266-6937

Roseburg National Cemetery
1770 Harvard Boulevard
Roseburg, OR 97470

PENNSYLVANIA

Indiantown Gap National Cemetery
RR 2, Box 484
Annville, PA 17003-9618

Philadelphia National Cemetery
Haines Street and Limekiln Pike
Philadelphia, PA 19138

National Cemetery of the Alleghenies
1158 Morgan Road
Bridgeville, PA 15017

PUERTO RICO

Puerto Rico National Cemetery
Avenida Cementerio Nacional 50
Barrio Hato Tejas
Bayamon, PR 00960

RHODE ISLAND

There are no national cemeteries in Rhode Island.

SOUTH CAROLINA

Beaufort National Cemetery
1601 Boundary Street
Beaufort, SC 29902-3947

Florence National Cemetery
803 E. National Cemetery Road
Florence, SC 29506

SOUTH DAKOTA

Black Hills National Cemetery
20901 Pleasant Valley Drive
Sturgis, SD 57785

Hot Springs National Cemetery
VA Medical Center
Hot Springs, SD 57747

Fort Meade National Cemetery
Old Stone Road
Sturgis, SD 57785

TENNESSEE

Chattanooga National Cemetery
1200 Bailey Avenue
Chattanooga, TN 37404

Memphis National Cemetery
3568 Townes Avenue
Memphis, TN 38122

Knoxville National Cemetery
939 Tyson Street, NW
Knoxville, TN 37917

Mountain Home National Cemetery
P.O. Box 8
Mountain Home, TN 37684

Nashville National Cemetery
1420 Gallatin Road, South
Madison, TN 37115-4619

TEXAS

Dallas-Fort Worth National Cemetery
2000 Mountain Creek Parkway
Dallas, TX 75211

Houston National Cemetery
10410 Veterans Memorial Drive
Houston, TX 77038

Fort Bliss National Cemetery
5200 Fred Wilson Boulevard
P.O. Box 6342
Fort Bliss, TX 79906

Kerrville National Cemetery
VAMC, 3600 Memorial Boulevard
Kerrville, TX 78028

Fort Sam Houston National Cemetery
1520 Harry Wurzbach Road
San Antonio, TX 78209

San Antonio National Cemetery
517 Paso Hondo Street
San Antonio, TX 78202

UTAH

There are no national cemeteries in Utah.

VERMONT

There are no national cemeteries in Vermont.

VIRGINIA

Alexandria National Cemetery
1450 Wilkes Street
Alexandria, VA 22314

City Point National Cemetery
10th Avenue and Davis Street
Hopewell, VA 23860

Ball's Bluff National Cemetery
Route 7
Leesburg, VA 22075

Cold Harbor National Cemetery
6038 Cold Harbor Road
Mechanicsville, VA 23111

Culpeper National Cemetery
305 U.S. Avenue
Culpeper, VA 22701

Danville National Cemetery
721 Lee Street
Danville, VA 24541

Fort Harrison National Cemetery
8620 Varina Road
Richmond, VA 23231

Glendale National Cemetery
8301 Willis Church Road
Richmond, VA 23231

Hampton National Cemetery
Cemetery Road at Marshall Avenue
Hampton, VA 23669

Hampton VA National Cemetery
VAMC, Emancipation Drive
Hampton, VA 23667

Quantico National Cemetery
18424 Joplin Road (Route 619)
Triangle, VA 22172

Richmond National Cemetery
1701 Williamsburg Road
Richmond, VA 23231

Seven Pines National Cemetery
400 E. Williamsburg Road
Sandston, VA 23150

Staunton National Cemetery
901 Richmond Avenue
Staunton, VA 24401

Winchester National Cemetery
401 National Avenue
Winchester, VA 22601

WASHINGTON

Tahoma National Cemetery
18600 S. E. 240th Street
Kent, WA 98042-4868

WEST VIRGINIA

Grafton National Cemetery
431 Walnut Street
Grafton, WV 26354

West Virginia National Cemetery
Route 2, Box 127
Grafton, WV 26354

WISCONSIN

Wood National Cemetery
5000 West National Avenue,
Building 1301
Milwaukee, WI 53295-4000

WYOMING

There are no national cemeteries in Wyoming.

State Veterans Affairs Cemeteries

ARIZONA

Southern Arizona Veterans' Memorial Cemetery
1300 Buffalo Soldier Trail
Sierra Vista, AZ 85635

ARKANSAS

Arkansas Veterans Cemetery
1501 W. Maryland Avenue
North Little Rock, AR 72120

CALIFORNIA

Northern California Veterans Cemetery
P.O. Box 76
11800 Gas Point Road
Igo, CA 96047-0076

Veterans Memorial Grove Cemetery
Veterans Home of California
Yountville, CA 94599

COLORADO

Colorado State Veterans Center at Homelake
3749 Sherman Avenue
Monte Vista, CO 81144

Veterans Memorial Cemetery of Western Colorado
2830 D Road
Grand Junction, CO 8150

CONNECTICUT

Department of Veterans Affairs (Veterans Home and Hospital)
287 West Street
Rocky Hill, CT 06067

Spring Grove Veterans Cemetery (Closed)
Darien, CT

Middletown Veterans Cemetery
Bow Lane
Middletown, CT 06457

DELAWARE

Delaware Veterans Memorial Cemetery
2465 Chesapeake City Road
Bear, DE 19701-2344

Delaware Veterans Memorial Cemetery—Sussex County
26669 Patriots Way
Millsboro, DE 19966-1694

GEORGIA

Georgia Veterans' Memorial Cemetery
2617 Vinson Highway
Milledgeville, GA 31061

HAWAII

East Hawaii Veterans Cemetery—No. I (Closed)
Home Iani Lane
Hilo, HI 96720

Hawaii State Veterans Cemetery
45-349 Kamehameha Highway
Kaneohe, HI 96744

East Hawaii Veterans Cemetery—No. II
County of Hawaii (Island of Hawaii)
Home lani Lane
Hilo, HI 96720

Kauai Veterans Cemetery
County of Kauai (Island of Kauai)
4331 Lele Road
Hanapepe, HI 96716

Lanai Veterans Cemetery
Maui County (Island of Lanai)
Lanido Road
Lanai City, HI 96763

Molokai Veterans Cemetery
County of Maui (Island of Molokai)
2725 Lihi Pali Avenue
Hoolehua, HI 96748

Maui Veterans Cemetery
County of Maui (Island of Maui)
Baldwin Avenue
Makawao, HI 96786

West Hawaii State Veterans Cemetery
County of Hawaii (Island of Hawaii)
Queen Kaahumano Highway
Kailua-Kona, HI 96740

IDAHO

Idaho Veterans Cemetery
10100 N. Horseshoe Bend Road
Boise, ID 83714

ILLINOIS

Sunset Cemetery
Illinois Veterans Home
1707 N. 12th Street
Quincy, IL 62301

INDIANA

Indiana State Soldiers' Home Cemetery
3851 N. River Road W.
Lafayette, IN 47906-3765

Indiana Veterans Memorial Cemetery
1415 North Gate Road
Madison, IN 47250

IOWA

Iowa Veteran's Home And Cemetery
13th and Summit Streets
Marshalltown, IA 50158

KANSAS

Kansas Veterans' Cemetery at Ft. Dodge
11560 U.S. Highway 400
Dodge City, KS 67801

Kansas Veterans' Cemetery at Winfield
1208 North College Street
Winfield, KS 67156

Kansas Veterans' Cemetery at Wakeeney
P.O. Box 185
4035 13th Street
Wakeeney, KS 67672

KENTUCKY

Kentucky Veterans Cemetery Central (In Design)
US Highway 31W
Radcliff, KY

Kentucky Veterans Cemetery-West
5817 Fort Campbell Boulevard
Hopkinsville, KY 42240

LOUISIANA (not open yet)

MAINE

Maine Veterans' Memorial Cemetery (Closed)
Civic Center Drive
Augusta, ME

Northern Maine Veterans' Cemetery—Caribou
37 Lombard Road
Caribou, ME 04736

Maine Veterans' Memorial Cemetery—Mt. Vernon Rd.
163 Mt. Vernon Road
Augusta, ME 04330

MARYLAND

Cheltenham Veterans Cemetery
11301 Crain Highway
Post Office Box 10
Cheltenham, MD 20623

Garrison Forest Veterans Cemetery
11501 Garrison Forest Road
Owings Mills, MD 21117

Crownsville Veterans Cemetery
1122 Sunrise Beach Road
Crownsville, MD 21032

Rocky Gap Veterans Cemetery
14205 Pleasant Valley Road, NE
Flintstone, MD 21530

Eastern Shore Veterans Cemetery
6827 E. New Market Ellwood Road
Hurlock, MD 21643

MASSACHUSETTS

Massachusetts State Veterans' Cemetery Agawam
1390 Main Street
Agawam, MA 01001

Winchendon Veterans' Cemetery
111 Glenallen Street
Winchendon, MA 01475

MICHIGAN

Grand Rapids Home for Veterans Cemetery
3000 Monroe, NW
Grand Rapids, MI 49505

MINNESOTA

Minnesota State Veterans Cemetery
15550 Highway 115
Little Falls, MN 56345

MISSOURI

Missouri State Veterans Cemetery Bloomfield, Mo
17357 Stars and Stripes Way
Bloomfield, MO 63825

Missouri Veterans Cemetery Springfield, Mo
5201 South Southwood Road
Springfield, MO 65804

Missouri State Veterans Cemetery in Higginsville, Mo
20109 Business Highway 13
Higginsville, MO 64037

St. James Missouri Veterans Home Cemetery
620 N. Jefferson
St. James, MO 65559

Missouri State Veterans Cemetery Jacksonville, Mo
1479 County Road 1675
Jacksonville, MO 65260

MONTANA

Eastern Montana State Veterans Cemetery
P.O. Box 1741
Highway 59 And Cemetery Road
Miles City, MT 59301

Montana Veterans Home Cemetery
P.O. Box 250
Columbia Falls, MT 59912

Montana State Veterans Cemetery
Fort William H. Harrison
P.O. Box 5715
Helena, MT 59604

NEBRASKA

Nebraska Veterans Home Cemetery
Burkett Station
2300 W. Capital Avenue
Grand Island, NE 68803

NEVADA

Northern Nevada Veterans Memorial Cemetery
P.O. Box 1919—14 Veterans Way
Fernley, NV 89408

Southern Nevada Veterans Memorial Cemetery
1900 Buchanan Boulevard
Boulder City, NV 89005

NEW HAMPSHIRE

New Hampshire State Veterans Cemetery
110 Daniel Webster Highway, Route 3
Boscawen, NH 03303

NEW JERSEY

Brigadier General William C. Doyle Veterans Memorial Cemetery
350 Provenceline Road, Route 2
Wrightstown, NJ 08562

New Jersey Memorial Home Cemetery (Closed)
524 N.W. Boulevard
Vineland, NJ 08360

NORTH CAROLINA

Coastal Carolina State Veterans Cemetery
P.O. Box 1486
Jacksonville, NC 28541

Western Carolina State Veterans Cemetery
962 Old US 70 Highway
Black Mountain, NC 28711

Sandhills State Veterans Cemetery
P.O. Box 39 (Mail)
400 Murchison Road
Spring Lake, NC 28390

NORTH DAKOTA

North Dakota Veterans Cemetery
1825 46th Street
Mandan, ND 58554

OHIO

Ohio Veterans Home Cemetery
3416 Columbus Avenue
Sandusky, OII 44870

OKLAHOMA

Oklahoma Veterans Cemetery (closed)
3501 Military Circle
Oklahoma City, OK 73111-4398

PENNSYLVANIA

Pennsylvania Soldiers' and Sailors' Home Cemetery
P.O. Box 6239
560 E. Third Street
Erie, PA 16512-6239

RHODE ISLAND

Rhode Island Veterans Cemetery
301 S. County Trail
Exeter, RI 02822-9712

SOUTH DAKOTA

South Dakota Veterans Home Cemetery
2500 Minnekahta Avenue
Hot Springs, SD 57747-1199

TENNESSEE

East Tennesse State Veterans Cemetery
5901 Lyons View Pike
Knoxville, TN 37919

Middle Tennessee Veterans Cemetery
7931 McCrory Lane
Nashvile, TN 37221

West Tennessee Veterans Cemetery
4000 Forest Hill/Irene Road
Memphis, TN 38125

TEXAS

Central Texas State Veterans Cemetery
11463 S. Highway 195
Killeen, TX 76542

UTAH

Utah State Veterans Cemetery
17111 S. Camp Williams Road
Bluffdale, UT 84065

VERMONT

Vermont Veterans Home War Memorial Cemetery
325 North Street
Bennington, VT 05620-4401

Vermont Veterans' Memorial Cemetery
487 Furnace Road
Randolph Center, VT 05061

VIRGINIA

Albert G. Horton, Jr. Memorial Veterans Cemetery
5310 Milner's Road
Suffolk, VA 23434

Virginia Veterans Cemetery at Amelia
10300 Pridesville Road
Amelia, VA 23002

WASHINGTON

Washington Soldiers Home Colony And Cemetery
1301 Orting-Kapowsin Highway
Orting, WA 98360

Washington Veterans Home
P.O. Box 698
Retsil, WA 98378

WISCONSIN

Central Wisconsin Veterans Memorial Cemetery
Wisconsin Veterans Home
N2665, Highway QQ
King, WI 54946

Southern Wisconsin Veterans Memorial Cemetery
21731 Spring Street
Union Grove, WI 53182

Northern Wisconsin Veterans Memorial Cemetery
N4063 Veterans Way
Spooner, WI 54801

WYOMING

Oregon Trail Veterans Cemetery
89 Cemetery Road, Box 669
Evansville, WY 82636

Territories

GUAM

Guam Veterans Cemetery
Veterans Affairs Office
490 Chalan Palayso
Agatna Heights, Guam 96910

SAIPAN

CNMI Veterans Cemetery
Military/Veterans Affairs
P.O. Box 503416
Saipan, MP 96950

APPENDIX G

Veterans Service Organizations

These are some of the largest Veterans Service Organizations (VSOs). You can find a fuller list of VSOs in Chapter 4.

Air Force Association

1501 Lee Highway
Arlington, VA 22209-1198
800-727-3337
service@afa.org
www.afa.org

The Air Force Association (AFA) is a civilian education organization promoting public understanding of aerospace and the role it plays in the security of the nation. AFA publishes *Air Force Magazine*, conducts national symposia, and disseminates information through outreach programs. AFA presents scholarships and grants to Air Force active duty, Air National Guard, and Air Force Reserve members and their dependents; and awards educator grants to promote science and math education at the elementary and secondary school level.

American Ex-Prisioners of War

3201 E. Pioneer Parkway, Suite 40
Arlington, TX 76010
817-649-2979
hq@axpow.org
www.axpow.org

The American Ex-Prisoners of War organization is a national organization for American citizens who were captured by the enemy. Membership is open to all former prisoners of war from any theater in any war, all former civilian internees, and the families of such persons. The organization of former POWs (military and civilian), their spouses, families, and civilian internees has helped those affected by their capture deal with the trauma through friendship of those who shared a common experience.

American G.I. Forum

2870 N. Speer Boulevard, Suite 102
Denver, CO 80211
303-458-1700
agifnat@agifnat.ipmail.att.net
www.agif.us

The American G. I. Forum (AGIF) is a congressionally chartered Hispanic/Latino veterans and civil rights organization. AGIF currently operates chapters throughout the United States, with a focus on veterans' issues, education, and civil rights. Initially formed to request services for World War II veterans of Mexican descent, it soon spread into non-veterans' issues such as voting rights, jury selection, and education desegregation, advocating for the civil rights of all Mexican Americans.

The American Gulf War Veterans Association (AGWVA)

P.O. Box 85
Versailles, MO 65084
800-231-7631
webmaster@gulfwarvets.com
www.gulfwarvets.com

The American Gulf War Veterans Association (AGWVA) was established to obtain treatment for those service members and their families who experience symptoms collectively known as the "Gulf War Illness" and to obtain justice and compensation for all those affected by these illnesses.

American Legion

700 N. Pennsylvania Street
P.O. Box 1055
Indianapolis, IN 46206
317-630-1200
www.legion.org

The American Legion is an organization of veterans of the United States Armed Forces who served in wartime. In addition to organizing commemorative events and volunteer activities, the American Legion is active in lobbying for the interests of veterans, including support for veterans benefits, such as pensions and the Veterans Affairs hospital system.

American Veterans—AMVETS

4647 Forbes Boulevard
Lanham, MD 20706-4380
301-459-9600
amvets@amvets.org
www.amvets.org

American Veterans, AMVETS, is a volunteer-led organization that accepts honorably discharged veterans as members. AMVETS provides support for veterans and the active military in procuring their earned entitlements, as well as offers community services. To be eligible for membership in Amvets, you must:

- Be actively serving or have served in the U.S. Armed Forces, including the National Guard and Reserves, anytime after September 15, 1940.
- Unless still serving, your discharge must have been under honorable conditions.

Additionally, if you served as an American citizen in the armed forces of an allied nation, under honorable conditions, between September 15, 1940, and May 8, 1975, you are also eligible, as are wartime members of the Merchant Marine. Proof of eligibility can be DD Form 214, an honorable discharge certificate, or other appropriate document.

Blinded Veterans Association

477 H Street, NW
Washington, DC 20001-2694
202-371-8880
bva@bva.org
www.bva.org

Blinded Veterans Association is an organization established to promote the welfare of blinded veterans through service programs, groups, and benefits. There is no charge for services and all legally blind veterans are eligible for BVA's help, whether they became blind during or after active duty.

Catholic War Veterans of the USA

441 N. Lee Street
Alexandria, VA 22314
703-549-3622
www.cwv.org

The Catholic War Veterans addresses issues related to God, country, and home. You can obtain information on VA benefits and information on CWV programs. An applicant shall be a member of the Catholic Church, enlisted, drafted, inducted, or commissioned into any branch of the United States Army, Navy, Marine Corps, Coast Guard, Air Force, and/or including the National Guard or Reserve components and was discharged under honorable conditions.

Cold War Veterans Association

P.O. Box 13042
Overland Park, KS 66282-3042
www.coldwarveterans.com

The mission of the Cold War Veterans Association is to fight for the rights of Cold War Veterans; to educate people as to why the Cold War was fought and won and why vigilance must be maintained; and to provide a fraternal community for men and women whose patriotism binds them together. CWVA is open to honorably discharged veterans and active-duty personnel who served at any time during the Cold War period—September 2, 1945, to December 26, 1991.

Disabled American Veterans

3725 Alexandria Pike
Cold Spring, KY 41076
877-426-2838
www.dav.org

The Disabled American Veterans, or DAV, offers professional services that include help with disability compensation, VA pension, death benefits, VA medical care, Social Security disability benefits, veterans' job programs, and more. Membership is open for any man or woman who was wounded, gassed, injured, or disabled in the line of duty during time of war, while in the service of either the military or naval forces of the United States of America, and who has not been dishonorably discharged or separated from such service, or who may still be in active service in the armed forces.

Fleet Reserve Association

125 N. West Street
Alexandria, VA 22314
703-663-1400
www.fra.org

FRA works to preserve and enhance benefits and quality-of-life programs for members of the Navy, Marine Corps, and Coast Guard. They represent the enlisted perspective to members of Congress, giving voice to the members' concerns. FRA also provides information on legislation, health care, education benefits and enhancements, veterans' services, and survivors' benefits.

Foundation for American Veterans, Inc.

7473 Wilshire
West Bloomfield, MI 48322
248-661-9365
fav@fav.org
www.fav.org

FAV, a nonprofit organization, was established to provide various benefits for all veterans through the veterans hospitals, homeless programs, educational programs, crisis programs, etc.

Iraq and Afghanistan Veterans of America

770 Broadway, 2nd Floor
New York, NY 10003
212-982-9699
info@iava.org
ww.iava.org

Iraq and Afghanistan Veterans of America, or IAVA, is the nation's first and largest group dedicated to the troops and veterans of the wars in Iraq and Afghanistan, and the civilian supporters of those troops and veterans. IAVA is a nonprofit organization responding to body and HMMWV armor shortage, the challenges of Post-Traumatic Stress Disorder, and inadequate funding for veterans' health care.

Iraq War Veterans Organization

P.O. Box 571
Yucaipa, CA 92399
info@iranwarveterans.org
www.iraqwarveterans.org

The Iraq War Veterans Organization, or IWVO, provides information and support for Operation Iraqi Freedom Veterans, Global War on Terror Veterans, Operation Enduring Freedom Veterans, active military personnel and family members related to pre-deployment, deployment, and post-deployment issues.

Jewish War Veterans

1811 R Street
Washington, DC 20009
202-265-6280
www.jwv.org

JWV works for veterans by advocating for veteran health and employment benefits, through hospital, rehabilitation, and veterans' service programs; supports the underprivileged, homeless, and handicapped through civic betterment projects. To be eligible for membership you must:

- Be a person of the Jewish faith of good character who is a citizen of the United States and served on active duty in the armed forces (including National Guard and Reserves) in any of its wars, campaigns, or conflicts AND
- Be honorably discharged

Military Officers Association of America

201 N. Washington Street
Alexandria, VA 22314
800-234-6622
www.moaa.org

MOAA is an independent, nonprofit, polically nonpartisan organization with members from every branch of service, representing the interests of military officers at every stage of their careers.

National Amputation Foundation, Inc.

40 Church Street
Malverne, NY 11565
516-887-3600
amps76@aol.com
www.nationalamputation.org

The Foundation is dedicated to helping all veteran amputees. It sponsors an Amp-to-Amp program to visit with new amputees.

National Association for Black Veterans, Inc.

P.O. Box 11432
Milwaukee, WI 53211
877-622-8387
www.nabvets.com

NABVETS will provide personal advocacy on behalf of veterans seeking claims against the United States Department of Veterans Affairs; advocacy for youth in all matters required for successful passage into adulthood; advocacy on behalf of families; with community involvement, provide advocacy in creating positive lifestyles for veterans; and to generate and preserve the historical record.

National Coalition for Homeless Veterans

333½ Pennsylvania Avenue, SE
Washington, DC 20003-1148
800-VET.HELP (838-4357)
nchv@nchv.org
www.nchv.org

The National Coalition for Homeless Veterans, or NCHV, is a resource and technical assistance center to provide emergency and supportive housing, food, health services, job training, and placement assistance, legal aid, and case management support for homeless veterans.

National Guard Association of the United States

1 Massachusetts Avenue, NW
Washington, DC 20001
202-289-0031
ngaus@ngaus.org
www.ngaus.org

NGAUS is a non-partisan organization representing current and former Army and Air National Guard officers. NGAUS is focused on procuring better equipment, standardized training, and a more combat-ready force by petitioning Congress for resources.

National Veterans Legal Services Program

P.O. Box 65762
Washington, DC 20035
202-265-8305
info@nvlsp.org
www.nvlsp.org

An independent veterans service organization providing veterans organizations, service officers, and attorneys with training to enable them to help veterans and their dependents obtain benefits that they deserve. They represent veterans and their dependents who are seeking benefits before the U.S. Department of Veterans Affairs and in court.

Navy Mutual Aid Association

Henderson Hall
29 Carpenter Road
Arlington, VA 22212
800-628-6011
info@navymutual.org
www.navymutual.org

The purpose of the association is to aid its members and their dependents or beneficiaries, by providing a substantial sum for their relief through insurance plans at as near the actual net cost as possible. The association assists, without charge, dependents and beneficiaries in securing the Federal benefits to which they may be legally entitled. The association serves all uniformed personnel of the Navy, Marine Corps, Coast Guard, National Oceanic and Atmospheric Administration, and U.S. Public Health Service, including all enlisted and officer grades, regular, reserve, and retired.

Non-Commissioned Officers Association

610 Madison Street
Alexandria, VA 22314
703-549-0311
veterans@ncoadc.org
www.ncoausa.org

NCOA was established in 1960 to enhance and maintain the quality of life for non-commissioned and petty officers in all branches of the armed forces, National Guard, and Reserves. The association offers its members a wide range of benefits and services designed especially for current and former enlisted servicemembers and their families. Those benefits include social improvement programs to help ensure well-being during the servicemember's active military career, transition to civilian life and throughout retirement, and to serve as a legislative advocate on issues that affect NCOA members.

Paralyzed Veterans of America

801 Eighteenth Street, NW
Washington, DC 20006-3517
800-424-8200
info@pva.org
www.pva.org

Paralyzed Veterans of America (PVA) is an advocate for quality health care, research, and education addressing spinal cord injury and dysfunction, benefits availability, and opportunities for independence for veterans.

Veterans for America

1025 Vermont Avenue, 7th Floor
Washington, DC 20005
202-637-2064
www.veteransforamerica.org

Veterans for America, formerly the Vietnam Veterans of America Foundation, is an advocacy and humanitarian organization. Veterans for America works with its affiliate organization, the Justice Project, to engage the American public in support of policies addressing the needs of veterans, those currently in the military, victims of war overseas, as well as initiatives to make the world more secure.

Veterans Assistance Foundation, Inc.

P.O. Box 109
Newburg, WI 53060
877-823-9433
www.veteransassistance.org

The Veterans Assistance Foundation (VAF) was established to operate transitional housing programs for military veterans who are homeless or at risk of becoming homeless and is dedicated to veterans advocacy. VAF and California Veterans Assistance Foundation (CVAF) provide supportive services and transitional housing for veterans from all over the United States. Services provided include health care assessment, wellness education, referrals for psychological assessment, veterans benefits counseling, GED program, vocational assessment and training, sobriety maintenance and referrals for Post-Traumatic Stress Disorder and housing assistance upon completing program.

Veterans of Foreign Wars

National Headquarters
406 W. 34th Street
Kansas City, MO 64111
816-756-3390
vfw@vfw.org
www.vfw.org

The Veterans of Foreign Wars of the United States, or simply VFW, is an American organization whose members are current or former members of the U.S. Armed Forces. To be eligible for membership, an individual must have earned a United States government-issued overseas expeditionary or campaign medal, or have one of the following:

- Combat Infantryman Badge
- Combat Medical Badge, Combat Action Badge
- Combat Action Ribbon
- Korea Defense Service Medal
- Air Force Expeditionary Service Ribbon with gold border
- U.S. Navy SSBN Deterrent Patrol Insignia
- Service in Korea from June 30, 1949, for 30 consecutive, or 60 non-consecutive days to present
- Hostile fire-imminent danger pay records

In addition, they must either currently be on active duty or in a reserve component, or have been honorably discharged from the U.S. Armed Forces. DD Form 214 or World War II era discharge paper with campaign medals, and or badges printed on back is used to verify membership eligibility. A member must also be a U.S. citizen.

Vietnam Veterans of America

8605 Cameron Street
Silver Springs, MD 20910
301-587-4110
www.vva.org

The Vietnam Veterans of America was organized to promote and support the full range of issues important to Vietnam veterans, to create a new identity for this generation of veteran, and to change public perception of Vietnam veterans.

Women's Army Corps Veterans Association

info@armywomen.org

Chapter projects include monetary donations to all types of charity organization and collections such as eye glasses, stamps for the wounded, coupons, clothing, and food for food banks. Eligible for membership in the Women's Army Corps Veterans Association are those women who can provide evidence that they are current, former or retired women members of the Army who have served honorably on active duty in the Army of the United States (AUS), Regular Army (RA), Army National Guard (ANG) and the United States Army Reserve (USAR) the Army Nurse Corps (ANC), the Women's Army Auxiliary Corps (WAAC), or the Women's Army Corps (WAC) in commissioned, warrant, non-commissioned or enlisted status for 90 days or more, after May, 14 1942. To be eligible you must have Verification of Eligibility in the form of:

- Honorable Discharge/Certificate of Service
- DD Form 214 (Report of Separation)
- Official Retirement Order
- Active Duty—provide a statement from custodian of personnel records, that service is being performed under Honorable Conditions (facsimile of Army Identification Card).
- United States Army Reserve and United States National Guard—provide a statement from custodian of personnel records, that service is being performed under Honorable Conditions (facsimile of Army Identification Card).

APPENDIX H

Department of Veterans Affairs by State/Territory

Each state has a Department of Veterans Affairs.

Alabama Department of Veterans Affairs
RSA Plaza Building, Suite 530
770 Washington Avenue
Montgomery, AL 36130-2755
334-242-5077
www.va.state.al.us

Alaska Department of Military & Veterans Affairs
P.O. Box 5800, Camp Denali
Fort Richardson, AK 99505-5800
907-428-6003
www.ak-prepared.com/dmva

American Samoa Veteran Affairs
P.O. Box 8586
Pago Pago, American Samoa 96799
(001) 684-633-4206
www.nasdva.com/americansamoa.html

Arizona Department of Veterans' Services
4141 N. Third Street, Suite 200
Phoenix, AZ 85012
602-255-3373
www.azdvs.gov

Arkansas Department of Veterans Affairs
2200 Fort Roots. Drive
Building 65, Room 119
North Little Rock, AR 72114
501-370-3820
www.nasdva.com/arkansas.html

California Department of Veterans Affairs
1227 O Street
Sacramento, CA 95814
800-952-5626
www.cdva.ca.gov/cdva/contactus.asp

Colorado Department of Military and Veterans Affairs
789 Sherman Street, Suite 200
Denver, CO 80203-1714
303-894-7474
www.dmva.state.co.us

State of Connecticut Department of Veterans' Affairs
287 West Street
Rocky Hill, CT 06067
860-529-2571
www.ct.gov/ctva

Delaware Commission of Veterans Affairs
Robbins Building
802 Silver Lake Boulevard, Suite 100
Dover, DE 19904
302-739-2792
www.state.de.us/veteran/

District of Columbia Office of Veterans Affairs
441 4th Street, NW, Suite 570 S.
Washington, DC 20001
202-724-5454
www.dc.gov/agencies/detail.asp?id=1043

Florida Department of Veterans' Affairs
Florida Department of Veterans' Affairs
4040 Esplanade Way, Suite 152
Tallahassee, FL 32399-0950
850-487-1533
www.floridavets.org

Georgia Department of Veterans Service
Floyd Veterans Memorial Building
Suite E-970
Atlanta, Georgia 30334-4800
404-656-2300
www.sdvs.georgia.gov

Guam Veterans Affairs Office
P.O. Box 3279
Agana, Guam 96932
671-475-4222
www.nasdva.com/guam.html

Hawaii Office of Veterans Services
459 Patterson Road
E-Wing, Room 1-A103
Honolulu, HI 96819
808-433-0420
www.dod.state.hi.us/ovs

Idaho State Veterans Services
320 Collins Road
Boise, ID 83702
208-334-3513
www.veterans.idaho.gov

Illinois Department of Veterans' Affairs
833 South Spring Street
P.O. Box 19432
Springfield, IL 62794-9432
217-782-6641
www.state.il.us/agency/dva

Indiana Department of Veterans Affairs
302 W. Washington Street, Room E120
Indianapolis, IN 46204-2738
317-232-3910
www.ai.org/veteran

Iowa Department of Veterans Affairs
Camp Dodge, Building A6A
7105 NW 70th Avenue
Johnston, IA 50131-1824
515-242-5331
www.iowava.org

Kansas Commission on Veterans' Affairs
Jayhawk Tower
700 SW Jackson, Suite 701
Topeka, KS 66603-3743
785-296-3976
www.kcva.org

Kentucky Department of Veterans Affairs
1111 Louisville Road
Frankfort, KY 40601
502-564-9203
www.kdva.net

Louisiana Department of Veterans Affairs
1885 Wooddale Boulevard
P.O. Box 94095
Baton Rouge, LA 70804-9095
225-922-0500
www.vetaffairs.com

Maine Bureau of Veterans' Services
117 State House Station
Augusta, ME 04333-0117
207-626-4464
www.maine.gov/dvem/bvs

Maryland Department of Veterans Affairs
The Jeffrey Building, 4th Floor
16 Francis Street
Annapolis, MD 21401
410-260-3838
www.mdva.state.md.us

Commonwealth of Massachusetts
Department of Veterans' Services
600 Washington Street, Suite 1100
Boston, MA 02111
617-210-5480
www.mass.gov/veterans

Michigan Department of Military and Veterans Affairs
Michigan Army and Air National Guard
Joint Public Affairs Office
3411 Martin Luther King Jr. Boulevard
Lansing, MI 48906
517-481-8000
www.michigan.gov/dmva

Minnesota Department of Veterans Affairs
Veterans Service Building
2nd Floor—Room 206-C
20 W. 12th Street
St. Paul, MN 55155-2006
651-296-2562
www.mdva.state.mn.us

Mississippi State Veterans Affairs Board
P.O. Box 5947
Pearl, MS 39288-5947
601-576-4850
www.vab.state.ms.us

Missouri Veterans Commission
1719 Southridge Drive
Jefferson City, MO 65102-0147
573-751-3779
www.mvc.dps.mo.gov

Montana Veterans' Affairs
P.O. Box 4789
Fort Harrison, MT 59636-4789
406-324-3000
www.dma.mt.gov/mvad

Nebraska Department of Veterans' Affairs
P.O. Box 95083
301 Centennial Mall South, 6th Floor
Lincoln, NE 68509-5083
402-471-2458
www.vets.state.ne.us

Nevada Office of Veterans Services
1201 Terminal Way, Room 215
Reno, NV 89502
775-688-1653
www.veterans.nv.gov

New Hampshire State Veterans Council
275 Chestnut Street, Room 577
Manchester, NH 03101-2411
603-624-9230
www.nh.gov/nhveterans

State of New Jersey Department of Military & Veterans Affairs
P.O. Box 340
Trenton, NJ 08625-0340
888-8NJ-VETS
www.nj.gov/military/veterans

New Mexico Department of Veterans Services
Bataan Memorial Building
300 Galisteo, Room 142
Santa Fe, NM 87504
505-827-6300
www.dvs.state.nm.us

New York Division of Veterans' Affairs
5 Empire State Plaza, Suite 2836
Albany, NY 12223-1551
888-838-7697
www.veterans.state.ny.us

North Carolina Division of Veterans Affairs
1315 Mail Service Center
Albemarle Building, Suite 1065
Raleigh, NC 27699-1315
919-733-3851
www.doa.state.nc.us/vets/va.htm

North Dakota Department of Veterans' Affairs
P.O. Box 9003
Fargo, ND 58106-9003
701-239-7165
www.nd.gov/veterans

Ohio Governor's Office of Veterans Affairs
77 S. High Street
30th Floor
Columbus, OH 43215
614-644-0898
www.veteransaffairs.ohio.gov/contact.htm

Oklahoma Department of Veterans Affairs
2311 N. Central
Oklahoma City, OK 73105
405-521-3684
www.odva.state.ok.us

Oregon Department of Veterans' Affairs
700 Summer Street NE
Salem, OR 97301-1285
503-373-2000
www.odva.state.or.us

Pennsylvania Bureau for Veterans Affairs
Building S-0-47, FTIG
Annville, PA 17003
800-547-2838
www.dmva.state.pa.us

Puerto Rico Public Advocate for Veterans Affairs
Apartado 11737
Fernandez Juncos Station
San Juan, PR 00910-1737
787-758-5760
www.nasdva.com/puertorico.html

Rhode Island Division of Veterans Affairs
480 Metacom Avenue
Bristol, RI 02809
401-462-0324
www.dhs.state.ri.us/dhs/dvetaff.htm

South Carolina Office of Veterans' Affairs
1205 Pendleton Street, Suite 369
Columbia, SC 29201
803-734-0200
www.govoepp.state.sc.us/va/contact.html

South Dakota Department of Military & Veterans Affairs
425 E. Capitol Avenue
Pierre, SD 57501-5070
605-773-3269
www.state.sd.us/applications/MV91MVAInternetRewrite/default.asp

Tennessee Department of Veterans Affairs
215 Eighth Avenue North
Nashville, TN 37243
615-741-6663
www.state.tn.us/veteran

Texas Veterans Commission
P.O. Box 12277
Austin, TX 78711-2277
800-252-8387
www.tvc.state.tx.us

Utah Division of Veteran's Affairs
550 Foothill Boulevard Suite 202
Salt Lake City, UT 84108
801-326-2372
www.veterans.utah.gov

Vermont Office of Veterans Affairs
118 State Street
Montpelier, VT 05620
802-828-3379
www.va.state.vt.us

Virgin Islands Division of Veterans' Affairs
1013 Estate Richmond
Christiansted, St. Croix, VI 00820-4349
340-773-6663
www.nasdva.com/usvirginislands.html

Virginia Department of Veterans Services
900 E. Main Street
Richmond, VA 23219
804-786-0286
www.dvs.virginia.gov

Washington State Department of Veterans Affairs
P.O. Box 41150
Olympia, WA 98504
360-725-2200
www.dva.wa.gov

West Virginia Division of Veterans' Affairs
1321 Plaza East, Suite 101
Charleston, WV 25301-1400
304-558-3661
www.wvs.state.wv.us/va/

Wisconsin Department of Veterans Affairs
30 W. Mifflin Street
Madison, WI 53703
608-266-1311
www.dva.state.wi.us

Wyoming Veterans Commission
5905 CY Avenue
Casper, WY 82604
307-265-7372
www.wy.ngb.army.mil/veterans.asp

APPENDIX I

VA State Approving Agencies

In order for a veteran to use his Montgomery GI Bill benefits for education, the school and specific program must have been approved by the applicable VA State Approving Agency. For more information on education benefits, see Chapter 9.

Alabama Department of Postsecondary Education
401 Adams Avenue, Suite 280
P.O. Box 302130
Montgomery, AL 36130-2130
334-242-2979

Alaska DMVA Department of Veterans Affairs
Alaska State Approving Agency
P.O. Box 5800
Fort Richardson, AK 99505-5800
907-428-6513

Arizona Department of Veterans' Services
3839 N. 3rd Street, Suite 108
Phoenix, AZ 85012-2068
602-255-5395

Arkansas State Approving Agency for Veterans Training Department of Workforce Education
Luther S. Hardin Building, 6th Floor
Three Capitol Mall
Little Rock, AR 72201-1083
501-324-9473

State of California; Bureau of Private Postsecondary and Vocational Education
1625 N. Market Boulevard, Suite S-202
Sacramento, CA 95834
916-574-7779

Colorado State Approving Agency
Veterans Education and Training
9101 E. Lowry Boulevard
Denver, CO 80230-6011
303-595-1622

Connecticut Department of Higher Education
61 Woodland Street
Hartford, CT 06105-2326
860-947-1816

Delaware State Approving Agency; Professional Accountability
Department of Education
401 Federal Street, Suite 2
Dover, DE 19901
302-739-4686

District of Columbia
VA Regional Office
1722 I Street NW
Washington, DC 20421
202-530-9102

Florida Bureau of State Approving for Veterans' Training
Florida Department of Veterans' Affairs
9500 Bay Pines Boulevard, Room 214;
P.O. Box 31003
St. Petersburg, FL 33731
727-319-7401

Georgia State Approving Agency
Department of Veterans' Services
Floyd Veterans' Memorial Building, Suite E-960
Atlanta, GA 30334-4800
404-656-2306

Hawaii State Post-Secondary Education Commission
State Approving Agency for Veterans Training
Administrative Service Building 1, Room 105
2442 Campus Road
Honolulu, HI 96822
808-956-6624

Idaho State Department of Education
Veterans Education/Proprietary Schools
650 W. State Street
P.O. Box 83720
Boise, ID 83720-0027
208-332-6977

Illinois Department of Veterans' Affairs
833 South Spring Street
P.O. Box 19432
Springfield, IL 62794-9432
217-782-7838

Indiana Department of Veterans Affairs
302 Washington Street, Room E120
Indianapolis, IN 46204-2738
317-232-3917

Iowa Veterans and Military Education
Iowa Department of Education
Grimes State Office Building
E. 14th and Grand
Des Moines, IA 50319-0146
515-281-3516

Kansas Commission on Veterans' Affairs
Jayhawk Towers, Suite 701
700 Jackson Street
Topeka, KS 66603
785-296-7465

Kentucky Approving Agency for Veterans Education
300 N. Main Street
Versailles, KY 40383
859-256-3242

Louisiana Department of Veterans Affairs
Veterans Education and Training/ SAA
1885 Wooddale Boulevard
P.O. Box 94095
Baton Rouge, LA 70804-9095
225-922-0500, Ext. 207

Maine State Approving Agency for Veterans Education Program
University of Maine System
10F Cross Road
P.O. Box 355
Winthrop, ME 04364
207-377-4661

Maryland Higher Education Commission
839 Bestgate Road, Suite 400
Annapolis, MD 21401-3013
410-260-4532

Massachusetts Board of Higher Education
Office of Veterans Education
454 Broadway, Suite 200
Revere, MA 02151
617-727-9420, Ext. 1325

Michigan Department of Labor and Economic Growth
Office of Postsecondary Services
Victor Office Center, 3rd Floor
201 North Washington Square
Lansing, MI 48913
517-241-6806

Minnesota Department of Labor & Industry
Division of Apprenticeship
443 Lafayette Road N.
St. Paul, MN 55155-4303
651-296-1038

Mississippi State Veterans Affairs Commission
3466 Highway 80 E.
P.O. Box 5947
Pearl, MS 39288-5947
601-576-4867

Missouri Veterans' Education and Training Section
State Department of Elementary & Secondary Education
P.O. Box 480
Jefferson City, MO 65102-0480
573-751-3487

Montana Veterans Education
Office of Public Instruction
P.O. Box 202501
Helena, MT 59620-2501
406-444-4437

Nebraska Private Postsecondary Career Schools & Veterans Education
Nebraska Department of Education
301 Centennial Mall South
P.O. Box 94987
Lincoln, NE 68509-4987
402-471-4825

Nevada Commission on Postsecondary Education
1820 E. Sahara Avenue, Suite 111
Las Vegas, NV 89104
702-486-7330

State of New Hampshire Postsecondary Education Commission
Veterans State Approvals; Career School Licensing
3 Barrell Court, Suite 300
Concord, NH 03301-8543
603-271-2555, Ext. 353

New Jersey Department of Military and Veterans Affairs/SAA
Eggert Crossing Road
P.O. Box 340
Trenton, NJ 08625-0340
609-530-6849/6852

New Mexico Department of Veterans' Services
State Approving Agency for Veterans Education
500 Gold SW
Albuquerque, NM 87102
505-346-4873

New York Bureau of Veterans Education
Division of Veterans Affairs
116 W. 32nd Street, 5th Floor
New York, NY 10001
212-564-8414

North Carolina State Approving Agency
120 Penmarc Drive, Suite 103
Raleigh, NC 27603-2434
919-733-7535

North Dakota State Approving Agency
Kirkwood Office Tower, Suite 206
919 S. 7th Street
Bismarck, ND 58504-5881
701-328-9661

Ohio Department of Education
Division of Career-Technical & Adult Education State Approving Agency for Veterans Training
25 S. Front Street, Mail Stop 615
Columbus, OH 43215-4183
614-466-8722

Oklahoma State Accrediting Agency
P.O. Box 53067; Capitol Station
Oklahoma City, OK 73152
405 521 3156

Oregon Office of Educational Improvement & Innovation
Oregon Department of Education
Public Service Building
255 Capitol Street NE
Salem, OR 97310
503-947-5727

Pennsylvania Division of Veterans/Military Education
Pennsylvania Department of Education
333 Market Street, 12th Floor
Harrisburg, PA 17126-0333
717-787-2414

Puerto Rico State Approving Agency
Department of Education
P.O. Box 190759
San Juan, PR 00919-0759
787-754-0884

Rhode Island Proprietary/Veterans Education
Office of Higher Education
301 Promenade Street
Providence, RI 02908-5748
401-222-6560, Ext. 134

South Carolina Student Services Division
South Carolina Commission of Higher Education
1333 Main Street, Suite 200
Columbia, SC 29201
803-737-2244

South Dakota Veterans' Education
South Dakota Division of Veterans Affairs
Sailors Building
500 E. Capitol Avenue
Pierre, SD 57501-5070
605-773-3648

Tennessee Veterans' Education
Higher Education Commission
Parkway Towers, Suite 1900
404 James Robertson Parkway
Nashville, TN 37243-0830
615-741-7569

Texas Career Schools and Veterans Education
Texas Workforce Commission
101 E. 15th Street, Room 202-T
Austin, TX 78778-0001
877-898-3833

Utah State Approving Agency for Veterans Education
Utah State Board of Regents
60 S. 400 West
Salt Lake City, UT 84101-1284
801-321-7133

Vermont Department of Education
State Office Building
120 State Street
Montpelier, VT 05620-2501
802-828-5139

Virginia Department of Veterans Services
900 E. Main Street; Ground Floor, East Wing
Richmond, VA 23219
804-225-2721

Washington Higher Education Coordinating Board
917 Lakeridge Way
P.O. Box 43450
Olympia, WA 98504-3430
360-753-7866

West Virginia Veterans State Approving Agency
Higher Education Policy Commission
1018 Kanawha Boulevard E, Suite 700
Charleston, WV 25301
304-558-0263

Wisconsin Department of Workforce Development
Division of Workforce Excellence Bureau of Apprenticeship Standards
201 E. Washington Avenue, Room 229
P.O. Box 7972
Madison, WI 53707
608-266-3133

Wyoming Office of the Adjutant General
5500 Bishop Boulevard
Cheyenne, WY 82009-3320
307-772-5053

APPENDIX J

SBA Veteran Business Development Offices

The Small Business Administration has state offices to assist veterans who want to pursue entrepreneur opportunities. For more information, see Chapter 11.

Alabama

Alabama District Office
801 Tom Martin Drive, Suite 201
Birmingham, AL 35211
205-290-7805

Alaska

Alaska District Office
510 L Street, Suite 310
Anchorage, AK 99501-3192
907-271-4841

Arizona

Arizona District Office
2828 N. Central Avenue, Suite 800
Phoenix, AZ 85004-1903
602-745-7230

Arkansas

Arkansas District Office
2120 River Front Drive, Room 100
Little Rock, AR 72202
501-324-5871, Ext. 239

California

Fresno District Office
2719 N. Air Fresno Drive, Suite 200
Fresno, CA 93727-1547
559-487-5791, Ext. 104

Los Angeles District Office
330 N. Brand Boulevard, Suite 1200
Glendale, CA 91203-2304
818-552-3224

Sacramento District Office
650 Capitol Mall, Suite 7-500
Sacramento, CA 65814
916-930-3721

San Diego District Office
550 W. C Street, Suite 550
San Diego, CA 92101-3500
619-557-7250, Ext. 1159

San Francisco District Office
455 Market Street, 6th Floor
San Francisco, CA 94105
415-744-8477

Santa Ana District Office
200 W. Santa Ana Boulevard, Suite 700
Santa Ana, CA 92701
714-560-7455

Colorado

Colorado District Office
721 19th Street, Suite 426
Denver, CO 80202
303-844-2607, Ext. 226

Connecticut

Connecticut District Office
330 Main Street, 2nd Floor
Hartford, CT 06106-1800
860-240-4657

Delaware

Delaware District Office
1007 N. Orange Street, Suite 1120
Wilmington, DE 19801-1239
302-573-6294, Ext. 223

District of Columbia

Washington District Office
740 15th Street, NW
Washington, DC 20005
202-272-0361

Florida

North Florida District Office
7825 Baymeadows Way
Suite 100B
Jacksonville, FL 32256-7504
904-443-1922

Miami District Office
100 S. Biscayne Boulevard; 7th Floor
Miami, FL 33131
305-536-5521

Georgia

Georgia District Office
Harris Tower
233 Peachtree Street, Suite 1900
Atlanta, GA 30303
404-331-0100, Ext. 609

Guam

Guam Branch Office
400 Route 8, Suite 302
Hagatna, Guam 96910-2003
671-472-7277

Hawaii

Hawaii District Office
300 Ala Moana Boulevard, Room 2-235
Honolulu, HI 96850-4981
808-541-3024

Idaho

Boise District Office
380 E. Parkcenter Boulevard, Suite 380
Boise, ID 83706
208-334-1696, Ext. 333

Illinois

Chicago District Office
500 W. Madison Street, Room 1250
Chicago, IL 60661
312-886-4208

Indiana

Indiana District Office
8500 Keyston Crossing, Suite 400
Indianapolis, IN 46240
317-226-7272, Ext. 232

Iowa

Des Moines District Office
210 Walnut Street, Room 749
Des Moines, IA 50309-2186
515-284-4554

Kansas

Wichita District Office
271 W. 3rd Street, N
Suite 2500
Wichita, KS 67202-1212
316-269-6273, Ext. 252

Kentucky

Louisville District Office
Romano Mazzoli Federal Bldg, Room 188
600 Dr. Martin Luther King Jr. Place
Louisville, KY 40202-2254
502-582-5588, Ext. 237

Louisiana

Louisiana District Office
365 Canal Street, Suite 2820
New Orleans, LA 70130
504-589-6685

Maine

Maine District Office
Edmund S. Muskie Federal Building, Room 512
68 Sewall Street
Augusta, ME 04330
207-622-8555

Maryland

Baltimore District Office
10 S. Howard Street, Suite 6220
Baltimore, MD 21201-2525
410-962-6195, Ext. 337

Massachusetts

Massachusetts District Office
10 Causeway Street, Room 265
Boston, MA 02222-1093
617-565-5562

Michigan

Michigan District Office
477 Michigan Avenue, Room 515
Detroit, MI 48266
313-226-6075, Ext. 221

Minnesota

Minnesota District Office
100 N. 6th Street, Suite 210-C
Minneapolis, MN 55403-1525
612-370-2334

Mississippi

Gulfport Branch Office
Hancock Bank Plaza
2510 14th Street, Suite 101
Gulfport, MS 39501
228-863-4449, Ext. 23

Missouri

Kansas City District Office
323 W. 8th Street, Suite 501
Kansas City, MO 64105
816-426-4907

Springfield District Office
830 E. Primrose Street, Suite 101
Springfield, MO 65807-5254
417-890-8501, Ext. 209

St. Louis District Office
200 N. Broadway, Suite 1500
St. Louis, MO 63102
314-539-6600, Ext. 245

Montana

Montana District Office
10 W. 15th Street, Suite 1100
Helena, MT 59626
406-441-1084, Ext. 130

Nebraska

Nebraska District Office
11145 Mill Valley
Omaha, NE 68154-3949
402-221-7208, Ext. 252

Nevada

Veterans Business Development Office
400 S. Fourth Street, Suite 250
Las Vegas, NV 89101
702-388-6684

New Hampshire

New Hampshire District Office
JC Cleveland Federal Building
55 Pleasant Street, Suite 3101
Concord, NH 03301
603-225-1601

New Jersey

New Jersey District Office
Two Gateway Center, 15th Floor
Newark, NJ 07102
973-645-6049

New Mexico

New Mexico District Office
625 Silver SW, Suite 320
Albuquerque, NM 87102
505-248-8238

New York

Albany District Office
Chamber of Commerce
1 Computer Drive S.
Albany, NY 12205
518-446-1118, Ext. 231

Elmira Branch Office
333 E. Water Street, 4th Floor
Elmira, NY 14901
607-734-8130, Ext. 30

Buffalo District Office
130 S. Elmwood Avenue, Suite 540
Buffalo, NY 14202
716-551-4301, Ext. 307

New York District Office
26 Federal Plaza, Room 3100
New York, NY 10278
212-264-2846

Syracuse District Office
401 S. Salina Street, 5th Floor
Syracuse, NY 13203-2413
315-471-9393, Ext. 252

North Carolina

North Carolina District Office
6302 Fairview Road, Suite 300
Charlotte, NC 28210-2227
704-344-6585, Ext. 1122

North Dakota

North Dakota District Office
P.O. Box 3086
Fargo, ND 58108-3086
701-239-5131, Ext. 215

Ohio

Cleveland District Office
1350 Euclid Avenue, Room 211
Cleveland, OH 44115-1815
216-522-4180, Ext. 212

Columbus District Office
401 N. Front Street, Suite 200
Columbus, OH 43215
614-469-6860, Ext. 241

Cincinnati District Office
550 Main Street, Room 2-522
Cincinnati, OH 45202
513-684-2814, Ext. 205

Oklahoma

Oklahoma District Office
301 N.W. 6th Street, Suite 116
Oklahoma City, OK 73102
405-609-8011

Oregon

Portland District Office
ODS Building
601 SW 2nd Avenue, Suite 950
Portland, OR 97204-3192
503-326-2586

Pennsylvania

Philadelphia District Office
Robert N.C. Nix Federal Building
900 Market Street, 5th Floor
Philadelphia, PA 19107
215-580-2706

Wilkes-Barre District Office
Stegmaier Building, Suite 407
Wilkes-Barre, PA 18702
215-580-2706

Pittsburgh District Office
411 7th Avenue, Suite 1450
Pittsburgh, PA 15219
412-395-6560, Ext. 106

Puerto Rico

Puerto Rico District Office
CitiBank Tower
252 Ponce De Leon Avenue, Suite 201
San Juan, PR 00918
787-766-5422

Rhode Island

Rhode Island District Office
380 Westminster Street, Room 511
Providence, RI 02903
401-528-4561, Ext. 4576

South Carolina

South Carolina District Office
1835 Assembly Street, Room 1425
Columbia, SC 29201
803-765-5339

South Dakota

South Dakota District Office
2329 N. Career Avenue, Suite 105
Sioux Falls, SD 57107
605-330-4243, Ext. 39

Tennessee

Tennessee District Office
50 Vantage Way, Suite 201
Nashville, TN 37228
615-736-7176

Texas

El Paso District Office
10737 Gateway West, Suite 320
El Paso, TX 79935
915-633-7025

Dallas/Fort Worth District Office
4300 Amon Carter Boulevard,
Suite 114
Fort Worth, TX 76155
817-684-5517

Houston District Office
8701 S. Gessner Drive, Suite 1200
Houston, TX 77074
713-773-6500, Ext. 242

Lower Rio Grande Valley District Office
222 E. Van Buren, Suite 500
Harlingen, TX 78550-6855
956-427-8533, Ext. 225

Lubbock District Office
1205 Texas Avenue, Room 408
Lubbock, TX 79401-2693
806-472-7462, Ext. 110

San Antonio District Office
17319 San Pedro Building 2, Suite 200
San Antonio, TX 78232
210-403-5926

Utah

Utah District Office
125 S. State Street, Room 2231
Salt Lake City, UT 84138
801-524-3218

Vermont

Montpelier Vermont District Office
87 State Street, Room 205
Montpelier, VT 05602
802-828-4422, Ext. 207

Virginia

Richmond District Office
400 N. 8th Street, Suite 1150
Richmond, VA 23240
804-771-2400, Ext. 132

Washington

Seattle District Office
2401 4th Avenue, Suite 450
Seattle, WA, 98121
206-553-7082

Spokane District Office
801 W. Riverside Avenue, Suite 200
Spokane, WA 99201-0901
206-553-7082

West Virginia

Charleston District Office
320 W. Pike Street, Suite 330
Clarksburg, WV 26301
304-623-5631, Ext. 231

Wisconsin

Wisconsin District—Milwaukee Office
310 W. Wisconsin Street, Suite 400
Milwaukee, WI 53203
414-297-1178

Wyoming

Wyoming District Office
100 E. B Street, Room 4001
P.O. Box 44001
Casper, WY 82604
307-261-6523

APPENDIX K

State Benefits and Discounts Offered to Veterans

Following is an overview of the benefits and discounts offered by individual states to resident veterans. For more information, see the websites of the state VA offices, Appendix H.

Alabama

G.I. Dependents' Scholarship Program

Entitlement: Four standard academic years or part-time equivalent at any Alabama *state-supported institution* of higher learning or a prescribed course of study at any Alabama state-supported technical school without payment of any tuition, required textbooks, or instructional fees.

Alaska

Veterans Land Discount/Purchase Preference

The Veterans Land Discount program allows certain veterans to a 25 percent discount on the purchase price of state residential/recreational land. A fact sheet is available on benefits administered by the Alaska Department of Natural Resources, Division of Mining, Land and Water Management: www.dnr.state.ak.us/mlw/factsht/vet prog.pdf.

Property Tax Exemptions

Real property owned and occupied as the primary residence and permanent place of abode by a qualified disabled veteran, whose disability was incurred or aggravated in the line of duty and whose disability has been rated as 50 percent or more by the military service or VA, is exempt from taxation on the first $150,000 of assessed valuation. Contact your local municipal tax assessor's office by March 15 for exemption for current year.

Veteran Housing and Residential Loans

The Alaska Housing Finance Corporation (AHFC) administers the Veterans Mortgage Program, which offers financing for qualified veterans at lower interest rates. For details see www.AHFC.state.ak.us (go to Loan Programs, then select Veterans Mortgage Program).

Hunting and Fishing Licenses

Resident hunting and sport fishing licenses are available at no charge to honorably discharged veterans with a 50 percent or greater service-connected disability and Alaska residency. Applicants must have lived in Alaska for 12 consecutive months immediately preceding the application. Veterans may obtain an application by calling 907-465-2376, or writing State of Alaska, Department of Fish and Game, Licensing Section, P.O. Box 25525, Juneau, AK 99802.

State Camping Pass

The legislature granted Disabled Alaskan Veterans (DAV) the right to receive one Alaska State Park Camping Pass free of charge. The DAV Camping Pass, which is valid in all developed Alaska State Park campgrounds, is good for two years. To receive a free DAV camping pass, an eligible disabled veteran must present proof of a service-connected disability and Alaska residency at either the Anchorage or Fairbanks DNR Public Information centers. Information on obtaining either the card or the letter can be found through the local Veterans' Affairs office or calling 1-800-827-1000.

Alaska Marine Highway Pass

A one-year pass on the ferries of the Alaska Marine Highway is available for veterans having a service-related disability. This pass entitles the disabled passenger and an attendant (if required by a physician) to travel at 50 percent of the regular passenger fare, between Alaska ports only, on all vessels, year-round. To request a pass application, call 1-800-642-0066 or write Alaska Marine Highway System, Attention: Pass Desk, 1591 Glacier Avenue, Juneau, Alaska 99801.

Free Tuition for Spouse or Dependent of Armed Services Member

The spouse or dependent of an armed services member who died in the line of duty or who died as a result of injuries sustained while in the line of duty or who was listed by the Department of Defense as a Prisoner of War or as Missing in Action is entitled to a waiver of undergraduate tuition and fees. The students must be in good standing in a state-supported educational institution physically located within Alaska. Contact: University of Alaska Anchorage, 3901 Old Seward Highway, Anchorage, AK 99508, 907-786-1586; University of Alaska Fairbanks, P.O. Box 756630, Fairbanks, AK 99775, 907-474-7256; University of Alaska Southeast, 11120 Glacier Highway, Juneau, AK 99801, 907-465-6255.

Arkansas

Homestead and Personal Property Tax Exemption

Arkansas veterans who have been rated, by the VA, as 100 percent service-connected disabled (permanent and total) or awarded Special Monthly Compensation for loss or loss of use of one or more limbs, and/or total blindness in one or both eyes, are entitled to exemption of homestead and personal property tax. Widows, so long as they do not remarry, dependent children, during their minority, continue this entitlement. Widows, so long as they do not remarry, dependent children, during their minority, are also eligible for this entitlement if the veteran was killed or died in the scope of his military duties, is missing in action, or died from service-connected causes as certified by the VA.

Gross Receipt of Tax Exemption

Tax exemption on gross proceeds derived from the sale of motor vehicles and adaptive equipment to disabled veterans who have purchased the vehicles or equipment with the financial assistance of the VA as provided under 38 U. S. C. 1901-1905 (AR Code 26-52-401 (7) et. seq.).

Income Tax Exemption

Provides an exemption of the first $6,000 of service pay or retired pay for members of the armed forces to include Reserve components or for retired members who are residents of the State of Arkansas.

Arkansas Department of Parks and Tourism

Arkansas resident veterans permanently service-connected at a 100 percent disability rate may camp for half price in Arkansas state parks.

Arkansas Game and Fish Commission

Resident three-year Disability Fishing License—RDC ($10.50) entitles all 100 percent totally and permanently disabled persons privileges of the Resident Sportsman's License (hunting) and the Resident Fisheries Conservation License (fishing).

Educational Benefits

Arkansas Department of Higher Education (ADHE) has the authority to provide free tuition and fees at any state-supported college, university, technical school, or vocational school; to the wife and children of any Arkansan who has been declared to be a prisoner of war or placed in a missing-in-action status since January 1, 1960. The same provisions apply to the surviving spouse and children of any Arkansas resident killed in action since 1960.

License Plates

The Revenue Division will provide (upon receipt of proper certification letters) a number of special privileges and benefits for Arkansas residents, including special license plates for Congressional Medal of Honor recipients, Purple Heart recipients, Ex-Prisoners of War, Disabled Veterans, Pearl Harbor Survivors, Armed Forces Retired, and Military Reserve.

California

College Tuition Fee Waivers for Veterans' Dependents

Waiver of mandatory system-wide tuition and fees at any State of California community college, California state university, or university of California campus. The spouse, registered domestic partner, child (under the age of 27) or unmarried surviving spouse of a veteran who is totally service-connected disabled, or who has died of service-connected causes may qualify. The child of a veteran who has a permanent service-connected disability also qualifies, although the child's income and value of support provided by a parent cannot exceed the national poverty level. Information and an application form is available on this site at www.cdva.ca.gov/service/feewaiver.asp.

Property Tax Exemptions

Property tax exemptions on the assessed value of a home of: (a) up to $103,107 if the total household income from all sources is over $46,302 per year, or (b) up to $154,661 if the total household income from all sources is under $46,302 per year. Those eligible are wartime veterans who are in receipt of service-connected disability compensation at the totally disabled rate; unmarried surviving spouses or registered domestic partners of veterans who are in receipt of service-connected death benefits; wartime veterans who are service-connected for loss of the use of two or more limbs; wartime veterans who are service-connected for blindness.

Motor Vehicle Registration Fees Waived

Waiver of registration fees and free license plates for one passenger motor vehicle, or one motorcycle, or one commercial motor vehicle of less than 8,001 pounds unladen weight. Medal of Honor recipients, American ex-prisoners of war, and disabled veterans are eligible. Applications and necessary documentation should be mailed to Department of Motor Vehicles, P.O. Box 932345, Sacramento, CA 94232, 1-800-777-0133, www.dmv.ca.gov.

Fishing and Hunting Licenses

Reduced annual fees for fishing and hunting licenses. Any veteran with a 50 percent or greater service-connected disability is eligible. First-time applicants must submit proof of their service-connected disability from the USDVA to: The California Department of Fish and Game, License and Revenue Branch, 3211 S Street, Sacramento, CA 95815, 916-227-2245, www.dfg.ca.gov/.

State Parks and Recreation Pass

A lifetime State of California Parks pass for only $3.50. Any veteran with a service-connected disability rated at 50 percent or greater, or a former prisoner of war is eligible. To apply by mail, a veteran should submit (1) a completed Department of Parks and Recreation form DPR 619; (2) a letter from the USDVA verifying a service-connected disability rated at 50 percent or greater, or former Prisoner of War status; (3) a copy of the veteran's drivers license to verify California residency; and (4) a check or money order for $3.50 made payable to the Department of Parks and Recreation. California Department of Parks and Recreation, Field Services Division, P.O. Box 942896, Sacramento, CA 94296-0001, 916-653-4272, www.parks.ca.gov/.

Colorado

Tax Exemption

There is excluded from gross income, retirement pay received by members of the armed forces, to the extent it is excluded from Federal income tax and not to exceed $20,000 in any one taxable year.

License Plates

The state provides plates at no cost to certain veterans, including: recipients of the Medal of Honor, recipients of the Purple Heart, to certain disabled wartime veterans, special disabled veterans license plates, and special license plates for former POWs. Plates for honorably discharged veterans may be purchased for nominal fee.

Motor Vehicles

No fee shall be charged to certain disabled veterans or ex-POWs who have established their right to benefits under public laws. Applies to subsequent vehicles, but only one at a time.

Fishing license

No fee to a member of the armed forces stationed as a resident patient at a military hospital or convalescent station, or any resident patient at a USDVA hospital located within the state, nor for any veteran who is permanently and totally disabled.

Small Game Hunting and Fishing License

Resident veteran with a service-connected disability of 60 percent or more is eligible for a free lifetime combination small game hunting and fishing license.

Florida

Property tax discount on homestead property owned by eligible veterans. To be eligible, a veteran must have an honorable discharge from military service, be at least 65 years old, be partially disabled with a permanent service-connected disability all or a portion of which must be combat related, and must have been a Florida resident at the time of entering military service. This discount is in addition to any other exemptions veterans now receive.

Georgia

Free Driver's License

A driver's license or state ID card is issued free to veterans who were Georgia residents when they entered active-duty status and are Georgia residents at the time of application or who have been residents of Georgia for at least two years immediately preceding the date of application for the license.

Homestead Tax

Certain disabled veterans and certain widows/widowers, or minor children, are allowed the maximum amount, which may be granted under Section 2102 of Title 38 of the United States Code.

Sales Tax on Vehicles

A disabled veteran who receives a VA grant for the purchase and special adapting of a vehicle is exempt from paying the state sales tax on the vehicle (only on the original grant).

Ad Valorem Tax on Vehicles

Exempt are veterans who are verified by VA to be 100 percent totally and permanently service-connected disabled and veterans who are receiving or who are entitled to receive statutory awards from VA for: (1) loss or permanent loss of use of one or both feet, (2) loss or permanent loss of use of one or both hands, (3) loss of sight in one or both eyes, or (4) permanent impairment of vision of both eyes to a prescribed degree. Exemption is granted on the vehicle the veteran owns or leases and upon which the free Handicapped Veterans (HV) motor vehicle license plate is attached.

Hunting and Fishing Licenses

Any veteran who is a legal resident of Georgia and who files with the Game and Fish Division, Department of Natural Resources, a letter from VA or a certificate from the Social Security Administration, Medicaid, Medicare, Railroad Retirement System, or a unit of Federal, state, or local government recognized by the Board of Natural Resources by rule or regulation stating that he or she is a totally and permanently disabled veteran is entitled to a lifetime honorary hunting and fishing license allowing the veteran to fish and hunt within the state without the payment of any fee. Persons who are at least 65 years old or who are rated totally blind also qualify.

Medal of Honor Tags

Special license plates are issued free to a veteran who is a legal resident of Georgia and who is a recipient of the Medal of Honor.

State Park Reduced Fees for Disabled Veterans

Any service-connected disabled veteran who was discharged under honorable conditions can visit/use state parks, historical sites and recreational areas at reduced rates.

Hawaii

Special Housing for Disabled Veterans

Payment by the state of up to $5,000 to each qualified, totally disabled veteran for the purpose of purchasing or remodeling a home to improve handicapped accessibility.

License Plates

For the same cost as regular license plates, qualified veterans can acquire distinctive veterans' license plates for their car or motorcycle.

Tax Exemptions

Applies to real property that is owned and occupied as a home by a totally disabled veteran or their widow(er). Also applies to passenger cars when they are owned by totally disabled veterans and subsidized by the Department of Veterans Affairs.

Illinois

Camping Fees

On any day of the week, disabled veterans or former prisoners of war will be charged reduced or no camping fee, depending on campsite.

Hunting and Fishing License

There is no fee for the hunting and fishing license for disabled veterans. The veteran may obtain this license by providing documentation of disability to the Illinois Department of Veterans' Affairs.

Indiana

Disabled Veteran Plates

Disabled veteran plates are the same as handicap plates in the State of Indiana. These are strictly limited to those individuals who have a serious mobility impairment due to a service-connected disability. Applications may be obtained from either the Bureau of Motor Vehicles (BMV) or the Indiana Department of Veterans Affairs. The Indiana Department of Veterans Affairs must verify the veteran's eligibility.

Ex-Prisoner of War Plates

The POW license plate is available to all ex–prisoners of war or to the surviving spouse of a deceased POW. Applications for these plates are available from the Indiana Department of Veterans Affairs. The Indiana Department of Veterans Affairs must verify the eligibility of the applicant.

Purple Heart Plates

Any Hoosier Veteran who has received the Purple Heart is authorized to have these special license plates. Applications may be obtained at the DMV or from the Indiana Department of Veterans Affairs. The veteran must present official documentation of the award, and the Indiana Department of Veterans Affairs must verify the veteran's eligibility.

Property Tax Deductions

Property tax deductions are available to disabled Hoosier Veterans under the following conditions: A $12,480 dollar deduction is available to veterans who served at least 90 days of honorable service AND are totally disabled (not necessarily service-connected but the disability must be evidenced by a U.S. Department of Veterans Affairs pension certificate) OR are at least 62 years old and 10 percent service-connected disabled. Note: This deduction is not available if the assessed value of the real property owned by the veteran is in excess of $113,000. A $24,960 tax deduction is available for veterans who served honorably in the armed forces during any period of wartime AND are at least 10 percent service-connected disabled. A $37,440 tax deduction is available for any veteran who (a) served honorably during any period of wartime, (b) is 100 percent service-connected-disabled, or (c) is at least 62 years of age with at least a 10 percent service-connected disability.

Remission of Fees (Free Tuition) for the Child(ren) of a Disabled Veteran

The natural or legally adopted child(ren) of a disabled veteran may be eligible for remission of fees (free tuition) at any state-supported postsecondary school or university in the State of Indiana. This applies at any age as long as the child was adopted by age 24 and the child is a resident of Indiana. The Remission of Fees is good for 124 semester hours of education and may be used for either undergraduate or graduate level work. The amount remitted is 100 percent of tuition and all mandatory fees.

Resident Veteran Hunting and Fishing License

Any Indiana resident who is classified as service-connected disabled by the U.S. Department of Veterans Affairs may purchase a license to hunt and fish in the State of Indiana for a reduced fee.

Louisiana

Free Hunting/Fishing Licenses

Louisiana statutes provide disabled veterans classified with a service-connected permanent disability, rated 50 percent or higher, and who are Louisiana residents, to be issued licenses to fish and hunt free of charge. Applications may be obtained and certified by contacting the local Parish Veterans Service Office.

Free Entrance to State Parks

Any Louisiana resident who is a veteran of the armed forces of the United States and who has suffered the amputation of a limb or who at any time has been awarded an allowance toward the purchase of an automobile by the U.S. Government or any Louisiana resident who is a veteran of the armed forces of the United States who, as the result of a service-connected disability, has been classified as 50 percent or more permanently disabled or permanent and total as a result of non-service-connected disabilities, shall be exempt from paying the day use entrance fee to any

Louisiana state park. Applications for this exemption may be obtained by contacting the local Parish Veterans Service Office.

Free "Purple Heart" License Plates

Free License Plate for recipients of the Purple Heart medal to be used in lieu of the regular motor vehicle registration plates. The recipient may be issued only one plate and such plate shall not be subject to renewal requirements applicable to regular numbered plates. A written request submitted with proof of receiving the Purple Heart should be sent to the Department of Public Safety. The surviving spouse may retain this plate in the event of the recipient's death. Vehicle Registration Bureau, P.O. Box 64886, Baton Rouge, LA 70896.

Maine

Hunting and Fishing License

A Maine resident who is a veteran with a service-connected disability evaluated at 100 percent, or is a veteran with a service-connected disability evaluated at 70 percent who has served in a combat zone during any armed conflict in which participants were exposed to war risk hazards, can obtain a complimentary license to fish, trap, or hunt (including archery, muzzle-loading, and pheasant stamps). The license can only be obtained from IF&W's main office in Augusta.

Disabled Veterans Access to State Parks

Any disabled veteran displaying on the veteran's motor vehicle special designating plates or placards issued in accordance with Title 29-A, section 523, subsections 1 and 2 is not required to pay a fee for admission to any state-owned park, camping area, or beach.

Massachusetts

Tuition Waiver for all Massachusetts Veterans to all State Colleges and Universities

Veterans of Massachusetts, as defined by M.G.L. ch. 4, s.7, clause 43, can be eligible for a tuition waiver at any state-supported course in an undergraduate degree program offered by a public college or university. To be eligible, a veteran must also be a legal resident of Massachusetts and he or she must not be in default of any Federal student loans.

Property Tax

Eligible veterans, spouses, and parents. To qualify, all *veterans* (and spouses where applicable) must

- Be certified at least 10 percent disabled by the U.S. Department of Veterans Affairs
- Be legal residents of Massachusetts
- Be occupying the property as his or her domicile on July 1 in the year of application
- Have lived in Massachusetts for at least six months prior to entering the service (spouses exempted) or
- Have lived in Massachusetts for five consecutive years immediately prior to filing for a property tax exemption.

Mississippi

Ad Valorem Tax

Service-connected, totally disabled (100 percent) American veterans who were honorably discharged from military service are exempt from all ad valorem taxes on homesteads of $7,500 or less in assessed value.

Hunting and Fishing Licenses

Veterans who have a total service-connected disability from the VA are not required to purchase a hunting or fishing license, but must have on their person proof of age, residency, and disability status while engaged in hunting or fishing.

State Retirement

Members of the State Public Employees Retirement System who served in the armed forces of the United States or who served in maritime service during periods of hostility during World War II shall be entitled to up to four (4) years credit for active duty in the armed forces or in such maritime service, provided they entered state service after discharge from the armed forces or after completion of such maritime service. Credit may be extended beyond four (4) years for those persons who can provide positive proof that they were retained in the armed forces or such maritime service during World War II by causes beyond his control and without opportunity for discharge.

Missouri

Free Automobile License Plates

Eligible include veterans who are rated 100 percent for service-connected disabilities, or in need of adaptive equipment, as well as Medal of Honor recipients, former POWs and widows of former POWs. Other veteran plates are available for a $15 fee.

Free Hunting/Fishing Licenses

For 60 percent or more rated service-connected veterans.

Tuition-Free Scholarships

Legislation passed in 1991 provides that certain surviving widows and children of Vietnam veterans may qualify to receive tuition-free scholarships to attend institutions of post-secondary education in Missouri. The veteran's death must be attributable to illness that could possibly be a result of exposure to toxic chemicals such as Agent Orange during the Vietnam conflict in order for the survivor to qualify.

Montana

Special Veteran Vehicle License Plate

Honorably discharged veterans and un-remarried deceased-veteran spouses are eligible. "Veteran" license plates are available for all U.S. military services, as well as plates denoting unique statuses such as a Purple Heart medal recipient, ex–prisoner of war, Pearl Harbor survivor, Legion of Valor, and certain levels of veteran disability. "Veteran" license plate sales fund the operations and maintenance for Montana's state veterans cemeteries.

Nebraska

Waiver of Tuition

The University of Nebraska, the state colleges, and community colleges on behalf of any eligible child, spouse, widow or widower that meets the following requirements may waive tuition. He or she is a resident of this state and meets the appropriate institutions' requirements for paying in-state tuition. He or she has a parent, stepparent, or spouse who was a member of the armed forces of the United States and who: (1) died of a service-connected disability, (2) died subsequent to discharge as a result of injury or illness sustained while in service, (3) is permanently and totally disabled as a result of military service, or (4) is classified as missing in action or as a prisoner of war during armed hostilities after August 4, 1964. The waiver shall be valid for one degree, diploma, or certificate from a community college and one baccalaureate degree. Applications are submitted to the Department of Veterans' Affairs by contacting the county Veterans Service Officer nearest the applicant's place of residence.

Nevada

Hunting and Fishing License

The State of Nevada Wildlife Division will issue free hunting and fishing licenses to any honorably separated veteran who has a service-connected disability of 50 percent or more. For more information, contact the Nevada Wildlife Division at 775-688-1500 in Reno, 702-486-5127 in Las Vegas, and 775-738-5332 in Elko.

Veterans Tax Exemption

An annual tax exemption is available to any veteran with wartime service (including in-theater service during the Persian Gulf War, Afghanistan, and Iraqi wars). To obtain this exemption, take a copy of your DD214 or discharge papers to your local county assessor. The exemption can be applied to a veteran's vehicle privilege tax or real property tax. The exemption cannot be split between the two. To obtain the exact amount of this benefit, contact your county assessor. Nevada offers a property tax exemption to any veteran with a service-connected disability of 60 percent or more. The amounts of exemption that are or will be available to disabled veterans varies from $6,250 to $20,000 of assessed valuation, depending on the percentage of disability and the year filed. To qualify, the veteran must have an honorable separation from the service and be a resident of Nevada. The widow or widower of a disabled veteran, who was eligible for this exemption at the time of his or her death, may also be eligible to receive this exemption.

New Hampshire

Education

The child of a missing person who was domiciled in this state serving in or with the U.S. Armed Forces after February 28, 1961, is entitled to free tuition at vocational-technical college as long as said missing person is so reported/listed as missing, captured, and so forth. Children of military members who die in service during wartime, and children of certain wartime veterans who die from a service-connected disability, may qualify for free tuition at New Hampshire public institutions of higher learning. A scholarship for board, room, rent, books, and supplies up to $2,500 per year for a period of no more than four years at such educational institutions may be furnished to these children if they are in need of financial assistance.

License Fee Exemption

Honorably discharged veterans who are residents of New Hampshire and who are permanently and totally disabled from service-connected disability may be issued a free perpetual Fish and Game License.

State Park Admission

NH veterans with any VA service-connected disability rating shall not be charged a fee for day-use admission to NH state parks.

Tax Exemption

Property owned and operated by certain veterans' organizations or departments, local chapters or posts shall be exempt from taxation. Certain wartime veterans, their wives or widows may be eligible for a property tax credit of $50 ($100 if both are eligible veterans). Cities/towns may vote to adopt a higher tax credit of up to $500. The widow of a veteran who was killed while on active duty in the military may be eligible for a tax credit of between $700 and $2,000 on real estate or personal property. There is a $700 tax credit on real estate occupied as principal place of abode by a permanently and totally disabled service-connected veteran, double amputee or paraplegic, or un-remarried surviving spouse. Cities and towns may vote to adopt a higher tax credit of up to $2,000. A permanently and totally disabled veteran who is blind, paraplegic, or a double amputee as a result of service connection and who owns a specially adapted homestead acquired with the assistance of the U.S. Department of Veterans Affairs, or with proceeds from the sale of any previous homestead acquired with the assistance of the U.S. Department of Veterans Affairs, shall be exempt from all taxation on the homestead. The veteran's surviving spouse shall also be exempt from all taxation on the homestead.

Training

Qualified veterans will be granted priority in obtaining training that is funded in whole or part by the Federal government or the State of New Hampshire.

Veterans License Plate

Veterans honorably discharged from the U.S. Armed Forces may be issued a special license plate.

New Jersey

POW and MIA Tuition Benefits

Free undergraduate college tuition is available to any child born or adopted before, during, or after the period of time his or her parent was officially declared a prisoner of war (POW) or person missing in action (MIA) after January 1, 1960. The POW-MIA must have been a New Jersey resident at the time he or she entered the service or whose official residence is in New Jersey. The child must attend either a public or private institution in New Jersey.

War Orphans Tuition Assistance

Children of those service personnel who died while in the military or due to service-connected disabilities, or who are officially listed as missing in action by the U.S. Department of Defense may claim $500 per year for four years of college or equivalent training. To qualify, the child must be a resident of New Jersey for at least one year immediately preceding the filing of the application and be between the ages of 16 and 21 at the time of application. The veteran must have been a state resident.

Vietnam Veterans Tuition Credit Program

The Vietnam Veterans Tuition Credit Program provides additional education benefits to veterans eligible for Federally funded education programs and who served on active duty from December 31, 1960, to May 7, 1975, and who were legal residents of New Jersey at the time of induction into the armed forces or at the time of discharge from active service or for a period not less than one year prior to making application. The amount of the award is $400 annually or $200 per semester for full-time attendance and $100 per semester for part-time.

Tuition Assistance

Pays up to 75 percent of tuition costs at accredited schools only with a maximum of $100 per undergraduate credit and a maximum of $170 per graduate credit. Tuition assistance may *not* be used together with any other Federal program (i.e., the GI Bill).

Fishing and Hunting Licenses

The NJ Division of Fish and Wildlife will annually issue the following items free to each qualified disabled veteran: licenses for a firearm, bow and arrow, fishing or all around hunting license, a pheasant and quail stamp, a state duck stamp, and a trout stamp. In addition, disabled veterans may apply for free permits: one bow and arrow deer permit, one firearm (muzzleloader or shotgun) deer permit, one spring and one fall turkey permit for use during applicable hunting season. (Note: Special deer and turkey permit applications will be available by mail from the Trenton office. All rules and regulations pertaining to the lottery system and laws for each season still apply.)

No Fee Automobile Registration for Medal of Honor Recipients

Recipients of the Medal of Honor are eligible for a no-fee registration and will receive special license plates noting their award. For information call 1-888-486-3339.

New Mexico

Veterans' Property Tax Exemption

Any veteran who served a minimum of 90 days consecutive active duty (other than for training), has an honorable discharge, and is a legal resident of New Mexico qualifies for a $4,000 reduction in the taxable value of their real property for county taxation purposes. This benefit can also be used for a one-third discount when registering a vehicle in New Mexico. The benefit is also available to the un-remarried surviving spouse of a veteran who would have otherwise qualified for this benefit.

Disabled Veteran Property Tax Exemption

Any veteran who has been rated 100 percent service-connected disabled by the U.S. Department of Veterans Affairs, and is a legal resident of New Mexico, qualifies for a complete property tax waiver on their primary residence.

Hunting & Fishing License

Any veteran rated 100 percent service-connected disabled qualifies for a free lifetime small game hunting and fishing license in the State of New Mexico.

Park Permits

New Mexico veterans with a permanent 100 percent service-connected disability may obtain one non-transferable annual day-use permit at no charge for personal use only. To obtain a permit, an eligible veteran shall present to the NM Parks Division a photocopy of the VA award letter indicating the veteran has a 100 percent service-connected disability; and proof of New Mexico residency, such as a New Mexico driver's license, or other state of New Mexico–issued identification.

Vehicle Tax

Any veteran who has suffered the loss or complete loss of use of one or more limbs due to their service in the military, shall be exempted from excise taxes when purchasing a new vehicle.

New York

Automobile

Auto registration, Thruway permits furnished free to qualified, seriously disabled veterans who receive a VA adaptive vehicle grant.

New York State Blind Annuity

Paid in monthly installments (2007 rate is $1,103.33 annually—$91.94 monthly) is available to visually impaired wartime veterans and certain unremarried spouses.

Burial Allowance

A supplemental burial allowance of up to $6,000 is authorized for certain military personnel killed in combat or while on active duty in hostile or imminent danger locations on or after September 29, 2003.

Veterans Tuition Award

Provides up to $1,000 per semester for full-time study or $500 per semester for part-time study to eligible New York State residents discharged under other than dishonorable conditions from the U.S. Armed Forces and are: Vietnam veterans who served in Indochina between December 22, 1961, and May 7, 1975; Persian Gulf veterans who served in the Persian Gulf on or after August 2, 1990. Afghanistan veterans who served in Afghanistan during hostilities on or after September 11, 2001.

Awards for Children of Veterans (CV)

Provides to eligible children of deceased veterans or those service-connected disabled of 40 percent or greater a non-competitive award of $450 a year.

Licenses and Permits

Veterans with a 40 percent or greater disability rating are eligible for low-cost hunting and fishing licenses, and free use of state parks, historic sites, and recreation sites.

Property Tax Exemption

Partial exemption from real property taxes is based on condition of service, with additional benefits based upon degree of service-connected disability. Applications must be filed before Taxable Status Day. Qualifying widow(er)s may file for benefit based on their spouse's service. Exemption applies to local and county property taxes.

North Carolina

Scholarships

A four-year scholarship program at North Carolina–approved schools has been established for the qualifying children of certain deceased, disabled, combat, or POW/MIA veterans.

Hunting and Fishing License

All 50 percent or more disabled veterans may obtain a lifetime hunting-fishing license upon the payment of $10.

Property Tax Relief

Certain Vehicles. A motor vehicle owned by a disabled veteran that is altered with special equipment to accommodate a service-connected disability. *Specially Adapted Housing.* Disabled veterans who receive U.S. Government assistance under Title 38, United States Code Annotated for the acquisition of specially adapted housing are eligible for an exclusion from ad valorem taxation on the first $38,000 in assessed value of housing together with the necessary land therefore that is owned and used as a residence by the disabled veteran.

North Dakota

Licenses

Special license plates for disabled veterans with loss of use, and former prisoners of war veterans (POW) are issued by the motor vehicle department upon the payment of $5.

Tax Exemptions

Property tax exemptions granted to paraplegic veterans up to net assessed valuation of $10,000 and lesser exemption to other service-connected veterans (or their un-remarried spouse) if veteran has over 50 percent service-connected disability and meets income limitation.

Loan Program

Loans to eligible resident veterans for temporary financial emergencies may be granted to honorably discharged veterans in amounts up to $5,000. Eight percent interest is charged. One-half of the interest is refunded if the loan is repaid in timely payments. The loan can be granted for periods of 6 to 48 months. Unremarried widow or widower of eligible veterans and National Guard members who meet certain active duty requirements are also eligible for a loan.

Ohio

Hunting and Fishing License

Veterans displaying license plates with the international wheelchair symbol, as well as certain other permanently disabled veterans, may apply for free hunting and fishing licenses, fur-taker permits, deer permits, wild turkey permits, and wetlands habitat stamps from the ODNR Division of Wildlife. Former prisoners of war may also apply for free hunting and fishing licenses, fur-taker permits, and wetlands habitat stamps. Applications for free permits are available from Division of Wildlife district offices in Columbus, Akron, Athens, Findlay, and Xenia; or by calling 1-800-WILDLIFE.

Watercraft Permits

All disabled veterans and former prisoners of war—as well as all Congressional Medal of Honor recipients—are eligible to apply to the ODNR Division of Watercraft to register their watercraft free of charge. The ODNR Division of Watercraft has details of the program at 1-877-4BOATER.

Camp Permits

All honorably discharged Ohio veterans who have been determined by the Department of Veterans Affairs to be permanently and totally disabled (and who receive a VA pension or compensation) are entitled to camp free of charge in Ohio state parks campgrounds. Former prisoners of war may also camp free in Ohio state parks. For more information on ODNR's outdoor recreational benefits for veterans, call the Department of Veterans Affairs in Ohio at 1-800-827-1000.

Oregon

Hunting and Fishing Licenses (Permanent Combination License)

A free hunting and angling license for disabled war veterans rated at 25 percent or more with the U.S. Department of Veterans Affairs. Veteran must be an Oregon resident for at least six months. Application requires proof in the form of a letter from the U.S. Department of Veterans Affairs. The letter must state the veteran's service-connected disability percentage. Call 1-800-827-1000 to order your letter. The letter should be submitted with the Department of Fish and Wildlife application to: Oregon Department of Fish and Wildlife, 3406 Cherry Avenue NE, Salem, OR 97303, 503-947-6101.

Disabilities Permit for Hunting and Fishing

The "Oregon Disabilities Hunting and Fishing Permit" is available to disabled veterans rated at 65 percent or more with the U.S. Department of Veterans Affairs. The disabilities permit is not a license or tag. Veterans must also obtain a Permanent Combination License. Application requires proof in the form of a letter from the U.S. Department of Veterans Affairs. The letter must state the veteran's service-connected disability percentage. Call 1-800-827-1000 to order your letter. The letter should be submitted with the Department of Fish and Wildlife Application to: Oregon Department of Fish and Wildlife, 3406 Cherry Avenue NE, Salem, OR 97303, 503-947-6101.

Home Loan Program for Oregon Veterans

ODVA offers a state veterans' home loan that is an additional and distinctively separate benefit from the USDVA (Federal VA) Home Loan Guaranty Program. The maximum loan amount for honorably discharged veterans is presently $417,000 (effective January 2, 2006). In some cases states can loan up to 100 percent of the appraised property value. Interest rates generally run about 1 percent below market—call to get a rate quote. All loans are made at fixed rates and veterans may choose up to a maximum loan term of 30 years.

Oregon Veterans' Education Aid

Educational benefits for Oregon veterans to pursue an approved course of study or professional training in or in connection with any accredited state or other public school or accredited private school or accredited college. Benefits are paid for as many months as the veteran spent in active service, up to a maximum of 36 months. Eligible veterans are entitled to receive up to $150 per month.

Veteran and Armed Forces Recognition License Plates

Service-connected disabled veterans qualify for a onetime registration fee for motor vehicle registration. Issued to honorably discharged veterans of the U.S. Armed Forces who have a service-connected disability rating from the U.S. Department of Veterans Affairs. Application requires proof in the form of a letter from the U.S. Department of Veterans Affairs. Call 1-800-827-1000 to order your letter. The letter should be submitted with the Oregon license plate application for service-connected disabled veterans.

Property Tax Exemption for Disabled War Veteran or Surviving Spouse

If you are a 40 percent or more disabled war veteran, you may be entitled to exempt a portion of your homestead property's assessed value from property taxes. If you are a disabled war veteran or the surviving spouse of a war veteran, you may be entitled to exempt $15,450 or $18,540 of your homestead property's assessed value from property taxes. The exemption amount increases by 3 percent each year.

Oregon Veterans' Home

The Oregon Veterans' Home is a skilled nursing care facility for Oregon veterans, their spouses or surviving spouses, and parents whose children died while serving in the U.S. Armed Forces. For information, call 1-800-846-8460.

Oregon State Park Use Permits

Service-connected disabled veterans have free day-use parking and free overnight rental of RV and tent campsites for up to five consecutive days and no more than 10 days total in a calendar month.

Rhode Island

Tax Exemption

Veterans of wartime service and Gold Star parents are eligible for a $1,000 to $5,000 property tax exemption. Additional exemptions are also available for the blind veterans and disabled veterans requiring "special adapted housing."

Free License Plates

The State of Rhode Island offers free license plates for former prisoners of war.

South Carolina

Income Tax Exemption on Retirement Pay

Any person retired from the uniformed services or their surviving spouse shall be allowed an exemption from the S.C. State Income Tax of $3,000 until age 65. At age 65, $10,000 of retirement pay is exempt.

Property Taxes—Homestead Exemption

All persons who have been declared permanently and totally disabled by the Social Security Administration, U.S. Department of Veterans Affairs, other state or Federal agencies are eligible for a homestead exemption in an amount set by the General Assembly. This also applies to persons over age 65.

Free Hunting and Fishing Licenses

Provides for free hunting/fishing licenses to veterans who are totally disabled. License must be applied for directly from SC Department of Natural Resources showing proof of disability. SCDNR phone 803-734-3838.

State Parks Totally Disabled Persons

Provides that any South Carolina resident who is a permanently and totally disabled veteran may enter any state park at a reduced rate upon presentation of supporting disability documentation. The veteran may also apply for a reduced fee "Palmetto Passport." Certain services may require an additional fee. For more information dial (888)-88PARKS (887-2757) or 803-734-0161.

Property Tax Exemption

Provides that the dwelling house where a veteran resides who has been rated as permanently and totally disabled by the U.S. Department of Veterans Affairs may be tax exempt. The tax exemption may be transferred when purchasing another dwelling.

Specially Adapted Housing

Provides for the exemption of state, county, and municipal taxes on the residence of veterans who have lost the use of their lower extremities or who have paralysis of one lateral half of the body.

Tax Exemption for Compensation, Pension, Disability Retirement Pay, and VA Payments

Provides that Federal tax-exempt moneys received from pension or compensation provided by the U.S. Department of Veterans Affairs, or disability pay from the armed forces, will not be included in SC tax.

Free Tuition/Education Assistance (Free Tuition for Certain Veterans' Children)

Provides for free tuition to the children of certain war veterans attending South Carolina state-supported colleges and universities as well as state-supported post high school technical education institutions. Certain residency requirements apply. For questions or to apply contact 803-255-4255.

South Dakota

Free Tuition for Veterans

Certain veterans are eligible to take undergraduate courses at a state university without the payment of tuition provided they are not eligible for educational payments under the GI Bill or any other Federal educational program. To qualify the veteran must have been discharged under honorable conditions; be a current resident of South Dakota and qualify for in-state tuition; meet one of the following criteria: served on active duty at any time between August 2, 1990, and a date to be determined; received an armed forces Expeditionary medal, Southwest Asia Service medal, or other United States campaign or service medal for participation in combat operations against hostile forces outside the boundaries of the United States; has a service-connected disability rated 10 percent or more, disabling. Eligible veterans may receive one month of free tuition for each month of "qualifying service" with a minimum of one, up to a maximum of four, academic years. Qualifying service is defined as the amount of time served on active duty between the beginning and ending dates of the particular period of conflict or hostilities during which the veteran earned eligibility for this program. Under the free tuition program, the veteran has twenty (20) years from the ending date of the specific period of service during which he or she served and met the eligibility criteria, or, twenty (20) years after the date that he or she was rated 10 percent, or more, disabled by the DVA.

Free Tuition for Children of Veterans Who Die During Service

Children who are under the age of 25, are residents of South Dakota, and whose mother or father was killed in action or died of other causes while on active duty are eligible for free tuition at a state-supported school, if the deceased parent was a bona fide resident of this state for at least six months immediately preceding entry into active service.

Free Tuition for Dependents of POW's and MIA's

Children and spouses of prisoners of war, or of persons listed as missing in action, are entitled to attend a state-supported school without the payment of tuition or mandatory fees provided they are not eligible for equal or greater Federal benefits.

Hunting and Fishing Cards for Disabled Veterans

Certain resident veterans may receive a hunting and fishing card, which is valid for four years. Upon purchase of an annual basic game and fish license, the card becomes the equivalency of a resident fishing license, small game stamp and habitat stamp until the expiration of the basic game and fish license. To qualify the veteran must be rated as totally disabled from service-connected injuries or be in receipt of the VA "K" award or, have been held as a prisoner of war or, be in receipt of Social Security benefits because of a total disability. Application forms are available from the Game, Fish and Parks Regional Office. The application, along with verification of eligibility, are submitted to Game, Fish and Parks, 412 West Missouri, Pierre, SD 57501.

Free Admission and Reduced Camping Fees for Veterans

Certain resident veterans may obtain free admission to any South Dakota state park and are eligible for a 50 percent discount on any camping fee or associated electrical fee. To qualify the veteran must be totally disabled from service-connected disabilities, or be in receipt of the VA "K" award, or have been held as a prisoner of war. Application forms may be obtained from the local park manager or through the Game, Fish and Parks office in Pierre.

Property Tax Exemption for Veterans and Their Widow or Widower

Dwellings or parts of multiple family dwellings that are specifically designed for use by paraplegics as wheelchair homes and which are owned and occupied by veterans with the loss, or loss of use, of both lower extremities, or by the unremarried widow or widower of such veteran, are exempt from taxation. The dwelling must be owned and occupied by the veteran for one full calendar year before the exemption becomes effective. For purposes of this statute, the term "dwelling" generally means real estate in an amount not to exceed one acre upon which the building is located.

Tennessee

License Plates

Free for 100 percent service-connected disabled veterans, Ex-POW's, and recipients of MOH, DSC, NC, or AFC.

Property Tax Relief

For combat-related 100 percent totally disabled veterans and/or their surviving spouses. For additional information, go to www.comptroller.state.tn.us/pa/patxrvet.htm.

Hunting and Fishing Licenses

Free for veterans with 30 percent or more war service-connected disabilities, after an initial onetime fee of $10.

Motor Vehicle Privilege Tax Exemption

For 100 percent disabled veterans.

Texas

Free Drivers License for Disabled Veterans

Texas drivers licenses may be furnished free of charge to veterans who have service-connected disabilities rated 60 percent or more by the VA or by a branch of the armed forces of the U.S. Application must be made prior to the time present driver's license expires. Application forms may be obtained from Department of Public Safety's license examining offices located throughout the state. Application forms should be completed by the veteran and forwarded to the VA for verification of service-connected rating of 60 percent or more. If a veteran was disability retired from military service and has no VA claim file, proof of disability must come from their respective branch of military service.

Fishing and Hunting Licenses for Disabled Veterans

Disabled veterans are eligible for special hunting and fishing licenses, at a reduced cost. A disabled veteran of the armed forces of the United States is one who has a service-connected disability, as defined by the Department of Veterans Affairs, consisting of the loss of use of a lower extremity or of a disability rating of 60 percent or more, and who is receiving compensation from the United States for the disability. A resident veteran as described in the law may hunt wild turkey and deer without a resident hunting license if he has acquired a resident exemption-hunting license.

Free Park Admission for Disabled Veterans

Free admission to Texas state parks is available to any veteran who has a service-connected disability, which is rated 60 percent or more by VA, or a service-connected disability, which has resulted in the loss of a lower extremity. Application may be made at the headquarters office of any Texas state park by providing satisfactory evidence of service-connected disability. If such evidence is not readily available, it can be obtained from the VA regional office where the claims folder is located. The Texas State Parklands Passport is available to any veteran who meets the disability requirements, whether or not he or she resides in Texas. The passport provides only free admission to the state parks, and does not exempt anyone from payment of other charges, such as camping fees and so forth.

Tax Exemption for Veterans

Disabled veterans who meet certain requirements, their surviving spouses, and the spouses and minor children of a person who dies on active duty in the U.S. Armed Forces are eligible for property tax exemptions on the appraised value of their property. The exemption is mandatory and applies to taxes levied by all taxing authorities in the state. A veteran, whose service-connected disabilities are rated less than 10 percent by the Department of Veterans Affairs, or a branch of the armed forces, is not entitled to a property tax exemption.

Utah

Property Tax Abatement

A Utah permanent place-of-residence property tax exemption equivalent to the military service-connected disability rating percentage is provided for disabled veterans or for their unremarried widows or minor orphans. Veteran's disability rating must be at least 10 percent. The maximum property tax exemption, rated at 100 percent military service-connected disability, is $214,263. To apply for Utah Disabled Veterans Property Tax Exemption, request VA Form 20-5455 from U.S. Department of Veterans Affairs (VA) at 1-800-827-1000, then file VA Form 20-5455, along with a copy of the veteran's U.S. military active duty release/discharge certificate or other satisfactory evidence of eligible military service, and the tax exemption application, on or before September 1st, to the applicable county treasurer, tax assessor, or clerk/recorder located in the county courthouse or county government building of each county seat. Effective January 1, 2008, disabled veterans will only be required to file for property tax abatement one time. After the initial filing it will automatically renew each year. However, veterans will have to re-file if all or a portion of their abatement is used toward tangible personal property, if their service-connected disability percentage changes, the veteran dies, sells the property or no longer claims that property as their primary place of residence.

Fishing License Privileges

Utah Disabled Veteran Fishing Licenses are available for veterans, free of charge, from the Utah Division of Wildlife Resources. To qualify a veteran must have obvious physical handicaps, such as permanently confined to a wheelchair, paraplegic, minus at least one limb, permanently requiring crutches, or blind.

Special Fun Tags

Free of charge to disabled veterans and other disabled persons are Utah Special Fun Tags, which allow free admission to most of the 41 state-controlled parks, campgrounds, and other recreation areas throughout Utah. The Utah Special Fun Tags also allow a $2 off camping fee discount Monday through Thursday, excluding holidays. Utah Special Fun Tags are available to disabled veterans upon application to the Utah Division of Parks and Recreation, along with a VA letter documenting 10 percent or greater military service-connected disability rating. Please call the State Parks and Recreation office at 801-538-7220 to have an application mailed to you or log on to www.stateparks.utah.gov to download an application.

Vermont

Vermont Veterans License Plate

Veterans can receive a Vermont Veterans License Plate when they register their vehicle. Veterans can have a Vermont Veterans License Plate on each of their cars. The Department of Motor Vehicles will charge $10 the first time a vehicle is registered with the plate. Of this fee, $5 goes toward the Office of Veterans Affairs to fund their activities.

Hunting and Fishing Licenses; Green Mountain Pass

Veterans with a Department of Veterans Affairs service-connected disability rating of 100 percent can receive a free lifetime hunting and fishing license. They can also receive a free Green Mountain Pass, which provides free access to state parks. For the hunting and fishing license, you will need to obtain a verification letter from the White River Junction Benefits office (1-800-827-1000). Submit the verification letter with a standard license application and send it to the Fish and Wildlife Department in Waterbury. Call 802-241-3700 for more information. Applications for the Green Mountain Pass are found at your town clerk's office.

Virginia

Virginia Military Survivors and Dependents Education Program

The Military Survivors and Dependents Program (MSDEP) provides education benefits to spouses and children of military servicemembers killed, missing in action, taken prisoner, or who became at least 90 percent disabled as a result of military service in an armed conflict. This program may pay for tuition and fees at any state-supported college or university. This program waives tuition and fees in Virginia. Benefits are available for up to four years.

License Plates

The Virginia Department of Motor Vehicles (DMV) offers a variety of veteran and military-related license plates.

Virginia Department of Game and Inland Fisheries (VDGIF)

The VDGIF offers a lifetime hunting and fishing license to service-connected, totally and permanently disabled veterans for only $10.

Washington

Washington State Parks Pass

Disabled Veteran Lifetime Pass at no charge; free camping/moorage; campsite reservations through state parks central reservations system; watercraft launching; trailer dump. Valid year-round. Offered to Washington state residents with a documented service-connected disability of at least 30 percent.

West Virginia

Tax Exemption

Partial exemption of military retirement pay and certain other types of retirement or annuity benefits from the Federal adjusted gross income for the purpose of computing state income tax.

Homestead Exemption

For certain eligible veterans. Specific information is available through the local county assessor's office.

Free Vehicle Registration

For veterans who are drawing 100 percent service-connected compensation from USDVA, in receipt of an auto grant from the USDVA, a former POW. Free license for recipients of Purple Heart and Pearl Harbor survivors. Free hunting and fishing privileges for 100 percent service-connected veterans or those in receipt of USDVA auto grant.

Wisconsin

Education

Wisconsin G.I. Bill provides a waiver of tuition and fees for eligible veterans and their dependents for up to eight full-time semesters or 128 credits at any University of Wisconsin System (UWS) or Wisconsin Technical College System (WTCS) institution. The Wisconsin G.I. Bill is a state program that is entirely separate from the Federal Montgomery GI Bill.

Disabled Veterans Reduced-Fee Fishing License

Wisconsin disabled veterans with a combined service-connected disability rating by the U.S. Department of Veterans Affairs (VA) of 70 percent or greater are eligible for a disabled veteran reduced-fee fishing license. The fishing license must be renewed annually, and does not exempt the holder from the need to purchase required fishing stamps. When purchasing the license at a DNR or county clerk's office, the applicant must provide a copy of a letter from the VA that indicates receipt of VA disability benefits and specifies the percentage of disability.

Wisconsin Veterans and Surviving Spouses Property Tax Credit

The Wisconsin Veterans and Surviving Spouses Property Tax Credit program provides a refundable property tax credit for the primary residence (in-state) via the state income tax form for: eligible veterans age 65 or older who entered service from Wisconsin and have a combined VA service-connected disability rating of 100 percent. The un-remarried surviving spouse of an eligible veteran. The un-remarried surviving spouse of a veteran who entered active duty as a Wisconsin resident, died in the line of duty, and was a Wisconsin resident at the time of death.

Index